The Canadian and American Constitutions in Comparative Perspective

The Canadian and American Constitutions in Comparative Perspective

edited by

Marian C. McKenna

University of Calgary Press

University of Calgary Press
2500 University Drive N.W.
Calgary, Alberta, Canada T2N 1N4

Canadian Cataloguing in Publication Data

Main entry under title:

The Canadian and American Constitutions in
   comparative perspective

   Includes bibliographical references and index.
   ISBN 1-895176-26-3

   1. Canada—Constitutional history. 2. United States—
Constitutional history. 3. Canada—Politics and government.
4. United States—Politics and government. 5. Comparative
government. I. McKenna, Marian C. (Marian Cecilia), 1926–

JF51.C35 1993   320.3'0971   C93-091361-2

The Alberta
Foundation
for the Arts

Financial support provided by the Alberta Foundation for the Arts,
a beneficiary of the Lottery Fund of the Government of Alberta

Providing a foundation for the arts

Cover design by Jon Paine
Printed in Canada by Hignell Printing Limited

∞ This book is printed on acid-free paper.

Table of Contents

I. The Constitution and Religion

II. Federalism in Canada and the United States

III. The Politics of Rights

IV. The Judiciary and Public Policy Issues

V. Conclusion

Preface

This book of essays originated in a conference titled "Canadian Reflections on the American Constitution," held at the Unversity of Calgary in the autumn of 1987 in observance of the Bicentennial of the American Constitution (1787–1987). The conference was made possible through the generosity of the following sponsors: the University Research Grants Committee, the Special Projects Fund, the Departments of History and Political Science, and the Office of the Dean of Social Science—all of the University of Calgary. Further assistance was provided by the United States Information Service, through the special efforts of Jack Hols, now of Spokane, and the Social Science and Humanities Research Council of Canada.

The principal speakers at the conference were: David Flaherty, George Graham, J. Woodford Howard, Harold Hyman, Harry V. Jaffa, Michael Kammen, F.L. (Ted) Morton, Jennifer Smith, and Mr. Justice Walter Tarnopolsky. Several of the original conference speakers agreed to revise their papers for publication, and to these have been added essays by Madam Justice Rosalie Abella, Madame Justice Claire L'Heureux Dubé, Roger Gibbins, Peter Holland, Thomas Pangle, and Peter Russell, to form the present collection.

Seeing this project through to completion has been a long, exasperating business, with many difficulties and delays. I am heavily indebted to the contributors for their understanding and patience. The initial encouragement of Thomas Flanagan, both for the conference and for the eventual publication of some of its papers, made the subsequent ordeal seem worth the effort. At all stages in the process, Thomas Flanagan, Roger Gibbins, and Holger Herwig have offered helpful editorial advice and critical comments. To Olga Leskiw, Laurie Dellemonache, and Joyce Woods, I extend thanks for their help in the preparation of the final manuscript.

Linda Cameron, former director of the University of Calgary Press took an immediate and lively interest in this project and this may be the appropriate place to acknowledge her steady support. I would also like to thank Shirley Onn, director of the University of Calgary Press for her enthusiasm and encouragement, and John King, production editor, who has given generously of his time to see this book through to final publication. Without the cooperation and assistance of the staff of the University of Calgary Press, and especially copyeditor Peter Enman, the publication of this book would not have been possible.

I acknowledge the following journals for granting permission to reproduce material that first appeared within their pages: Madam Justice Rosalie Silberman Abella, *The McGill Law Journal* 34 (1989): 1021; J. Woodford Howard, Jr., *The Journal of Law and Politics* 7:3 (1991): 481–523; Peter H. Russell, *The Canadian Journal of Political Science* 24:4 (1991): 691–709; Jennifer Smith, *The Canadian Journal of Political Science* 21:3 (1988): 443–63.

Publication has been facilitated by a grant from the Endowment Fund of the University of Calgary. This book has been published with the help of a grant from the Canadian Federation for the Humanities, using funds provided by the Social Sciences and Humanities Research Council of Canada.

Introduction: A Legacy of Questions

In observance of the bicentennial of the American Constitution (1787–1987) a distinguished group of scholars from Canada and the United States gathered in September 1987 on the campus of the University of Calgary for a conference at which a dozen invited papers were presented examining different aspects of the two constitutions. Their objective, while utilizing the comparative method, was to probe the respective origins and frameworks of the two constitutions, to consider their merits and defects over time, and to single out their common core of enduring principles as they relate to historical and contemporary problems. Wherever possible, the conference participants were engaged in an exercise designed to stimulate interest in the constitutional problems facing the two countries, and to suggest ways in which each of the two current constitutional arrangements compare and contrast. An overall objective of the conference and the papers selected from it for publication was to generate a better understanding of the constitutional problems facing the two countries, always bearing in mind that civic education is one of the most important charges that the members of any society can undertake.

The emphasis on the comparative approach in the essays that follow was prompted by a variety of considerations. The most basic of these incentives arose from the assumption that interest in comparison is a part of all intellectual inquiry, curiosity and intelligent analysis. It should therefore form a part of the study of constitutional history and development. Gradually, social scientists are compensating for the long neglect of the North American continental experience in constitution-making and the social laboratory it provides as a natural resource in their respective disciplines. Political scientists in past decades have taken the lead in making cross-border comparative studies the subject of periodical articles, monographs and essays, realizing that scholarly inquiry can and should transcend national boundaries. In political science, comparative work in fact constitutes one of the most visible and prolific activities in this, the youngest discipline in what we call the social sciences. Here, comparative analyses comprise a large and occasionally dominant subdivision. It is therefore no accident that in this collection, essays representing the discipline of political science predominate.

The bicentennial of 1987 was utilized as a point of departure to provide what was considered an appropriate opportunity to examine some of the fundamental questions that have persisted over the years about the origins, functioning, transformation and implications for the future of the two working constitutional systems. We asked ourselves such questions as: What are the central ideas embodied in the Canadian and American constitutions? What elements, if any, are common to each? What elements in each are of enduring importance and utility? How was the older American Constitution perceived in the 1860s by its British North American neighbor? What were the concerns that led to the *Constitution Act, 1867* and the contemporary *Constitution Act, 1982* with the *Canadian Charter of Rights and Freedoms* entrenched in it? And what changes and political implications for Canada's future as a sovereign and unified nation did these developments bring with them? These were only some of the questions raised in reflecting on a common past, present and future as neighboring nations.

So far as we were aware, no such conference had ever been held before either in Canada or the United States. Looking at these complex problems from a comparative perspective wherever feasible was unique to the undertaking. By putting these ideas and views in writing, we have been made only too well aware that in the present political climate and changing constitutional scene, especially in Canada, constitutional discussion is an emotional minefield, to be avoided by those wishing to be prudent.

Up to World War II, and for a decade or so thereafter, the differences between the Canadian and American constitutional experiences were greater than their similarities. But even in the nineteenth century apt comparisons can be drawn between them, and in more recent times parallels are more numerous and revealing than has been generally thought. It was this awareness of the rich possibilities for analysis that the comparative approach offered that provided the conceptual framework for this volume of essays.

What few of the authors in this volume could have anticipated in 1987 is the heat that has been generated in the ongoing debate during recent decades in Canada, accompanying the crisis in constitutional arrangements between the federal and provincial governments which has preoccupied the populace and all levels of authority. Never has that debate been more heated or critical than in the 1990s, a mere decade after the *Constitution Act, 1982*. This was the real catalyst which has sparked a whole new debate. It has produced a veritable explosion of new interest, inquiry, and publications covering virtually all aspects of past and present constitutional experience since Canadian Confederation. The debate is fuelled by contemporary questioning of the existing Canadian constitution, which has its roots in the spurt of nation-building and conflicting province-building following World War II. An additional source, and a strident voice in the debate, is the increasingly disenchanted Québécois view of recent years, which holds that the existing constitution restricts the process of nation-building in the Province of Quebec.

Even in the United States, as a result of the publicity surrounding the national unity debate, there has arisen a new interest in some circles in the gnawing questions agitating Canadian society. Do the present Canadian constitutional arrangements contribute to the country's unity or disunity? Are Canadians a united people, divided by their government, or are they a divided people whose fragile unity is a product of overarching constitutional arrangements?

THE AMERICAN CONSTITUTIONAL HERITAGE

Constitutional history, although its study is the preserve of a small contingent of scholars and specialists, is a thriving concern on both sides of the border. There was the expected upsurge of interest and a virtual explosion in constitution-related publications coincidental with the U.S. bicentennial celebrations. But in the intervening years since 1987 constitutional research, not to mention comparative research, has had a spotty career. The role of the American Constitution in national development, for example, has fallen into the cracks between more faddish specializations (e.g., gender, race, ethnic, quantitative and native studies), remaining largely unnoticed except by a few dedicated political scientists and historians. In what constitutional research is being produced in an ongoing fashion, emphasis is placed, rather unduly it would seem, on constitutional origins and the perennial fascination with the original intent of the Constitution's framers. Specialists have concerned themselves, to a much lesser extent, with the long-range significance of constitutionalism for evolving American society, or with how other societies have been influenced by the American constitutional example.

In contrast, Canadians, through the working out of the current constitutional crisis, are rediscovering their past and the complexities of the present. The future of the Canadian experiment is as yet in doubt, hanging suspended, like some patient in the hands of too many constitutional doctors. The dramatic events through which Canadians have recently passed give a foreboding sense that some great watershed (whether it be Meech Lake or the 1992 referendum results) has been reached. The comparative experiences chronicled in the following essays reflect the fact that the United States (Canada's proximate model in 1867) had only recently passed through its own constitutional crisis. After more than a century, that bloody American Civil War is still perceived as a milestone in the annals of humanity's struggle to create lasting civic polities.

The essays in this collection, some of which are concerned with the consensus and compromise embodied in constitution-making and change, emphasize the shaping force of law and government institutions in the unfolding direction taken by the new forms of social, political and economic change that characterize our times. The twin themes that give these essays coherence are: the impact of society and social forms on government and its institutions; and the impact of government, through constitutionalism, on society, especially on the political functions of society. Inevitably, each in its own way raises such other difficult questions as: What elements in the constitutional system under which we live are worth preserving, are of enduring importance? And which are in need of change? What changes, if any, might be considered? These are problems not easily resolved, but then there are few easy questions in the realm of contemporary constitutional inquiry.

Americans have enjoyed great good fortune in the benefits flowing from a rich constitutional heritage. The 1787 document, now entering upon its third century as the organic law, has successfully withstood the test of a fiery Civil War, severe economic depression, international wars and assorted crises. An essential element in the dynamism of the government created by the Constitution is the process of constitutional development made possible by judicial interpretation of the basic law. Reference in the essays which follow to the activity of the Supreme Court in such important problem areas of our time as religious freedom, racial equality and civil liberties is designed to demonstrate the workings of this process and to illuminate the Court's policy-making role in changing the law of the Constitution to meet the changing needs and aspirations of modern American society. Not to be overlooked are such other elements important to a smoothly functioning constitutional order as federal-state arrangements and the inclusion of a workable amending formula. The U.S. Constitution's flexible clauses and language have allowed the original text to survive with only a modest number of amendments. It is, however, in the work of the Supreme Court over more than two centuries that we find the vital instrument in the preservation of a "living" Constitution.

In every organized political community there must be some kind of system of fundamental principles and procedures for the preservation of order, the means by which a society is governed. In the West we call this a constitution. Certain of these are embodied in written documents, while others are moulded by custom. Some represent clear-cut blueprints, others only aspirations, and some are merely façades. The U.S. Constitution represents the ideals and aspirations of "We the people"; it also functions as the nation's basic law. Of the world's operative written constitutions, it is now the oldest.

The relationship between Americans and their Constitution has been a source of ongoing comment and some controversy over many years. In at least two ways American behavior continues to mystify people in other countries. The first is their tendency to discuss issues of public policy in terms of *their* Constitution exclusively, as if the United States were the center of the constitutional universe and its Constitution a document the rest of the world is expected to comprehend and, preferably, know in some detail. People in other lands tend naturally to look first to their own constitutional tradition (if they have one) to explain why certain things are done in certain ways in their own country. They do not generally expect others to understand in minute detail their own constitutional framework in all its peculiarities. Undoubtedly, this ethnocentric attitude on the part of Americans, considered in some quarters to be arrogance, derives from an inbred notion of the "superiority" of American political institutions, and in particular, the 1787 document.[1]

A second characteristic others might find difficult to understand about American behavior is the veneration of the Constitution and its Bill of Rights, along with the Declaration of Independence of 1776. Today these three documents are on display in the Exhibition Hall of the National Archives building in Washington, D.C. Every year many thousands of visitors line up to view the great charter which has played such a central role in American national life. Many people are deeply impressed by the display to which tour guides sometimes refer as a "shrine." In the domed hall, the documents are sealed inside bronze and glass cases and lowered at night into a massive vault beneath the floor. To outsiders, the reverence in which these icons are held seems somehow incongruous in a society so devoted, at least in constitutional principle, to the separation of church and state. In the absence of a monarchical tradition, these relics substitute for national symbols.

Until very recently, this near-reverence for the Constitution displayed by ordinary citizens was extended to the justices of the Supreme Court, the institution invested with the authority to interpret the Constitution's meaning. Leaders of public opinion around the turn of the century consecrated the Constitution and virtually deified the members of the high Court, who were considered to be the sacred document's "impersonal voices." Such an attitude had its roots in the first ages of judicial review, when the states challenged the Supreme Court's authority. Its Chief Justice, John Marshall, answered that challenge in a long line of decisions

---

1 These observations were advanced by David Flaherty, one of the original conference participants, in his review essay, "Constitution Worship," *Canadian Review of American Studies* 20 (1989), 81.

in which he firmly established the predominance of the national government over the states, at the same time establishing the authority, if not the supremacy, of the federal judiciary.[2] The Court was thought to hold the keys that unlocked the meaning of the Constitution, allowing for those laws and acts that passed the test of judicial scrutiny, and rejecting those that did not.

During the wave of riots that swept through the United States in the 1830s, aimed at eradicating a variety of social problems and grievances, Abraham Lincoln, in his first political act (his Springfield Lyceum Address of 1838), condemned them as a threat to American institutions, warning that rioting would destroy the people's attachment to the government. The future President insisted on respect for law and order as a safeguard of republican liberty and urged in his address that reverence for the Constitution and the law become "the political *religion* of the nation."[3] In the midst of a later crisis in the 1930s, Supreme Court Justice George Sutherland recalled how, as a youth, he had been taught that the Constitution was a "divinely inspired instrument." With no hesitation, he added: "I truly think so."[4]

This form of worship could not have been due to any reverend quality in the text of the document, made up as it is of words which, apart from the preamble, are not only secular but legalistic. This reverence for the Constitution, if it exists at all, must survive because it embodies or represents something greater than itself, greater even than the sum of its parts—an ideal or myth which somehow connects American politics with the eternal verities. As the redolence of its bicentennial attests, the 1787 American Constitution was one of those rare achievements embodying some of the most remarkable results of political debate and compromise. It was, as David Flaherty has noted, "a work of such extraordinary originality and insight, the product of such celebrated circumstances, that it is hardly surprising that otherwise rational people think of the Constitution as being divinely preordained."[5]

---

2 The leading Marshall Court decisions invoking national supremacy over the states include: *Martin* v. *Hunter's Lessee*, 1 Wheaton 304 (1816); *McCulloch* v. *Maryland*, 4 Wheaton 316 (1819); and *Cohens* v. *Virginia*, 6 Wheaton 264 (1821).

3 Address before the Young Men's Lyceum of Springfield, Illinois, 27 January 1837, *Abraham Lincoln: Complete Works*, 2 vols., John G. Nicolay and John Hay, eds. (New York: The Century Co., 1894), 1:12.

4 Quoted in Joel F. Paschal, *Mr. Justice Sutherland: A Man Against the State* (Princeton: Princeton University Press, 1951), 8.

5 Flaherty, "Constitution Worship," 81–82.

THE CANADIAN CONSTITUTIONAL HERITAGE

Referring to the fifteen years following World War II, the journalist Bruce Hutchison wrote: "Perhaps in this brief period no other nation has altered so much as Canada. It might be truer to say that Canada became a nation in mind, as it was long a nation by constitution, only yesterday or the day before, its inhabitants a distinct and distinguishable race." In the long journey undertaken in the 1950s to rediscover Canada, he encountered what he called a little-understood people with a surprising past and an indeterminate future. No one had as yet defined the Canadian in words. "But what of it?" asked Hutchison. What had so far been produced was as yet a character too young, and certainly "too reticent for definition." However, he found it to be hardening and assuming a definite shape distinct from other peoples, even the American neighbors next door.[6]

Historians record that an essentially negative and centrifugal movement, a recoil from the American Revolution, began the Canadian experiment. In Canada's constitutional beginnings its leaders deliberately chose to emulate the mother country, to whom the bulk of its citizens pledged their loyalty. As a result, Canada emerged as an autonomous dominion within the Empire under the *British North America Act, 1867* (now renamed the *Constitution Act, 1867*). The Canadian constitution is defined as a body of understandings which in turn define the basic institutions of government, the relationship between them, plus the relationships between governments in the federal system, and between the citizens and those governments.[7] The constitution has evolved in incremental stages as a series of practices worked out by successive ministries in succeeding generations. But more important than all of these is the role the courts have played.

The Canadian constitution has been viewed as a "living instrument of government," always considered to be wider in scope than the terms of the *British North America Act, 1867*, and not restricted to the intentions of the Fathers of Canadian Confederation. Thus, the settlement of 1867 was only the beginning, and has been under constant transformation since that time. (Although the *B.N.A. Act* was one of the key documents that went into the making of the Canadian constitution, care should be taken to distinguish between it and the constitution.)

---

6 Bruce Hutchison, *Canada: Tomorrow's Giant* (Toronto: Longmans, Green and Co., 1957), Foreword, i, and 3.

7 This is the definition that Alan Cairns gives the Canadian constitution. "The Living Canadian Constitution," in *Constitution, Government and Society in Canada: Selected Essays by Alan C. Cairns*, Douglas E. Williams, ed. (Toronto: McClelland and Stewart, 1989), 31.

In formulating the terms of their union, Canadians debated among themselves, but did not articulate their ideals, hopes and aspirations in any elaborate way for the rest of the world's consumption, as did the Americans. They acted pragmatically, almost by instinct. The leading figures in the debate were least given to theory, and were skeptical of nearly everything.

After passing through its seedtime as a cluster of northern colonies of Great Britain, Canada began its life as a nation, emerging as a Confederation officially proclaimed on 1 July 1867. The admiration so readily shown by other nations for the American constitutional model was not shared by the Fathers of Confederation, certainly not by Sir John A. Macdonald, the first Prime Minister. Canada's constitutional origins were different from those of the neighbor to the south.

Unlike the Constitution of 1787, the *B.N.A. Act* enshrined few if any eternal principles and is singularly devoid of inspirational content. The Canadian constitution was given birth in no revolutionary or populist context, and as one prominent political scientist has pointed out, it has acquired little symbolic aura in its subsequent history.[8] The movement toward Confederation was not so much a rejection of the United States or of Europe as it was a pragmatic response to a series of conditions and considerations that were at once political, economic, military and diplomatic.

The Canadian union patched together at Quebec and Charlottetown was more the product of a local governing and commercial elite in British North America, attempting to break the political and cultural deadlock resulting from the 1840 *Act of Union* between Upper Canada (Ontario) and Lower Canada (Quebec). The idea, at least in part, was to link up the Maritimes (Nova Scotia and New Brunswick) with the western provinces in a transcontinental union that would eventually stretch across the continent to what is today British Columbia.[9] The Fathers of Confederation displayed an understandable reluctance to follow the constitutional example of the Americans, who were just then emerging from a bloody Civil War. An underlying intention was to resist the perceived threat of expansion northward by a consolidated United States after its victory over the South in 1865.

---

8 Ibid., 27.

9 The origins of the federal arrangement in Canadian confederation is ably set forth in Ronald Watts, "The American Constitution in Comparative Perspective: A Comparison of Federalism in the United States and Canada," in *The Constitution and American Life*, a special issue of the *Journal of American History* 74:3 (December, 1987), 769–91. See 769–70 for the above. On the hotly debated consent issue in Nova Scotia, see J.G. Marshall, *An Examination of the Proposed Union of the North American Provinces* (Halifax, 1865), and Jennifer Smith, "Canadian Confederation and the Influence of American Federalism," in this volume.

It was a shaky union at best. Only a few months after Confederation Nova Scotia reconsidered and attempted, though unsuccessfully, to pull out. However there was as much common ground as differences. The union survived and was eventually able to reach an accommodation with the recently reunited nation to the south. Thereafter the two nations, which shared a common British heritage and colonial experience, grew in strength and maturity in close proximity one to the other, developed an intimate commercial relationship and coexisted peacefully along one of the longest borders shared between two nationalities.

Canada eschewed adopting a republican form of government, however attractive that idea may have seemed to some at the time of Confederation, or since. They opted instead for a parliamentary system patterned squarely on the older, more revered British model. The Confederation created in 1867 comprised several other features which distinguished it from the American union of states. There was no felt need or desire evident for the kind of political theorizing that accompanied the creation of the American polity. Ideology played a much larger role in American nation-building, not only at the time of the revolutionary movement but in considering existing models for the constitutional arrangement of 1787, resulting in the document that seems to have cast such a spell over succeeding generations.

The constitution Canada adopted, with the important exception of including in it a federal system, was similar in principle to that of the mother country. A constitutional monarchy within a parliamentary setting was and remains an integral part of Canadian constitutionalism. But the *Constitution Act, 1867* enshrined few if any broad principles of government. There were, for example, no such resounding assertions of human rights as Thomas Jefferson penned in 1776 to accompany the creation of the new American political entity.

What the 1867 federal arrangement did provide was a strong concentration of powers within the central government, combining a parliamentary system with a federalism that some observers, K.C. Wheare, for example, have considered only "quasi-federal." This concentration of powers was a deliberate move in reaction against the excesses of states' rights and secession which had led the United States to the catastrophe of the Civil War. Canada, it was determined, would choose a different path.[10]

Americans fought a revolution *against* colonialism in their attempt to throw off any semblance of British rule. They considered but rejected a parliamentary system. Canadians sought their political development

---

10 See his *Federal Government* (London, 1963); on the reaction to American circumstances at the time of Confederation, see William L. Morton, *The Critical Years: The Union of British North America, 1857–73* (Toronto: McClelland and Stewart, 1964).

within the British imperium. Their founding elite held a hazy vision of creating a federal-provincial relationship similar to that which had existed under the old colony-empire relationship. Implicit in this was the expectation of subordination of the provinces to the more powerful central government in important matters. The provinces, which grew from four to ten over time, with the addition of two territories, were made dependent on the central government for funds and more importantly, the assignment of the residual powers was made to the central government. This was just the opposite, at least in theory, of the federal arrangement in the Tenth Amendment in the American Constitution's Bill of Rights as initially construed.

The essays which follow have been grouped for convenience's sake into four sections, each of which deals with these broad areas of concern: the American Constitution and religious freedom; federalism in Canada and the United States; the politics of rights as it relates to the functioning of the new *Canadian Charter of Rights and Freedoms*; and the role of the judiciary in public policy issues. All the essays, without exception, take the common approach of viewing constitutions as living organisms. In this they heed the wise admonition of Associate Justice Oliver Wendell Holmes, whose eloquent statement reveals a perspective too often lacking in the jurisprudence of both countries:

> The provisions of the Constitution are not mathematical formulas having their essence in their form; they are organic living institutions transplanted from English soil. Their significance is vital, not formal; it is to be gathered not simply by taking the words and a dictionary, but by considering their origin and the line of their growth.

This understanding of a "living constitution" has led in the United States to the nearly hopeless dichotomy between judicial activism and "original intent," while in Canada it has often led to the mistaken belief that a constitution that is a century old must have outlived its usefulness. In another context Holmes wrote:

> When we are dealing with words that are also a constituent act, like the Constitution of the United States, we must realize that they have called into life a being the development of which could not have been foreseen completely by the most gifted of its begetters. It was enough for them to realize or to hope that they had created an organism; it has taken a century and has cost their successors much sweat and blood to prove that they created a nation. The case before us must be considered in the

light of our whole experience and not merely in that of what was said a hundred years ago.[11]

This helps to explain why, in his judicial decision-making, Holmes was able to demonstrate the rare art of combining his history, the demands of an ordered system, and practical results, in determining which rule to adopt.

As Alan Cairns has argued in a celebrated essay,

> Realistically speaking, all working constitutions are living constitutions, springing from, but not bound and gagged by history. . . . Positively, a functioning institution of ancient origin acquires the special credibility that derives from its continuing utility for the attainment of one or more specified human goals. In the Darwinian process of institutional competition for survival it has emerged triumphant. Negatively, it is placed on the defensive by the fact that the contemporary circumstances to which it now applies are significantly different from the circumstances to which it was originally a response. Hence, it appears to be tinged with mortality.[12]

Inadequate recognition of this, in Cairns' view, is a significant cause of the constitutional morass in which Canadians have found themselves. "We might say," he adds, "that the constitution has not failed us, so much as we, by our inadequate understanding of its living nature, have failed it."[13]

Herein lies the best rationale for a volume of this nature.

I. THE CONSTITUTION AND RELIGION

The specific characteristics of the peculiarly American approach to religion were suggested well over a century ago by the central subject of **THOMAS PANGLE**'s essay. In *Democracy in America*, Alexis de Tocqueville wrote:

> It must never be forgotten that religion gave birth to Anglo-American society. In the United States, religion is therefore mingled with all the habits of the nation and all the feelings of patriotism, whence it derives a peculiar force. To this reason another of no less power may be added: in America religion has, as it were, laid down its own limits. Religious institutions have remained wholly distinct from political institutions, so

---

11 As cited in Archibald Macleish and E.F. Pritchard, Jr., eds., *Law and Politics: Occasional Papers of Felix Frankfurter* (New York: Harcourt, Brace, 1939), 71.

12 "The Living Canadian Constitution," 28.

13 Ibid., 38.

that former laws have been easily changed while former belief has remained unshaken. Christianity has therefore retained a strong hold on the public mind in America: and I would more particularly remark that its sway is not only that of a philosophical doctrine which has been adopted upon inquiry, but of a religion which is believed without discussion. In the United States, Christian sects are infinitely diversified and perpetually modified; but Christianity itself is an established and irresistible fact, which no one undertakes either to attack or to defend.[14]

Tocqueville believed strongly in the ideas and values of the Christian tradition as the basis of a democratic faith. He recognized that faith is an integral element in human action and its most powerful dynamic. Throughout his philosophical and sociological inquiry into the implications of democracy, he comments at a number of points on the influence that religion has had on American society. But he was far more concerned with making an analysis of the relation between religious faith and democratic practice:

When the religion of a people is destroyed, doubt gets hold of the higher powers of the intellect and half paralyses all the others. . . . When there is no longer any principle of authority in religion any more than in politics, men are speedily frightened at the aspect of this unbounded independence. . . . For my own part, I doubt whether man can ever support at the same time complete religious independence and entire political freedom. And I am inclined to think that if faith be wanting in him, he must be subject, and if he be free, he must believe.[15]

Tocqueville doubted whether man can ever support at the same time complete independence from religion and entire political freedom. And, as Professor Pangle's essay points out, he notes the check to materialism that religion—not sectarianism or dogmatism—provides:

Most religions are only general, simple and practical means of teaching men the doctrine of the immortality of the soul. That is the greatest benefit which a democratic nation derives from its belief, and hence belief is more necessary to such a people than all others. When, therefore, any religion has struck its roots deep into a democracy beware that you do not disturb it; but rather watch it carefully, as the most precious bequest of aristocratic ages.[16]

---

14 As translated in the Henry Reeve text, and revised by Francis Bowen, with a historical essay by Phillips Bradley, ed. (New York: Vintage Books, 1945), 2:6–7.

15 Ibid., 2:22–23.

16 Ibid., 2:154–55.

The first part of the *Democracy* treats specific aspects of government and politics in America, including the federal Constitution and the workings of the federal government. Behind these more formal or structured elements of democratic government, Tocqueville explores such questions as the relations between religion and democracy.

Professor Pangle, who teaches political philosophy, is a mildly critical proponent of the ideas of Leo Strauss. In 1980, Pangle wrote: "It seems to me that Strauss points us toward a most helpful model for political allegiance in and to modern democracy. That model is Tocqueville." At that time and in that context, Pangle was interested in patriotism, loyalty, its wellsprings, as well as its usefulness in democratic society.[17]

In everything but law, the United States, at the opening of the twentieth century, was a Christian nation. Some states recognized Christianity as the official, though not the established, religion. Jurors were required to believe in God, teachers to read from the Bible, and in some states a religious observance of the "Lord's Day" was a legal obligation. "Almost a century earlier," historian Henry Steele Commager noted, "the perspicacious Tocqueville had remarked this unofficial establishment and rejoiced in it."

> There is no country in the whole world in which the Christian religion retains a greater influence over the souls of men than in America, and there can be no greater proof of its utility, and of its conformity to human nature, than that its influence is most powerfully felt over the most enlightened and free nation on earth. . . . In the United States religion exercises but little influence upon the laws and upon the details of public opinion, but it directs the manners of the community, and by regulating domestic life, it regulates the state.[18]

Tocqueville was an admirer of the democracy he found in America and he cherished it not so much because he found in it classical virtue or philosophy, but because he found there "the home of freedom," and of a Christianity that had finally come to terms with the human aspirations for earthly freedom and equality. "Freedom," as Pangle wrote earlier, "Tocqueville seems to have understood much as Thomas Jefferson and Clay and Lincoln understood it: not as subordinate to moral and contemplative virtue, but as an end to which these latter must themselves be subordinated."[19] In the essay which follows, Pangle uses Tocqueville as

---

17 Thomas Pangle, "Facing the Founders: Patriotism American Style," *National Review* (29 November 1985), 30–36.

18 Quoted in *The American Mind: An Interpretation of American Thought and Character Since the 1880s* (New Haven: Yale University Press, 1950), 163.

19 Thomas Pangle, 33.

his model for an analysis of religion in contemporary, as opposed to nineteenth-century American society.

The effect of pluralism on emerging constitutional values is nowhere better illustrated than in the sphere of church-state relations in the United States in the twentieth century. Although the First Amendment in the 1791 Bill of Rights was meant to protect freedom of religion, it also provided that the new American nation would not support a state church. As J. Woodford Howard, Jr. argues in his essay "The Robe and the Cloth," the religion clauses in the First Amendment, when carried to their logical conclusions, contradict each other, and long years of research have shown that the framers provided us with little information to help resolve this conflict.

For a variety of reasons, it was not until the twentieth century, and in a handful of cases that came to the Supreme Court after World War II, that the controversy surrounding the religion clauses began to ripen. Over the decades since then, church-state disputes in the United States have become a constitutional minefield. In their attempt to carve out a judicial policy in this troublesome area, the justices of the Supreme Court have spent lonely decades on the front line of American politics. More often than not their decisions have infuriated members of some or all denominations, secularists, logicians and legal craftsmen in the law schools. Many of the Court's more recent decisions can only be understood in *ad hoc* terms, i.e., as improvisations that are designed to hold the line until some new formulation can be consensually reached, until the issue goes away, or until a reluctant Congress decides to act.

In surveying the judiciary's treatment of these clauses in the twentieth century, Professor Howard finds the Supreme Court invariably reluctant to protect conduct based squarely on religious beliefs, other than that form of conduct involving free speech and freedom of the press—areas already protected by other clauses in the First Amendment. Turning to the Court's interpretation of the Establishment Clause, Howard finds Court doctrine not only controversial but confusing, as have many other Court observers. But he is sensitive to the multiple difficulties faced by the Court in these areas. Above all he recognizes that the Court has become a victim of historical discontinuity.[20]

Framers of the Constitution and the Bill of Rights simply could not have dreamed of, much less anticipated, how pluralistic American society was to become in the nineteenth and twentieth centuries, with their bewildering diversity of religious beliefs, the secularization of society,

---

20 Professor Howard's approach parallels that taken by Stephen Pepper in his essay, "The Constitution and Religious Pluralism," in Adolph H. Grundman, ed., *The Embattled Constitution* (Malabar, Fla.: Robert E. Krieger Co., 1986), 92–115.

and the intrusive nature of bureaucracy in American lives. When to all these are added the inherent conflict between the religion clauses and American misconceptions about the guarantees in the Bill of Rights, we can begin to appreciate the enormous complexity of the issues faced by the courts.

In recent decades the United States has been compared to the Roman Empire in the multiplicity of its religious sects.[21] In the beginning of the American democratic experiment there was the realization that diverse religions would require neutrality on the part of the federal government at least, if not the states, some of which still had a form of religious establishment until as late as 1833. In the early Republic, there was a certain candor displayed in extolling the virtues of religious toleration, but over the course of time sects continued to multiply and the United States came to exceed Rome in the minuteness of differences between them and in the scope of their elaborate organizations. Religion continued to flourish in the nation, but no particular religion has ever been in a position to dominate national life. The starting point in this, as in many other areas, has been diversity.

In its task of construing the First Amendment guarantees of religious freedom, the Supreme Court is obliged to confront the perplexing problem of determining what society may or may not do with "the disruptive messenger from God."[22] One solution that might have served in a limited number of cases was to apply the sanctions of the common law. In some instances this was done, and when it was, the religious zealot was treated as a public nuisance. Repudiation of the applicable sections of the criminal and civil codes as contrary to divine revelation was overruled, most notably in *Reynolds* v. *United States* (1879). In this case the polygamous rites of Mormons were ruled to be violations of the law regulating civil marriages. In the post-Civil War era, the United States Supreme Court found no constitutional protection for "crime masquerading as religion."[23]

In this century, the modern Supreme Court has tended to fashion accommodations between the rights of the community to peace and order and the right of the proselyte to the free exercise of religious belief. Jehovah's Witnesses are one of many groups to have benefited from this approach. The Court has ruled that Witness children are exempt from the compulsory flag salute in public schools, though not for strictly religious reasons, but rather because the practice can be regarded as an unconstitu-

---

21 Daniel J. Boorstin, *The Genius of American Politics* (Chicago: University of Chicago Press, 1953), 134–35.

22 John P. Roche, *Courts and Rights: The American Judiciary in Action* (New York: Random House, 1966), 79.

23 Ibid., 80. *Reynolds* v. *United States*, 98 U.S. 145 (1879).

tional regulation of thought.[24] Furthermore, it has been ruled that Witnesses can be restrained from ringing doorbells only if the homeowner has tacked up a "Do not disturb" sign on his door.[25]

As a general principle, the First Amendment forbids Congress (and, after the ratification of the Fourteenth Amendment, the states) either to favor or to penalize any single religious body in the enactment of public policy. However, in the effort to prevent religious organizations from becoming the intended beneficiaries of legislation, the principle has often been compromised beyond recognition. As John Roche explains:

> The Court . . . strains without much success to avoid granting special benefits to religious groups *per se*. In the nature of things, it is extremely difficult effectively to protect free exercise of religion without vaulting the wall separating church and state. It is particularly difficult if special benefits to religious bodies are defined as establishments of religion. In a sense, the only way out for the Court is to grant tacit protection to religion by safeguarding the more comprehensive freedom of speech (or silence).[26]

The Court's rulings in religion cases reflect the ambivalence of the country on church-state problems. In its attempt to protect the rights of proselytizing religious groups, it has developed a jurisprudence of disingenuous accommodations or exemptions from the police power of local communities. And at the same time it tries to protect the crusading rights of the anti-religious. Nonbelievers, basing their case on the supposedly secular import of the First Amendment, have been successful in recent times in persuading the Court to end prayer in the public schools, and when the New York State Board of Regents attempted to formulate a nonsectarian prayer (in effect addressed "To Whom it May Concern"), it too was invalidated as an unwarranted intrusion by the state into the realm of religion.[27] In yet another case, the Court struck down readings from the Bible in Maryland public schools, even those from the Old Testament.[28]

Most controversial of all is the ancient and ongoing battle over public support for religiously oriented schools, a growing concern in Canada, as well as in the United States. In the Canadian constitutional order, there is no separation of church and state; in several provinces, parochial

---

24 *West Virginia State Board of Education* v. *Barnette*, 319 U.S. 624 (1943). Witnesses claim that flag saluting is a divinely proscribed form of idol worship.

25 *Martin* v. *Struthers*, 319 U.S. 141 (1943).

26 Roche, *Courts and Rights*, 80.

27 *Engel* v. *Vitale*, 370 U.S. 421 (1962).

28 *Abington School District* v. *Schempp*, 374 U.S. 203 (1963).

schools are tax-supported at approximately the same levels as the public schools. Prayer in the public schools, however, has fared no better in Canada than in the United States; in 1992, Manitoba became the last holdout to strike down publicly mandated prayer in public schools.

In the United States, compromises were made during the administration of Lyndon B. Johnson, when the federal government moved more boldly than in the past to support the educational objectives of religious schools and colleges—while at the same time assuming it was possible to differentiate between educational and religious goals. Thus, one Court ruling held that state-supplied movie projectors could be used for instruction in parochial schools for science but not for religious teaching. Although the logic supporting such distinctions may have been somewhat tenuous, the question remained: how could anyone achieve standing to challenge the constitutionality of these benign, well-intentioned statutes?[29] Nevertheless, it soon became clear that one must never underestimate the resourcefulness of those wishing to make court challenges.

Professor Howard concludes his essay by offering some interesting and valuable suggestions that may help both courts and the American people to work their way through this constitutional maze. On essentials, however, he refrains from holding out any hope that there will ever be any settled meaning of the religion clauses in the First Amendment. The most that can be hoped for is that the courts will intelligently mediate between the objectives of the various religious groups in American society in this complex part of its culture.

II. FEDERALISM IN CANADA AND THE UNITED STATES

According to nearly all critics of the American framers, the supreme achievement of the federal Constitution was the duality of the system of government which it created—"an indestructible Union composed of indestructible states." The Constitution made an apportionment of governmental powers and functions between nation and states, on the principle of local government for local affairs and general government for general affairs only, and to preserve the equilibrium thus established, it created a Supreme Court. This duality, thus safeguarded in the document, was the novel feature which, more than any other, differentiated the new system from previous experiments in popular government. It offered the most promising solution as yet devised in any scheme of government for the problem of building a nation without at the same time tearing down local self-government.

---

29 Roche, *Courts and Rights*, 83. For a fuller treatment of these issues, see Leo Pfeffer, *Church, State and Freedom* (Boston, 1967).

The Canadian scheme of powersharing provides for a federal or con-federational form of government, dividing powers between a central government in Ottawa and provincial governments in a manner that gives substantial power to each. The initial novelty, federalism, it is generally conceded, is an American invention considered the most important contribution made by the American founders to the science of government. It is woven into the constitutions not only of Canada, but also of Mexico, India, Australia, Germany, and Switzerland. Federalism is America's primary government export.

As **JENNIFER SMITH** sets forth in her essay, when Canadians sat down in the mid–1860s to design their federal state, this and other aspects of the American Constitution were considered, and were regarded as impor-tant, but the American brand of federalism was looked upon as not necessarily one of its positive aspects or points of reference in the consti-tutional deliberations of the Fathers of Confederation. As Roger Gibbins notes, "the mere precedence of the American Constitution ensured Amer-ican influences in the Canadian debates, even if those influences were largely negative in character" (p. 132).

Gibbins makes an important distinction when he points out that while both societies opted for a federal form of government, in the Amer-ican case "federalism fit comfortably within, and indeed in some respects was a reflection of, other constitutional principles, such as the separation of powers embraced by the Founding Fathers. In the Canadian case, the adoption of federalism was a matter of necessity rather than choice, and the fit with other constitutional principles such as parliamentary suprem-acy and responsible government has never been an easy one" (p. 132n.5). This distinction will help to dispel for some the confusion, if not the complexity, in the parallel developments in adoption of federal arrange-ments.

Professor Smith's essay offers a new interpretation of the emergence of federalism in the Canadian constitution and explains the reasons behind the reluctance of its framers to adopt the American model as it had functioned (or malfunctioned) prior to 1860. The essay offers a helpful analysis of the contending interpretations developed by Canadian historians and political scientists in their reading of the 1864–67 debates and delegates' pronouncements.

The model forming the core of this essay is an interesting one. The views of the Canadian framers are measured against James Madison's conception of federalism, as set forth in *The Federalist*, No. 39.[30] The American founders had in mind creating a republic, a new form of representative government with a complicated set of restraints on the majority, indicating their basic distrust of popular majorities. Among those restraints was the division of governmental powers between the national and state governments, and the separation of power among the three branches—legislative, executive and judicial. The framers of the 1787 Constitution resolved the crisis of state legislative excesses during the years following the Revolution by erecting a new layer of government at the national level to form a counterweight to the power of the states and to restrict them in substantial ways. The framers were confronted by the problem of the existence of the thirteen states as powerful sovereignties. They got around this problem by denying certain powers to the states while giving broad powers to the federal government to encourage national integration and union. As Madison explained, the guiding principle of the constitutional convention was to provide a republican remedy for the "diseases most incident to republican government."[31]

Jennifer Smith's choice of the Madison model is a happy one. He was the first to recognize that the government created at Philadelphia was "partly national, and partly federal." That two authentic levels of government could exist in the same geographic area, resting on the same constituencies, was not only novel for the time but impossible to conceive of under older theories of sovereignty. It was the British conviction emphatically that sovereignty is indivisible. Federalism seemed a suspect principle, an arrangement that encouraged dissension, not unity. Critics dismissed it as illogical, as "a government within a government," which denied all reason. But this was precisely what was provided for in American federalism, and it was the doctrine of popular sovereignty that made it possible. If created by and for the people, state and federal governments could legislate and govern concurrently over the same population and territory. The differences between the two kinds of government lay in the purposes and powers assigned to each. Thus the compound scheme embodying the characteristics both of a confederation and a unitary government was to be the American answer to the problem of sovereignty.

Madison's *The Federalist*, No. 39 provided the most cogent argument on behalf of the proposed Constitution with the built-in federal arrange-

---

30 Alexander Hamilton, John Jay and James Madison, *The Federalist* (New York: Modern Library, 1937). This collection of eighty-five essays was written in support of the 1787 Constitution. The essays were influential in securing its adoption and in shaping later interpretations of it.

31 Alfred H. Kelly, Winfred A. Harbison and Herman Belz, *The American Constitution: Its Origins and Development* (New York: W.W. Norton, 1983), 91.

ment. A few specific powers were to be withdrawn from the states, but in general, he explained, they would retain their sovereign authority. On the other hand, the central government would blend the character of a unitary national government with the characteristics of a confederation, giving the states as distinct a role as possible in the new constitutional order.

It is well to remember that the chief purpose of *The Federalist* was to allay the apprehensions of state-minded men and to secure adoption of the new Constitution. Madison tried to assure them that the government would be a confederation as far as the source of its power was concerned. Ratification of the Constitution would rest firmly on the consent of "the people of America," which Madison said meant the people as citizens of the separate states rather than of a unitary nation.

The powers possessed by members of the House of Representatives rested directly on popular election, deriving their legitimacy from a unitary model, while those of the Senate, whose members were then chosen by state legislatures, derived their authority from the confederation model. Executive power derives from both through the electoral college. The new government combined characteristics of both types, yet its supporters referred to it as a federal plan, thus giving a new meaning to the term "federal." No one at the time knew the effect it would have on the states, or how future conflicts between the states and the federal government would be resolved.

The final answer came in 1861 with the outbreak of the Civil War. To the Fathers of Canadian Confederation, and especially John A. Macdonald, time and events had revealed grave defects in the American scheme, chief among them the relationships between the national and state governments. Macdonald identified state sovereignty as the weak link in the American Constitution and ultimately as the source of the Civil War. All in all, the events in the decades between 1830 and 1860 to the south provided an unfortunate prelude to the Canadian Confederation debates of 1864–67, and in the light of that experience the outcome of those debates, as described in Professor Smith's essay, is understandable.

In his essay on "Federalism in a North American Context," KENNETH HOLLAND opens the lens of observation and analysis to a wider angle to include Mexico along with the United States and Canada in assessing the contribution of the supreme courts of the three countries and the various conceptions of their respective federal arrangements as articulated by them. His overall purpose is to reflect on the effect their contemporary jurisprudence will have on the impending North American Free Trade Agreement (NAFTA), if it is ratified by the legislatures of the three countries. He ponders the question: Will it inhibit or facilitate the realization of the continental vision?

With the slow but steady evolution of the European Economic Community from a common market toward a political and military union, the question in many minds is: Will this lead in the coming decades to the economic and political integration of its counterpart in North America? Whether or not it is possible to give any plausible answer to this question, Kenneth Holland's thesis maintains that the history of federalism in Canada, Mexico and the United States shows how any movement toward economic and political union will inevitably be affected by the federal arrangements in each of the North American democracies. Using the supreme courts and their rulings as a model provides a unique approach in exploring those conceptions of the federal arrangement which pose greater obstacles to continental integration than do others.

He begins by recounting the six phases through which the U.S. Supreme Court's doctrinal approach to federalism in the United States has passed in the time since Chief Justice John Marshall first put the stamp of his judicial nationalism on that body. Always in the pursuit of the correct formula, the Court's doctrinal development has sought the proper balance under federalism between the exercise of powers within their proper sphere by state and national governments.

Professor Holland then treats the development of federalism in Canada, moving quickly over ground covered by Jennifer Smith in her discussion of its origins. Holland concludes that English-speaking Canadians at the outset showed no enthusiasm for the American federal system, preferring instead a modified version of the British unitary system of government. Like Americans before them, however, including Madison, Canadian centralists had to compromise their vision in order to win the participation in Confederation of French-speaking Quebec and the Maritime provinces. While it is true to say that a federal system was established within the *Constitution Act, 1867*, it was one with a far more powerful central government than the one established by Americans in 1787.

From that point on, the American and Canadian systems began to evolve in opposite directions. The trend in Canadian politics to concede more and more powers to the provinces was assisted by the judiciary in Britain, while in the United States the judicial nationalism of John Marshall and the tensions generated by southern secessionist agitation resulted first in the conflict of the 1860s and, subsequent to it, greater dominance over national affairs by the government in Washington than would have been possible to exert over the once powerful states in a loosely structured union.

The power of judicial review reverted to the Supreme Court of Canada from Great Britain's Judicial Committee of the Privy Council after

1949. Quebec then launched a campaign to check any future Supreme Court decisions which would in effect enhance federal power at the expense of the provinces. Changes were sought in the appointment process, giving Quebec three of the nine justices. Holland asserts that, as Quebecers feared, the Court supported federal over provincial claims in disputes over taxation, labor, commerce and economic planning. The role of the Canadian high court after 1949 he finds analogous to the nationalizing mission pursued by the U.S. Supreme Court in its formative years under the influence of Justices John Marshall and William Story.

But the agitation for decentralization (in particular by Quebec) continued unabated, taking Canada through one constitutional crisis after another up to the present. The Supreme Court bowed to this movement to a degree in the 1970s: in a majority of cases to which it was a party, Quebec won out from 1960 to 1975. During the same period, Holland states, the Supreme Court of Canada began to follow a more centralist approach with regard to the other provinces. This uneven treatment was the result of separatist threats from Quebec.

A clear line of demarcation in these trends is traceable to the initiatives taken by the Trudeau government to repatriate the constitution, culminating in the *Constitution Act, 1982*. Again the Supreme Court changed course and supported the federal government in this new move toward centralization. Meanwhile Quebec sovereigntists failed to win a majority in the 1980 referendum. In subsequent years, the Court has served as a brake on the movement toward province-building, and it became increasingly involved in cases interpreting the 1982 *Canadian Charter of Rights and Freedoms*. Now it became the Court's role to impose constitutional restraints on both the provinces *and* the federal government. As events would later prove, the Supreme Court of Canada showed itself to be even bolder than its U.S. and Mexican counterparts in striking down provincial acts.

Mexico, beginning with its constitution of 1824, followed the U.S. constitutional model more closely than Canada or most other countries, and from the outset emulated the liberalism they associated with it. The difficulty was with the instability of succeeding Mexican governments, beginning with the movement toward centralization of the 1830s which precipitated rebellion, the annexation of Texas by the United States, and the war which followed. However, the commitment to federalism survived the political and military turmoil of these and ensuing decades to become a basic feature of the 1917 constitution.

This is not to say, however, that there was thereafter smooth sailing toward a mutually agreeable division of powers between the two levels of government. Instability and endemic poverty are as characteristic of recent times as is a tendency for great power to be concentrated in the executive. In spite of this, the courts have to a large extent been able to maintain their independence and have been a force contributing to the evolution of a more healthy federal-state balance. Since the 1930s, however, the Court's independence has been adversely affected, with the advent of limited terms for justices, and in recent years the judiciary has seldom attempted to invalidate any major action by an incumbent president.

The future of NAFTA is as yet unsettled, but the need for hemispheric cooperation and the liberalization of trade policies will persist, whatever the outcome. As Kenneth Holland asserts, the increasing integration of Mexico and Canada into the international economy, and especially the economy of the United States, will proceed even if NAFTA is not achieved for all three powers.

We live in an age of rapid change and shifting loyalties. Some American critics are questioning the utility of federalism and, in pointing out the numerous flaws in the way it operates, are even suggesting its abandonment. These essays demonstrate that the task of maintaining a working balance between centralized and local power is formidable. They should also lead us to a less harsh assessment of a system that has worked reasonably well over the course of two centuries or more. In its essence federalism presupposes a constantly shifting and evolving pattern of relationships. As Holland's essay reveals, courts can play important roles as umpires in the inevitable conflicts that will arise and might also contribute to a deeper understanding of the nature and possibilities of the peculiarly complex federal arrangement.

III. THE POLITICS OF RIGHTS

In one fashion or another, the essays in this section, and others in this volume, underscore the extent to which Canada's *Constitution Act, 1982* and especially its *Canadian Charter of Rights and Freedoms* represent the profoundly different relationship that now exists between Canadians and their governments, as opposed to that which existed in the constitutional arrangements that they replaced, particularly federalism and parliamentary supremacy. In his essay, **F.L. (TED) MORTON** exposes to sharp scrutiny what he calls "the *Charter* myth" and its genesis in this comparative view of American rights-oriented jurisprudence. In an attempt to counter arguments which he considers inaccurate and misleading about constitutionalism and judicial review in the American context, he begins by surveying the evolution of judicial review in the United States, in the process offering ample evidence to show that it is not always exercised for benevolent purposes. The American Supreme Court has not always used its awesome power to champion the weak or the oppressed, nor has it always acted as a powerful agent of social reform. Here he effectively exposes "the darker, neglected side of American constitutional experience" in order to demystify "the heroic model" of the United States Supreme Court. His ultimate purpose is to chasten the misrepresentations of the "*Charter* myth."

The original role of the American Supreme Court was conservative, Morton argues, at least in a technical sense. It has been represented as being politically neutral, "conserving" traditionally recognized rights and freedoms. But that role has changed over time, if it ever really existed. The beginning of that change appeared in the post-Civil War years when the newly ratified Fourteenth Amendment provided the Court with the new instrument of "substantive due process" which was applied to the defense of corporate capitalism and private property rights as against regulatory reforms advocated by state legislatures, populists and progressive reformers. For Morton, this anti-reform bias serves as an object lesson in the consequences to be expected from a "politicization of the courts."

Next he treats the core issue of his essay—"the politics of rights." What the introduction of the *Charter* means to Canadian constitutionalism is not so much that it "guarantees" rights, old or new, but that it creates new ways to make decisions about rights in which the courts play a much more influential role. For Canadians, this means a major change in their legal and constitutional system—a new role for the judiciary. Previously, Canadian judges were largely responsible for the interpretation of the laws, and while that responsibility did not change, in and of itself, what really was occurring was a usurpation of the fundamental constitutional doctrine of parliamentary supremacy. Now the final say on *Charter* rights and legislative policy rests with the judiciary under s. 52 of the *Constitution Act, 1982*. What the Canadians achieved in judicial autonomy in 1949, in contrast to the previous arrangement of having parliamentary legislation subjected to review by the Judicial Committee of the Privy Council in Britain, was now transcended by a judicial centrality in the whole constitutional process. Canadians were beginning to grasp what Associate Justice Oliver Wendell Holmes had asserted long ago: courts do and must legislate.

This creation of a new locus of power in the political and constitutional system—the courts—has the effect of attracting interest groups looking for ways to influence public policy. In the American context, as Morton explains, this phenomenon has been appropriately described as the "politics of rights." Interest groups, he states, recast their policy goals in the rhetoric of rights, and then take them to the courts to be "enforced." Such a "politics of rights" was not possible in Canada prior to the entrenchment of the *Charter* in 1982. Its adoption opened the way for interest groups in Canada, adapting to American-style pressure tactics, to employ litigation to promote their objectives, which are often political. As a follow-up to this, Morton shows how in the politicization of the judiciary, as judges become more adept in the use of their interpretive discretion to change public policy, intense interest develops (as is now the case in the United States) in who is appointed to the bench. In recent years, the political struggles over judicial appointments in the United States have reached a new level of unseemliness. This American trend has not as yet carried over into Canada, but it sounds a warning about the price that might be exacted for using the courts as vehicles for political reform.

The final section of Morton's essay discusses the adoption of the "living constitution" or "living tree" analogy in the Canadian approach to interpreting the *Charter*. In this connection it is worth pointing out that neither the federal *Interpretation Act* nor its provincial counterpart are binding on the interpretation of a constitution. They might be persuasive, but will not be viewed as binding. It would be similarly pointless to rely on the *United Kingdom Interpretation Act*, in view of the symbolic significance of the act of patriation. These acts may be persuasive or relevant, but none are binding. Therefore, the judicial branch is free to proceed on its own instincts rather than be bound by any one particular instrument in interpreting the constitution.

One of the most important aspects of interpreting the new *Charter* was the question: What precedents are relevant and receivable by Canadian courts? Since there are language similarities between the *Charter* and the *Canadian Bill of Rights* of 1960, existing jurisprudence under it is relevant. In sections, the *Charter's* language is similar to the American Bill of Rights, which means that American jurisprudence and legal precedents are also relevant. In addition, certain clauses in the *Charter* that derive from international instruments (the United Nations Charter of 1945 and its Declaration of Human Rights of 1948) even make it possible for European precedents to assist a court in interpreting *Charter* provisions. An ongoing support for constitutionally entrenched rights, manifested earlier in John Diefenbaker's weak *Canadian Bill of Rights* of 1960, and much more decisively in the 1982 *Charter*, have thus made it inevitable that the United States Supreme Court and American jurisprudence will acquire a prominence for Canadians that has not existed before. This is what Roger Gibbins has in mind presumably when he discusses in his essay the ways in which the *Charter* opened up the Canadian constitution to American constitutional theory and experience. In order to conform to the "living tree" analogy, constitutions and their meaning must change as society changes, and the responsibility for bringing a constitution abreast of modern conditions is in large part vested in judges.

What parallels can be drawn between the "living tree" analogy as it is applied in Canada and the "living constitution/noninterpretivist" doctrine unfolding in American constitutionalism? Morton goes on to complete his analysis by demonstrating how different the two approaches appear in practice, and how central a role the latter doctrine has played in widening the rift in the United States in the liberal/conservative conflict over judicial selection and interpretation. Nor is there any likelihood that the advocates of original intent will retrieve the field any more than will progressive jurists counselling judicial self-restraint and deference to Congress—the original meaning of the "living constitution" doctrine in the United States. Morton concludes that in view of all this Canadians should rethink the application of the "living tree" doctrine to the *Charter* in light of the parallel American experience.

Roger Gibbins approaches his comparison of Canadian constitutional development with parallel American constitutional experience from a different perspective. He casts a wider net than other contributors to this volume in his comparison of the two societies and governmental structures in their contemporary aspect. His survey embraces cultural and economic as well as constitutional and legal practices. He admits that American constitutional principles have left a world-wide imprint on the evolution of democratic politics. It follows that there are certainly reflections of American constitutionalism in the historical evolution of the Canadian federal state.

However, in taking a closer look at the contours of political life in Canada, he shows that reflections of the American constitutional experience before the events of the 1980s are hard to find. Surveying the years from Confederation to the adoption of the *Charter*, Gibbins concludes that, during all that long period of development, Canadians have not generally been receptive to American political norms, institutions and values. They have been loath to borrow politically from the United States for a number of reasons, cultural as well as constitutional, and this has been the case even when American political experience may have been of some value or relevance. Broadly defined, contemporary Canadian society already reflects things American to an extensive (and, in the eyes of many Canadians, an alarming) degree. The message here is clear: there has been a decided determination in high quarters to keep American political and constitutional influences at arm's length.

The centerpiece of this essay is his examination of the course of Canadian constitutional change since 1945 and his attempt to determine to what extent that course has evolved in response to constitutional principles or developments imported from the United States. This section marshals evidence to establish that Canada and the United States were much more distinctive politically than in other ways, especially in the period following World War II. In this era American influence on political life in Canada was far more apparent than real. And during the long period of destabilization and debate that ensued, the Canadian constitutional system seems to have remained surprisingly immune from American influence.

The two countries, of course, are governed within a federal structure, and federalism remained a common element during this time. However, the post–1945 period transformed the two societies as a result of new postwar challenges and developments. This resulted in a blurring of the lines of authority and an obscuration of the former divisions of power in both federal systems.

Gibbins' argument insists that this parallel experience with federalism did not display similarities; on the contrary, the differences were in every respect stark. Fiscal federalism, the vigorous nationalist movement spawned in Quebec, and a spate of regional and intergovernmental conflicts were peculiar to Canada. They changed the face of Canadian society, producing tensions which found their expression in a prolonged constitutional debate that, beginning in the 1960s, has been carried through almost without interruption into the 1990s. In the words of Canadian novelist Robertson Davies: "This constitutional debate is our version of civil war. But dowdy and dispiriting though it may appear, it is the struggle for the nation's soul."

From its origins, American federalism has been significantly different from both the Australian and Canadian systems. The American states, in addition to their obligations under the Constitution's Article IV, ss. 1 and 2, are under other constraints. Since the Civil War, they are forbidden to settle their differences by force. Disputes are to be settled either by the Supreme Court or by an interstate compact, i.e., an agreement through which two or more states with a common problem establish a legally binding relationship aimed at a common solution. Before these compacts become effective, they must be approved by Congress, after which they are reinforceable by the Supreme Court.

Franklin Roosevelt's successor, Harry Truman, is the only one of the nine American presidents from 1945 through to Ronald Reagan who did not try to promote what has been called "the new federalism." And yet, with all the expenditure of effort and fanfare, what resulted as an end product remained substantially the same. "*Plus ça change, plus c'est la même chose.*" This was at least true so far as the basic structure was concerned. Competitive and dual federalism were replaced after 1937 by what political scientists in the United States called "picket fence federalism." The growth of big government, with the great welfare bureaucracy created by the New Deal, resulted in government at all levels—federal, state and local—pursuing common interests that often differed from those of elected officials. Each picket evidently was meant to represent some government policy on social welfare, highways, etc. Here, as in Canada, lines were blurred, for the pickets overlapped the respective spheres of national, state and local government.

In the meantime, and within this development, the seeds of cooperative federalism were beginning to sprout, and it bloomed in the 1960s and 1970s with a myriad of federal grant programs whose value rose by 1980 to $90 billion. Funding came from the federal government, while execution and administration remained in the hands of state and local governments.

All the while, the role of the national government in the federal system continued to inflate and expand until the administration of President Reagan, who, it appeared, was intent on spearheading a retreat from national government expansion, dictated in part by ideology and in large part by shrinking financial resources. The rationale behind decentralization was the administration's conviction that state and local governments needed strengthening. If Canadians took any notice at all of these developments, there can be little wonder that the shifting approaches held little appeal for them. The complex and diffused system of government provided by the American federal system led to serious questioning of its value among Americans themselves. Its intricate and ambiguous nature sometimes causes governmental confusion. And, as Roger Gibbins points out in his essay, in Canada, flux in the federal state was being driven throughout this time by a constitutional agenda that bore little if any resemblance to the problems being faced in the United States.

But it was the felt need for repatriation of the constitution, high on the agenda of the Trudeau Liberal government, that resulted in the proclamation in April 1982 of the *Constitution Act*, which marked the culmination of at least one phase of the constitutional debate. Up to this time that debate had featured the victory of the separatist Parti Québécois in 1976, the 1980 sovereignty-association referendum, and echoes of angry regional discord. The intense debate did not draw extensively from American models or experience in other countries, mainly because it addressed distinctively Canadian problems of power arrangements and national unity. However, after a brief lull, the debate was renewed in a more intensive form than ever, because the *Constitution Act, 1982* was silent on a number of controversial issues and on the burning question of Quebec's position within the Canadian federal state.

The *Canadian Charter of Rights and Freedoms* entrenched in the *Constitution Act, 1982*, whether intentionally or not, did inject American constitutionalism into Canadian constitutional culture and political life. Gibbins notes, rights were infused into the Canadian constitution and political discourse: "There is little question that it was the American constitutional ethos, and not that of other countries, which influenced the Canadian *Charter*."

If the *Charter* came to Canada largely by way of the United States, as Alan Cairns and others maintain, what then are the implications for future Canadian constitutional development? Will the rights entrenched in the *Charter* serve over the long run to "harmonize" Canadian and American political cultures? This seems even more likely, since the proposed North American Free Trade Agreement simultaneously promises to integrate the economies of the two countries, along with that of Mexico, in a closer association than has ever been known before. There are already signs that Canada is becoming more like the open society that the United States has long claimed to be. The vast American experience with the interplay of constitutional rights and public policy will, at least in a selective or limited way, inevitably be brought into play as diverse groups in Canada pursue political ends through judicial means, and as both lawyers and judges attempt to sort out the implications of the *Charter* for political life and public policy.

And finally, as Peter Russell argues in the concluding essay in this volume, and as Roger Gibbins makes clear, the *Charter* has provided a shift in the Canadian constitutional culture towards an acceptance of popular sovereignty, as citizens come to see the constitution as *theirs*, rather than as the exclusive property of federal and provincial governments and their surrogates. An increased citizen participation and reduced deference to governments and elites is seen as a healthy trend that will bring Canadian constitutional culture more in line with that in the United States. Whether or not this will be the main consequence of recent developments remains to be seen, but it is already clear that this change is at least partly responsible for the narrow defeat of the Meech Lake Accord of 1987, and the more resounding referendum defeat of the Charlottetown Accord of 1992, both of which Gibbins discusses in his essay.

Gibbins traces the decline (from the mid–1950s into the 1990s) of Canadian society's interest in a constitutional system that was almost exclusively governmental in character and suggests a more positive receptivity to American constitutional theory and practice. The 1982 *Charter* makes it virtually inevitable that the U.S. Supreme Court's example and American jurisprudence will acquire a more practical prominence for Canadians, something that Canadian constitutional life had previously lacked. Such a development implies that Canadian constitutional scholarship will become more comparative than it already is, with a growing emphasis on American experience.

One other root cause which it is believed has enhanced Canadian appreciation of American constitutional theory and practice springs from efforts to uncover some structural reason for the constitutional malaise which has been generating irresistible pressures for decentralization and devolution. Some thinkers, Donald Smiley among them, have argued that the crucial flaw in Canadian constitutional arrangements is the inability of the central government to represent, accommodate and tame provincial particularisms. Roger Gibbins is the most notable recent exponent of a view that sees the American congressional system, with its absence of a tight party discipline, as a useful means of facilitating interregional brokerage, thus strengthening the central government where such bargaining must originate.[32]

A resurgent provincialism, particularly in the western provinces of Canada, stimulated new interest in the capacity for regional accommodation of American congressional arrangements, a movement which in one form is pressing for reform of the Canadian Senate to make it more effective and provide for election rather than appointment of senators. Such a reform would help to eliminate some of the worst features of under-representation and regional disparities in the country. These and other developments discussed elsewhere in these essays and in related works make the theory and practice of American constitutionalism far more relevant to the kinds of constitutional choices confronting Canadians today than has ever been the case in the past.

IV. The Judiciary and Public Policy Issues

Once Canada's *Constitution Act, 1982*, with the *Charter* entrenched in it, went into effect, more attention than ever was focused on the Supreme Court of Canada. That is so in spite of the fact that for almost half a century, since appeals to Britain's Privy Council were abolished, the Supreme Court has been the court of last resort for the country. Yet until fairly recently, little has been known about the Court, in part because nominees to it face no confirmation process as do American Supreme Court nominees, and in part because of the nature of the Canadian political system prior to 1982.

In an interview in 1980, former Associate Justice Louis-Philippe Pigeon, stepping down after twelve years on the Supreme Court of Canada, discussed the reasons for some of the differences between the American and Canadian Supreme Courts.[33] Most Canadians in his day knew very little about the Supreme Court of Canada. They were unable to identify any of the justices and were unfamiliar with its work. Asked why this was so, Justice Pigeon blamed the media for ignoring the Court.

---

32 Cf. Donald Smiley, "The Structural Problem of Canadian Federalism," *Canadian Public Administration* 14 (1971), 326–43; and Roger Gibbins, *Regionalism: Territorial Politics in Canada and the United States* (Toronto: Butterworths, 1982). For a more general survey of the intrastate analysis, see Donald V. Smiley and Ronald L. Watts, *Interstate Federalism in Canada*, vol. 39 of the research studies of the Royal Commission on the Economic Union and Development Prospects for Canada (Toronto, 1985). See also Alan C. Cairns' essay, "International Influences on the Charter," in *Charter versus Federalism: The Dilemmas of Constitutional Reform* (Montreal: McGill-Queen's University Press, 1992), 22–23.

33 Interview, "The Highest Court North of the Border," *National Law Journal*, 2 June 1980, 13.

At that time there was not a single reporter covering the work of the Court, and, when appointments were made to it, they were treated as items of regional and not national news.

Another reason cited was the reputation the Court then had for making very narrow adjudications rather than taking the kind of activist or public policy approach then associated with the work of the U.S. Supreme Court. Nor were judgments of the American Court drafted in the same style as those of the Canadian high court.

Justice Pigeon went on to complain that there had been very little in the way of scholarly literature produced about the Court. "Academics are those who write scholarly works, and the academics generally have had a low opinion of the court. Most of them, in fact, have nothing but contempt." These were hard words, and, when Justice Pigeon was encouraged to elaborate on them, he went on to argue that academics admired the U.S. Supreme Court "and because we don't follow the same rules, the Canadian Supreme court doesn't measure up to their standards."[34]

If any part of this indictment of the media and academics is justified, much of what Justice Pigeon said back in 1980 has since changed dramatically and irrevocably. Even though the Supreme Court of Canada had for years been making judgments affecting virtually every part of Canadian life, its power and exposure to public attention and scrutiny has never been more evident than it became in the 1980s. In the fall of 1981, in the Constitutional Appeals, the Court delivered a landmark decision in which separate majorities held that the Trudeau government's constitutional proposals were legal, but violated convention. The *Constitution Act, 1982* came into being when, as a direct outgrowth of these decisions, the federal proposals were modified and the support of every province except Quebec was obtained. With it, of course, came the *Canadian Charter of Rights and Freedoms*, and constitutional and jurisprudential life in Canada would never be the same again.

No one has a better vantage point from which to observe and comment on the increasingly important and public nature of the Court's work than one of its sitting justices. **MADAME JUSTICE L'HEUREUX-DUBÉ** here offers the observations and comments of someone who has been a witness to and a participant in the exercise of the Court's new power during one of the most critical periods in its history. Before 1982, the Supreme Court of Canada functioned more or less in accordance with the prevailing notions of British constitutionalism. In former times, the role of the Court was a limited one; a good deal of its time was spent in very ordinary litigation. For example, any person who had more than $10,000 involved in a judgment had an automatic right to appeal to this Court.

---

34 Ibid.

Only subsequently have members of the Court instituted the leave-to-appeal right across the board.

In another interview, two years later, Mr. Justice Ronald Martland commented hesitatingly on the direction that court decisions had already begun to take on issues involving the 1960 *Canadian Bill of Rights*. (In *The Queen* v. *Drybones*, a 1970 case, the Court had ruled that the *Bill of Rights* overrode a federal law inconsistent with it.) Justice Martland was asked what happens when the popular will is manifestly unfair. If the judge's primary role is to adjudicate the case before him or her, and not to adopt a sort of legislative approach, how then are minorities protected? His reply took this form:

> Under the British parliamentary system . . . if the legislature of the day enacts legislation that may be unfair to the minority, or that fails to protect its position, our task is to deal with that legislation. It has to be applied, and we can't refuse to apply it merely because we don't like it.[35]

He referred directly to the extent to which individual judges feel they are endowed with a measure of legislative power and questioned whether they have a licence by means of judicial decision to create law. He added: "I rather share the view that it is not the task of judges to make law, but essentially it's to apply it as it exists, and leave it to the people's elected representatives to determine whether or not they want change."[36]

That same year, now recognized as a watershed in Canadian constitutional development, the people spoke, and their new constitution and *Charter* indicated they wanted change. As Madame Justice L'Heureux-Dubé points out, the result of that change was the new direction taken by the Supreme Court. It now began to hold legislation up against strict norms. And in engaging in this process of judicial review in the American mode, the Court may now invalidate legislation which, for one reason or another, does not pass muster against those norms.

Through selected examples in constitutional adjudication (issues of justiciability, cases involving imported doctrines of "political questions," free speech, affirmative action, etc.), she attempts to throw light upon the similarities and differences in the functionings of the two Supreme Courts and the manner in which each performs its tasks. The differences she uncovers are traced in part to the type of constitutional document each of the two courts is required to interpret and apply. Interestingly, the explicit authority given to the Supreme Court of Canada to undertake the

---

35 "The View from Inside the Supreme Court of Canada," interview with William Monopoli, senior editor for Legal Affairs, *The Financial Post*, 27 March 1982. *The Queen* v. *Drybones* [1970] S.C.R. 282.

36 Ibid.

process of judicial review is set in sharp contrast to the absence of such explicit authority in the American Constitution. This omission has been the subject in the United States of intensive (and endless) research into its historical origins and the intent of the framers, but it is now generally agreed that a majority of the delegates at the Philadelphia convention were in favor of judicial review and evidently believed that it was implied in the language used in the document, especially in Articles III and VI.

Along with other commentators in this volume, Madame Justice L'Heureux-Dubé reiterates how the *Charter* has altered the function of Canada's Supreme Court so that it no longer conforms, as it once did, to the British model under which Parliament, and not the judiciary, decided how the competing interests of the state and the individual are to be resolved. After 1982, the judiciary became the recognized guardian of the constitution. It is clear from the early jurisprudence that the Supreme Court of Canada was destined to play an unprecedented role in the life of the country. One sign of the new relationship with the American Supreme Court was revealed in the fact that Justices Estey and Dickson felt comfortable in quoting with approbation from Chief Justice Marshall's decision in *McCulloch* v. *Maryland*, and approved the constitutional approach advocated in it.[37] Such cross-border use of cases and precedents can be expected to increase over time.

With the advent of the Charter, the Court's role has been altered. It may not be an altogether different role, but, as one views the impact of the *Charter*, what may be described to a degree as a political or legislative role is now imposed on the Court. The consequence is that certain areas are now removed from the control of Parliament and the provincial legislatures. Their powers have been diminished. When a conflict between legislation and the *Charter* arises, it now becomes the job of the courts to resolve it. The *Charter* does include an escape hatch, as several writers in this volume, including Madame Justice L'Heureux-Dubé, have pointed out. It includes protective features (e.g., the "notwithstanding" clause) which give Parliament and the provincial legislatures some leeway in comparison with the rule followed in the United States.

It is pointed out in this essay that the use of American examples must be selective. Sections of the *Charter*, most notably s. 15(2) and s. 1 might serve better than any imported American constitutional provisions in avoiding such rancorous controversies as arose with adjudication in the *Bakke* case,[38] and will allow the Canadian high court to give a broader interpretation to the rights and freedoms which follow s. 1. Most, how-

---

37 *McCulloch* v. *Maryland*, 4 Wheaton 316 (1819).

38 *Bakke* v. *University of California*, 553 P. 2d 1152 (1976); *Regents of the University of California* v. *Bakke*, 438 U.S. 265 (1978).

ever, will agree with Madame Justice L'Heureux-Dubé when she states that "to reject the American experience out of hand and to refuse to engage in its examination, as at least a comparative exercise, would surely be [a great] mistake."

MADAM JUSTICE ABELLA's essay takes a very different approach, one that is more theoretical and less case-oriented. It illustrates the process by which judges, especially those on the Supreme Court, play their policy-making roles. Contrary to popular assumptions about the *Charter*'s bringing Canada's judges into some new role or partnership, judges, she argues, have always been involved in public policy. After defining her terms—law, judicial neutrality, and public policy—she moves on to show how policy-making is enmeshed in the judge's involvement in the development of law, whether in interpreting statutes or selectively applying precedents. After examining the traditional functions of judges in this light, along with the views of some of the philosopher–judges who have written about them, the author draws the conclusion that the *Charter* introduced in Canada in the *Constitution Act, 1982* has not changed anything in this regard.

The analysis hinges on several important assumptions. The first is that previous notions about judicial neutrality are naive, and in some quarters are now completely discredited. As she asserts, it may well be that any true neutrality is a myth, even though impartiality and an open mind are the first and most indispensable qualities sought after in the process of judicial selection. Moreover, judges must not be assumed to be guilty of usurpation of the political function traditionally reserved to legislative bodies. If the interpretive role judges play has the potential for interfering in Canada with parliamentary supremacy, or in the United States with the Court's becoming a third house of the legislature, Justice Abella assures us that it was always the case. Once we accept her premises that public policy forms the basis of law, and that judges are required to take public policy issues into consideration when attending to their duty of formulating the law, then it follows that judges cannot be accused of usurping the legislative function, and judicial neutrality need not be impaired by the application of public-policy considerations.

To speak or write of courts, judges and public policy in relation to politics may still strike some readers as irreverent. Until fairly recently, surveys of public opinion in the United States indicated that Americans thought that an association between courts and politics was a bad thing. Courts are supposed to be "above politics." In the United States, with its separation of powers, there has been a traditional jealousy over mixing the different processes of government, especially that of making law with that of saying what it is after it has been made. Like most of the good ideas which the framers of the Constitution of 1787 believed in, this one has a very sound basis, but it should not be made into an absolute rule. And in the light of recent experience, this distinction could not be rigidly enforced even if the will to do so existed.

A further issue concerns the meaning of the term "politics." If it is used in a pejorative sense to refer to horse-trading, jobbery or partisan manipulation, that is one usage, but there are others. Along with their discretion, judges also have power that fits nicely into Harold Lasswell's definition of politics as "who gets what, when and how." Individual judicial decisions can determine a great deal about who gets what from, and pays what to, the government system:

> Who owes taxes or military service, who is entitled to pensions, unemployment benefits, or welfare are matters that judges frequently decide, just as in civil . . . disputes between individuals, judges determine who owns a piece of property.[39]

It becomes obvious, in this light, that courts and judges are of necessity major players in these processes.

In sum, the process is interpretive for judges, and not blatantly political. Moreover, unlike the legislature, the judiciary is impervious to electoral judgment. Some think that is undemocratic; others do not. In Madam Justice Abella's view, it is a strong point in favor of a dispassionate and non-partisan outlook on the part of judges that cannot be a part of the legislature's role. Above all, she writes, the concept of public policy is value-laden.

The basic point is clear: judges do help shape public policy; they have always done so; and, in both the United States and Canada, they do it in ways that are substantive. In very recent years, the polity's reliance on judges to decide major issues of public policy has, if anything, increased. One illustration of this is found in the nervous attitude that public officials, leaders, interest groups and private citizens assumed while awaiting the U.S. Supreme Court's ruling in the case *University of California* v. *Bakke* in the spring of 1978, one of the cases discussed by Madame Justice L'Heureux-Dubé. They waited for the authoritative word on the legitimacy of hundreds of private and public affirmative action programs. The Court's decision insured continued judicial supervision of efforts to eradicate the effects of racial discrimination from American life, while at the same time ordering the University of California medical faculty at Davis to admit the white applicant, Bakke, who was fully qualified.

The effects of judicial decisions such as this one, even though they apparently concern only a single citizen and an institution or government

---

39 Walter F. Murphy and C. Herman Pritchett, *Courts, Judges, and Politics: An Introduction to the Judicial Process* (New York: Random House, 1979), 3.

agency, often radiate to large segments of the population, or perhaps even to the nation as a whole. Were it not for a section of the *Charter* which, as Madame Justice L'Heureux-Dubé points out, has the effect of precluding this kind of litigation in Canadian courts, that effect could, and sometimes does, spill over across the border.

In Canada, as well as in the United States, conventional wisdom has long held that legislatures or parliaments pass laws and the courts decide what they mean. The judge's role, though essential, was regarded as secondary to that of the real policy-formulating instruments of government, executive and legislature. As a result, judges have tended to be wary of appearing to be making policy judgments and have papered over their decisions with "a protective veil of adjectives." But whether they took on the form of disguise or not, their opinions had to consider, among other factors, logic, precedents, community standards or values, and the policy implications their legal conclusions represented. Judges have always been involved in evaluating, i.e., deciding which values or policies ought to be operational. All law is about values, values are about public policy, and both law and public policy are about morality.[40] Considering public policy, then, is an essential function of a court's legitimate role in legal interpretation.

What then has been the effect of the *Charter* on post–1982 jurisprudence in Canada? According to Madam Justice Abella, it has allowed public policy-making "to come out of the judicial closet" and to participate more openly than in the past in assuming that policy partnership of which it has been a part for centuries.

Judges have a duty, a constitutional duty, when a case is properly before them, to try to stop any institution, government agency, or individual or group, no matter how representative of the popular will, from doing forbidden things or from doing proper things in a forbidden way. These kinds of decisions, especially when justified by opinions that become a part of the national culture, can affect not only particular public policies; they can also help to shape and define more general values such as liberty, equality, fairness, security, privacy and the right to property—in short, the kinds of values that politics in a democratic society is all about.

CONCLUSION

The concluding essay in this volume, by one of Canada's eminent political scientists, asks the quintessential question: "Can the Canadians be a sovereign people?" With this synthesis of the events that have figured so

---

40 R.W.M. Dias, *Jurisprudence* (London: Butterworths, 1985), 196, and H.L.A. Hart, *The Concept of Law* (Oxford: Clarendon Press, 1961).

prominently in Canada's recent constitutional past, the story of Canada's constitutional odyssey comes full circle to the post-Meech Lake and post-referendum (1992) phase. In this essay, PETER RUSSELL provides students of Canadian politics, law and society with a much needed historical perspective on Canada's recent constitutional turmoil. Beginning with the central issue of popular sovereignty, and the deal-making process in the Confederation era, a process in which imperial officials and colonial political elites played key roles, the essay spans the pre- and post-Confederation debates over the sovereignty of governments and legislatures. Provincial rights advocates wrestled with centralists, resulting in the subsequent triumph—within their allotted sphere of jurisdiction—of winning significant powers for provincial legislatures.

The first watershed was reached in the long struggle by Canadians to take custody of their constitution in 1926, when the Balfour Declaration made Canada and the other self-governing Dominions autonomous communities. There followed the slow but steady progress toward constitutional self-government. Sovereignty then became muted in the long debate over the amending formula issue. Where did the power reside to change the constitution? The debate, however, was not altogether sterile. Out of it developed some valuable ideas and assumptions about the nature of Canada as a political community. Nevertheless, the country and its leaders continued for decades "to lean on the legal crutch of imperial sovereignty."

After World War II, Newfoundland's populace exercised the powers of a sovereign constituency through an elected convention and two referenda in its decision to join Canada (1949). The next milestone in the Canadian odyssey toward popular sovereignty came in 1964, but the amending formula initiated that year was considered too rigid, and its rejection plunged the country into five succeeding rounds of what Russell terms "macro-constitutional politics." The end is not yet in sight.

Nation-building under the Trudeau government occupied the next phase in the constitutional debate which was now deepening, and according to Russell, only beginning to broaden. This phase is marked by the groundswell of support building in the West and the Atlantic region for a stronger voice and more effective participation in the central government's institutions and decisions. A new voice was also being heard, heralding the foundation in law of aboriginal rights.

Russell's essay moves through two more decades of intense socio-political and constitutional debate—spanning the constitutional transformation from the election in Quebec of the Parti Québécois to the demise of the Meech Lake/Langevin Constitutional Accord. The defeat of the referendum on the subsequent Charlottetown Accord post-dated the writing of this essay. A trenchant analysis is applied, however, to the substance and process of the *Constitution Act, 1982*, the far-reaching impact of the *Canadian Charter of Rights and Freedoms*, and the hotly debated implications of the now-defunct Meech Lake Accord.

Professor Russell's question—"Can the Canadians be a sovereign people?"—(which Canadians may interpret in several different ways) remains unanswered at this writing. It was not settled in the fifth round of what he calls "macro-constitutional politics"—nor in the sixth which followed in 1992. And so the constitutional future of all Canadians, including its aboriginal peoples and the Québécois, is still in doubt.

What the future will bring no one can predict, but the essays in this volume point out some of the political mistakes of the past which, thus far, have impeded the overall progress of Canadian constitutional development. These essays, several of which appear here for the first time, and most of which have as yet received no widespread exposure, are designed to smooth the path of the constitutional journey on which Americans over two centuries ago, and Canadians a century later, embarked. More than in past decades, Americans and Canadians must begin to look beyond their own borders to ensure that the common elements of the past will help to bind together, and not to divide, our peoples in times of political crisis and constitutional turmoil. Having weathered one firestorm of Quebec separation, perhaps Canadians will succeed once again to resolve their differences and find answers to basic questions of constitutional structure and powers. The drama of the Canadian constitution's refounding may yet open the way to a new era of shared adventure in a renewal of the American and Canadian systems.

Marian C. McKenna
Calgary, March 1993

I

The Constitution and Religion

The Accommodation of Religion: A Tocquevillian Perspective

Thomas L. Pangle

There is perhaps no respect in which recent American and Canadian constitutional traditions differ so profoundly as in their posture toward the establishment of religion, or, more broadly expressed, the proper separation of church and state. And one can hardly imagine a more fundamental constitutional issue. Religion is that sphere of life in which human beings, as individuals and as societies, attempt to come to terms with the ultimate questions of existence, through the worship of, obedience to, and rumination upon divinity and the afterlife or eternity. It is difficult to avoid the conclusion that it is in its posture toward religion that a nation most fully and clearly defines itself.

Now a leading and well-known feature of the American Bill of Rights is the First Amendment prohibition on establishment of religion. That prohibition is stated in remarkably ambiguous language: "Congress shall make no law respecting an establishment of religion." The history and intended meaning of this sentence, and especially of the words "respecting" and "establishment," remain highly controversial and to some extent conjectural. It is plain from the evidence available to us that many of those in the First Congress who voted for these words did not for a moment intend them to outlaw existing, generally rather modest, forms of established religion in the various states; indeed, a plausible argument has been made that most Congressmen intended the language to *protect* the established religions in the states.[1] But what we may fairly term the

---

1 Michael Malbin, *Religion and the First Amendment: The Intentions of the Authors of the First Amendment* (Washington: American Enterprise Institute, 1978); see also Walter Berns, *The First Amendment and the Future of American Democracy* (New York: Basic Books, 1976), c. 1. The crucial sections of the Congressional debates are to be found in *Annals of the Congress of the United States; 1789–1824*, 42 vols. (Washington, D.C.: Gales and Seaton, 1834–56), 1:729–31, 755, 766 (hereinafter *Annals of Congress*). Especially revealing are the remarks of Congressmen Sylvester and Huntington as well as Madison on 15 August 1789.

"extreme left" on the establishment issue at the time of the Founding (Madison and Jefferson) has in the twentieth century carried the day. The Supreme Court, beginning with *Everson* v. *Board of Education* (1947), has read into the establishment clause Jefferson's "wall of separation between church and state."[2] In order to read this "wall" into the establishment clause, the Court has had to ignore much of what was said in the debates in the House of Representatives over the intended meaning of the First Amendment (15, 17, and 20 August 1789); in addition, the Court has had to pass over the explicit governmental support for religious education voted in the reenactment of the Northwest Ordinance by the same Congress that passed the Bill of Rights.[3] The Court has on the whole refused to be guided by George Washington's authoritative pronouncements, not only in his Farewell Address, but in his early Presidential Proclamation of 3 October 1789: "It is the duty of all nations to acknowledge the providence of Almighty God, to obey His will, to be grateful for His benefits, and humbly to implore His protection and favor."[4]

The Court has preferred to be guided by the "Memorial and Remonstrance" of 1785, in which Madison (supported by Jefferson) attacked a bill proposed in the Virginia legislature (supported by John Marshall, George Washington, and Patrick Henry, among others) that would have provided state funds to support "Teachers of the Christian Religion."[5] The same Madison later castigated as unconstitutional the appointment of Congressional chaplains, and voiced his disapproval of the Thanks-

---

2 *Everson* v. *Board of Education*, 330 U. S. 1 (1947); on state aid to church schools, see also *Lemon* v. *Kurtzman*, 403 U. S. 602 (1971), and the opinions on both sides of the decision in *Tilton* v. *Richardson*, 403 U. S. 672 (1971); on the issue of the constitutionality of released time from public schooling for attending church classes, see *Illinois ex rel. McCollum* v. *Board of Education*, 333 U. S. 203 (1948), which seems to be at some tension with *Zorach* v. *Clauson*, 343 U. S. 306 (1952). On the unconstitutionality of school prayers, see *Engel* v. *Vitale*, 370 U. S. 421 (1962); on the unconstitutionality of Bible readings in school, see *Abington School District* v. *Schempp*, 374 U. S. 203 (1963). The "wall of separation" phrase comes from Jefferson's letter to the Danbury Baptist Association, 1 January 1802, in A. Lipscomb and A. Bergh, eds., *The Writings of Thomas Jefferson*, 20 vols. (Washington: Thomas Jefferson Memorial Association, 1905), 16:281.

3 The text of the Northwest Ordinance may be found in Charles C. Tansill, ed., *Documents Illustrative of the Formation of the Union of the American States*, 69th Congress, 1st session, House Document No. 398 (Washington, D.C.: GPO, 1927), 47–54; see Art. 3: "religion, morality, and knowledge being necessary to good government and the happiness of mankind, schools and the means of education shall forever be encouraged."

4 James D. Richardson, comp., *A Compilation of the Messages and Papers of the Presidents, 1789–1897*, 10 vols. (Washington, D.C.: GPO, 1896–99), 1:64. See also Madison's very pious Presidential proclamation of 16 November 1814, ibid., 1:558.

5 The text and historical background may be found in Marvin Meyers, ed., *The Mind of the Founder* (Indianapolis: Bobbs-Merrill, 1973), 8–16.

giving holiday proclamations, tax exemption for churches, and the appointment of chaplains for the armed services.[6] Perhaps most revealing of all, Madison as President vetoed on constitutional grounds a bill incorporating the Episcopal Church in the District of Columbia, in part because the bill empowered the church to educate poor children.[7] In accordance with the Madisonian line, the United States Supreme Court has in the last two generations looked with grave reserve on any form of state aid for parochial schooling, and on any intrusion of "religious activity" into public schools.

In sharp contrast, the Canadian constitutional tradition, lacking of course an "establishment clause," has always made a legitimate place for state-supported and approved denominational schools. Moreover, the Canadian head of state remains the English monarch, who is entitled "Defender of the Faith." Most striking of all, the present Canadian constitution begins from the premise that "Canada is founded upon principles that recognize the supremacy of God." The American Constitution, of course, makes no reference whatsoever to such principles or to such a "supremacy." The American Constitution begins, not with a reference to God, but with a reference to "We the People" as supremely authoritative. On the other hand, throughout most of its history, and indeed until our lifetime, the American constitutional and political ethos remained much closer to the Canadian, as was somewhat reluctantly acknowledged by Justice Douglas, speaking for the Court in *Zorach* v. *Clauson*:[8] "We are a religious people whose institutions presuppose a Supreme Being." But in the last two generations, especially at the level of the legal elite, the traditional American ethos, lacking any explicit grounding in the text of the Constitution, has eroded, not to say evaporated. When leading legal scholars today speak of "Constitutional Faith," they have in mind postmodernist Heideggerianism or Rortyism, not the faith of the Founding Fathers.[9]

We must hasten to add that the predominant view we have just limned, in each country, is now under challenge. In Canada, there is a strong tendency amongst the legal elite to adopt or adapt what is pre-

6 Madison to Edward Livingston, 10 July 1822, in G. Hune, ed., *The Writings of James Madison*, 9 vols. (New York: G.P. Putnam's Sons, 1900–1910), 9:100–103; Madison, "Detached Memoranda ca. 1817," *William and Mary Quarterly*, 3d series, 3 (1946), 554–60.

7 The veto message, and the fierce debate it stirred in Congress as to the intended meaning of the establishment clause, may be found in *Annals of Congress* 22:982–87 (21 and 23 February 1811).

8 343 U.S. 306 at 313 (1952).

9 See Sanford Levinson, *Constitutional Faith* (Princeton: Princeton University Press, 1988), and my discussion in *The Ennobling of Democracy: The Challenge of the Postmodern Era* (Baltimore: Johns Hopkins University Press, 1992).

sumed to be the superior American consensus in almost all aspects of legal theory; and this tendency is likely to become steadily more evident in the legal elite's posture toward church-state relations. At the same time, the recent American consensus, at least as regards the establishment clause, is being increasingly shaken by a minority of scholars, judges and activists who doubt both the civic wisdom and the historical or legal legitimacy of the Madisonian–Jeffersonian doctrine.

In this situation of flux and reconsideration of fundamentals, we are prodded to ruminate, in the broadest possible context, on the relative merits of these two rather different contemporary constitutional attitudes toward the proper relation between church and state. I propose to contribute to this rumination by viewing the question from what I believe to be a most illuminating vantage point, transcending both the American and the Canadian perspectives: the vantage point afforded by Tocqueville's democratic theory. It is not my purpose to investigate which of the two contemporary constitutional outlooks Tocqueville would favor were he to be resurrected—though I am inclined to surmise he would prefer the Canadian. My aim is rather to enrich our understanding of what it is we should be thinking about, what it is we should see to be at stake, when we consider the merits and demerits of these two contrasting constitutional postures toward religion.

THE BASIC ISSUES

Tocqueville's meditation on the relation between religion and politics in modern democracy prompts, and helps us to come to grips with, the most important question which must be addressed in any thorough consideration of the relation: why are religious liberty, and the separation of church and state, good? Or to put the question another way, what ends ought we to have in view as we formulate, interpret, and administer laws and policies that foster and that limit religious liberty and the separation of church and state? Tocqueville thus allows us to shake free of the complacent illusion that separation of church and state, and religious liberty, may be treated as ends in themselves. He compels us to seek the more fundamental, principled basis for our attachment to religious liberty.

In the societies with which we and Tocqueville are most immediately concerned, religion means principally the Christian religion (Protestant and Roman Catholic), and secondarily the Judaic religion. While these religions conflict in important secondary teachings, they agree on still more important fundamentals: it suffices to mention the Ten Commandments, the commandments to love God and to love one's neighbor, and the afterlife in which judgment is rendered which sanctions these commandments. Every individual and every society must take a stand, one way or another, implicitly if not explicitly, toward these or kindred claims of religion to afford the decisive, authoritative guidance for life. We may then say, at the cost of leaving in the background many sorts of ambiguous compromise positions, but in order to clarify the basic issues, that religious liberty is supported, and defined or interpreted by its supporters, with a view either to: a) the opinion that such liberty, properly defined, will maintain or strengthen a certain degree of religious authority, which is seen as a good thing; or b) the opinion that such liberty will check or weaken religious authority, which is seen as a bad thing. The converse reasons are in play when religious liberty is opposed.

THE CAUSE OF RELIGIOUS LIBERTY IN THE FRENCH REVOLUTION

In his study of the French Revolution as it emerged out of the "Old Regime," Tocqueville analyzes a great political and intellectual movement which espoused religious liberty, the disestablishment of religion, and the separation of church and state in the name of the destruction of religion. The "philosophy of the eighteenth century," which was "one of the principal causes of the Revolution," was "profoundly irreligious"; "the philosophers of the eighteenth century opposed the church with a sort of fury; they attacked its clergy, its hierarchy, its institutions, its dogmas, and, so as to better overthrow these, they wished to rip up the very foundations of Christianity."[10] A few "searching and intrepid geniuses," carrying to an extreme the "examining spirit" induced by the Reformation, came to the conclusion that "not just some, but all" the Christian traditions were false: "the same spirit which, at the time of Luther, made several million Catholics leave Catholicism, pushed several isolated Christians each year out of Christianity itself."[11] But unlike their freethinking philosophic ancestors, the philosophers who accepted the premises of the modern Enlightenment did not remain "isolated." They spread their skepticism among masses of revolutionary followers with whom they appeared to share "a sort of new religion": a "faith" in the "perfectibility" and the "power" of mankind guiding itself by individual, autonomous reason.[12] The church "leaned principally on tradition," while the revolutionary writers "professed a great contempt for all institutions which founded themselves on respect for the past"; the church "recognized an authority

---

10 Alexis de Tocqueville, *L'Ancien régime et la révolution*, ed. J.-P. Mayer (Paris: Gallimard, 1967; revised ed. 1984), bk. 1, c. 2, p. 63 (cited as 1.2.63). Subsequent references will be to this edition, thus cited by book, chapter, and page. All translations are my own.

11 Ibid., 3.2.242.

12 Ibid., 3.2.251.

superior to the individual reason," while the promoters of the revolution "appealed to nothing but that reason itself."[13]

The philosophers of the Enlightenment opposed religion not only because they thought it to be false, but thought life guided by scientific truth to be precious for mankind at large, as well as for individual philosophers. They launched an attack on all existing political institutions in the name of more specific new doctrines of justice, including "the natural equality of men; the consequent abolition of all the privileges of castes, classes, professions; the sovereignty of the people; the omnipotence of the social power; the uniformity of rules, etc."[14] They saw the Christian church and its doctrines to be diametrically opposed to these new conceptions of justice. The church "founded itself on a hierarchy," but the new way of thinking "tended toward the confusion of ranks."[15] "In order to come to terms with one another, there would have been required on both sides a recognition that political society and religious society, being by nature essentially different, cannot govern themselves by similar principles; but at that time they were far from such recognition, and it appeared that, in order to mount the attack on the institutions of the state, it was necessary to destroy those of the church, which served the former as foundation and model."[16] Besides, the church "was itself then the first of political powers, and the most detested of all, even though it was not the most oppressive."[17]

Last but not least, the *philosophes* confronted in the church "precisely that part of the government that was the closest and the most directly opposed to them." The church, "being specially charged with surveillance over thought and censorship of writings, troubled them every day."[18] The philosophers of the French Enlightenment championed religious liberty against church authority as part of their crusade against censorship in all its forms. They were convinced that censorship, even of the limited sort that prevailed in France prior to the Revolution, was a grave obstacle to radical, independent writing and speaking, which they identified as the core of "the general liberties of the human spirit."[19]

Now Tocqueville argues that the *philosophes* were wrong in almost every aspect of this understanding of the relation between religion and democracy, and hence in their understanding of the value of religious

---

13 Ibid., 3.2.245.
14 Ibid., 1.2.63.
15 Ibid., 3.2.245.
16 Ibid., 3.2.245.
17 Ibid., 3.2.245–46.
18 Ibid., 3.2.246.
19 Ibid., 3.2.246.

liberty. Their errors come into sight, according to Tocqueville, not only in the subsequent history of the French Revolution and its aftermath, but even more clearly when one undertakes a comparative study of democracy as it has emerged in America, in contrast to the democratic movement as it emerged in France.

To begin with, religious liberty understood as entailing the abolition of censorship, does not in fact promote radical and independent writing as well as does a censorship of the sort that prevailed in France prior to the Revolution. Those who, like Tocqueville himself, espouse religious liberty entailing the abolition of censorship must resign themselves to this melancholy truth. The constriction of true religious, political, literary, and philosophic diversity and the diminution of radical independence of thought are severe costs of such religious liberty. The historical evidence proves that true intrepidity of thought and boldness of expression flourish where a limited degree of repression challenges and tests intellectual courage: "There are times when the oppression of writers can arrest the movement of thought, others when it animates that movement; but it has never been the case that a sort of policing such as that which was exercised in the eighteenth century has not multiplied a hundredfold the power of thought." The authors of the eighteenth century "suffered that species of check which animates the struggle, and not the heavy yoke that breaks it." Tocqueville appeals here to the authority of David Hume, who astonished Diderot by writing him in 1768 to the effect that French intolerance "was more favorable to the progress of the spirit" than the liberty of the English: "The Scotchman was right. Inhabiting a free country, he had experience; Diderot judged the thing as an intellectual, Hume judged it as a political man."[20]

The utter failure of the French intellectuals to understand the relation between freedom of the spirit and toleration, especially the toleration characteristic of modern democratic society, is for Tocqueville the most acute symptom of their general failure to understand the specific dangers to freedom and spirituality presented by modern democracy. Only if one

---

20 Ibid., 3.2.247–48. One may analogously compare the relative vitality of literary and spiritual life behind the Iron Curtain in the last twenty years and in the Free World; as Italo Calvino concluded, in a comparison of the life of the mind in Eastern and Western Europe, "this is the paradox of the power of literature: it seems that only when it is persecuted does it show its true powers, challenging authority, whereas in our permissive society it feels that it is being used merely to create the pleasing contrast to the general ballooning of verbiage"; or as Philip Roth put it after returning from eastern Europe in the 1980s, "in my situation, everything goes and nothing matters; in their situation, nothing goes and everything matters" (both authors quoted in *New York Times*, 8 February 1990, B1). Isaiah Berlin observed more generally that "integrity, love of truth, and fiery individualism grow at least as often in severely disciplined communities or under military discipline, as in more tolerant or indifferent societies": see *Two Concepts of Liberty* (Oxford: Oxford University Press, 1958), 13–15 and 48.

grasps those dangers with full clarity will one begin to think hard and seriously about remedies or ameliorations, and only then will one begin to appreciate the enormous value religious faith and authority have for modern democracy. At that point, Tocqueville teaches, one is in a position to recognize that religious liberty can and must be properly conceived as the means to the strengthening, within modern democracy, of politically responsible religious authority.

THE DANGERS OF DEMOCRACY AS SEEN IN AMERICA

Tocqueville identifies the "tyranny of the majority" as the gravest threat to the human spirit in the age of democracy.[21] Majority rule is basic to democracy. Majority domination is directly entailed in the fundamental democratic principles of equality and individual liberty: one man, one vote. But human beings hardly become more wise or virtuous simply by being gathered together in large groupings, or by discovering their collective political power. A majority can be at least as oppressive as any individual or minority. In a democracy, majoritarianism is therefore desperately in need of a moral education that humbles majority arrogance. In democracies, the dominant majority needs to be taught or induced to listen to, and even in some measure to respect, dissenting minorities or individuals. But education is not a sufficiently reliable limit on democratic majoritarianism. The majority also needs social, political, and economic competitors, whose power is not dependent on winning majority approval.

It is not easy to see where such education and such competition may come from in modern democracy. Citing the authority of Madison and Jefferson, Tocqueville expresses grave doubts as to whether the chiefly institutional checks and balances in the American Constitution effectively limit majoritarian tyranny at the political level.[22] The first volume of *Democracy in America* develops a complex and subtle diagnosis of the majoritarian ills of the democratic political process in America. Yet the most serious danger lies at a deeper level. The worst and fullest tyranny to which mankind tends to be enslaved is the tyranny over the mind, the tyranny over opinion, and above all the tyranny over *moral* opinion, opinion as to what is right and wrong. It is the *moral authority* of the

---

21 Alexis de Tocqueville, *De la Démocratie en Amérique*, ed. J.-P. Mayer (Paris: Gallimard, 1951), vol. 1, part 2, c. 7 (or 1.2.7). In quotations, I have used the translation by George Lawrence, edited by J.-P. Mayer (Garden City, N.Y.: Doubleday Anchor, 1969), frequently altering the translation to make it more literal; specific page references will be to this translation, to be cited as *Democracy in America*.

22 *Democracy in America*, 1.2.7, end (pp. 260–61): Tocqueville quotes Madison's *The Federalist*, No. 51 and Jefferson's letter to Madison of 15 March 1789.

majority in democracies that is most inescapable and overwhelming. The symptoms, in America, of this tyranny Tocqueville vividly describes in part 2, volume 1 of *Democracy in America* (chapter 7, in the section titled "The Power Exercised by the Majority in America Over Thought"). But I believe that he succeeds in fully plumbing the psychological roots and mechanism of democratic slavery only in his analysis of intellectual life in part 1, volume 2 of *Democracy in America*.

Tocqueville begins from the observation that the modern democratic spirit exemplified in America is decisively formed by a popularized, individualistic, and materialistic or down-to-earth philosophic outlook that is profoundly skeptical towards all authority, be it traditional or contemporary. This rationalist doubt of authority, though genuine and thoroughgoing in the hands of the rare geniuses who spawned it (e.g., Descartes and Bacon), became inevitably vulgarized as it was translated by the eighteenth century Enlightenment into a mass phenomenon. In modern democracy, the egalitarian rejection of authority is itself a new, authoritative moralism in disguise—and hence all the more insidious in its despotism. Americans are indoctrinated from early youth with the dogmas that they have a moral duty to think for themselves, that their dignity consists in their regarding themselves as intellectually equal individuals, and that they ought to be ashamed at appearing to bow to anyone's authority. Americans are certainly not taught to think skeptically about the social commitment to intellectual autonomy, or to examine the great pre-modern philosophic arguments against such a commitment. They are not induced to comprehend sympathetically the great virtues of, and arguments for, pre-modern, hierarchic, and more authoritarian societies. More generally, inhabitants of modern democracy tend not to understand democracy because they have no firm comparative basis for critical moral self-assessment. Even the intellectual elites of modern democracy simply assume, without demonstration or even argument, that democracy is superior and aristocracy inferior. Modern democrats tend to be deplorably ignorant of the distinctive virtues and vices, the characteristic strengths and weaknesses, the peculiar forms of freedom and slavery, that define, respectively, democratic and aristocratic societies. As a result of this massive moral prejudice, citizens of democracy tend to be woefully unaware of the herdlike limits on their pretended independence of opinion.

For the fact is, Tocqueville insists, that there is no such thing as a non-authoritarian society. "It can never happen that there are no dogmatic beliefs, that is to say, opinions which men take on trust and without discussion," because "without ideas in common, there is no common action, and, without common action, there may still exist human beings, but not a social entity."[23] The "spirits of all the citizens" have to be "held together by certain leading ideas." The question, then, "is not to ascertain whether there exists an intellectual authority in the democratic centuries, but only where it is lodged and what its limits are."

In *aristocratic* ages, people are "naturally inclined to take as the guide for their opinions the superior reason of a man or a class, while they are very little disposed to recognize any infallibility in the mass of men." Precisely "the contrary holds in centuries of equality." The "disposition to believe in the mass of men augments, and it is more and more public opinion that rules the world." When the person who inhabits democratic countries compares himself to all those who surround him, "he feels with pride that he is equal to each of them"; *but*, "when he comes to contemplate the *collectivity* of his fellows, and to place himself alongside this great body, he is overwhelmed by his own insignificance and weakness." In other words, "the *same* equality that renders him independent of each of his fellow citizens taken one by one leaves him isolated and defenseless in the face of the majority." "The public therefore," Tocqueville concludes, "has among democratic peoples a singular power, of which the aristocratic nations could not conceive."

Democratic public opinion does not typically achieve its sway by persuasion, but rather by a kind of moral imposition, "an immense pressure of the spirit of all on the intelligence of each." Public opinion holds sway in such a way as to dampen and even to morally condemn daring dissent. The tolerance of democratic public opinion exhibits an unhealthy, despotically egalitarian proclivity to degenerate, first, into the easygoing belief that all points of view are equally valid (or invalid)—and hence none is in need of searching critical argument or stalwart defense;[24] and then further into the strident belief that anyone who does insist on making judgments about others, or who argues passionately for the superiority of specific character traits, ways of life, conceptions of human nature and justice, etc., is somehow (as we hear nowadays) "exclusivist," "elitist," "intolerant," "antidemocratic," and hence immoral.

The sapping of the individual mind's capacity to think in genuine independence from a molasses-like public opinion goes hand in hand with a shrinking of the individual citizen's belief in and inclination toward meaningful civic action or significant involvement in public life. Tocqueville describes in the democratic way of life a specific new behavioral and emotional syndrome for which he invents a word: "individualism."

---

23 Quotations in this paragraph are taken from *Democracy in America*, 2.1.2, "On the Principal Source of Beliefs Among Democratic Peoples."

24 Cf. ibid., 2.1.5, p. 444: "Opinions are ill-defended or abandoned, and in despair of solving unaided the greatest problems of human destiny, men ignobly give up thinking about them."

To understand what Tocqueville means, we must follow him in sharply distinguishing "individualism" from selfishness or egoism. Passionate, excessive self-love is a vice coeval with human nature. It manifests itself in all societies, in various ways, and most vividly in active, ambitious competition with others. Individualism, on the other hand, "is a quiet and considered sentiment which disposes each citizen to isolate himself from the mass of his fellows and retire into the circle of family and friends."[25] Modern democratic society, with its anti-traditionalism, its opening of opportunity, its restless mobility, its stress on individual initiative and autonomy grounded in the moral principles of universal rights, uproots and detaches citizens one from another, steadily constricting the avenues and possibilities for any one person to shape or care for the lives of others. Modern democracy makes "the duties of each individual to the species much clearer, the devotion to another individual much rarer: the bond of human affection widens but weakens." "To the extent that conditions are equalized," Tocqueville points out, "there are more individuals who, not being rich enough or strong enough to exercise a great influence on the fate of their fellows, have nevertheless acquired or conserved enough enlightenment and wealth to be able to be self-sufficient." These individuals "owe nothing to anyone, they expect nothing, so to speak, from anyone; they habituate themselves to thinking of themselves always in isolation; they gladly imagine that their whole destiny is in their own hands." Thus, "democracy doesn't just make each person forget his ancestors, it hides from him his descendants and separates him from his contemporaries."

The powerful tendency of the democratic personality to withdraw into the narrow circle of immediate acquaintances is intensified by the inordinate taste for physical comfort that is yet another dangerous proclivity of modern democratic society. To grasp the peculiar character and intensity of this passion in modern democracy, Tocqueville again appeals to the contrast with aristocratic society. He states his basic premise as follows: "What most vividly seizes the human heart is not by any means the quiet possession of a precious object, it is the imperfectly satisfied desire to possess it accompanied by the incessant fear of losing it."[26] Now in aristocracy the few who are well off enjoy their hereditary comforts without having had to acquire them and without fear of losing them; while the vast majority who are poor lack the comforts of life without hope of acquiring them. In modern democracy, "when on the

---

25 Quotations in this paragraph are from ibid., 2.2.2, "On Individualism in Democratic Countries."

26 Quotations in this paragraph are from ibid., 2.2.10 and 11, "On the Taste for Material Well-Being in America," and "Particular Effects Produced by the Love of Material Enjoyments in Democratic Centuries."

contrary, the ranks are blurred and privileges destroyed, when patri-monies are divided and enlightenment and liberty spread, the longing to acquire well-being presents itself to the imagination of the poor and the fear of losing it haunts the spirit of the rich." What is more, "a multitude of middling fortunes are established, whose possessors have enough material enjoyments to acquire a taste for them, but not enough to be contented; they never procure the material enjoyments without effort and do not indulge in them without anxiety." Accordingly, "they ceaselessly attach themselves to pursuing or to retaining these material enjoyments that are so precious, so incomplete, and so fugitive." The "passion for material well-being," Tocqueville contends, is thus "essentially a passion of the middle class," with which it grows and extends itself and finally becomes preponderant. The objects of this passion are "petty, but the soul cleaves to them: it dwells on them, every day and very closely, until finally they hide from it the rest of existence."

The democratic soul tends to be characterized by an unprecedented truncation of its conception of the future. "When each strives ceaselessly to change his station, when an immense competition is open to all, when riches are accumulated and dissipated in a few instants amidst the tumult of democracy, the idea of a quick and easy fortune, the image of Luck, in all its forms, presents itself to the human spirit."[27] "The present bulks large; it hides the future, which is eclipsed, and men no longer think beyond tomorrow." The result is not only spiritual barrenness and moral irresponsibility, but also an economically unhealthy disregard for long range consequences.

From the strange force of democratic man's passionate attachment to the petty and evanescent grows what Tocqueville calls "the secret anxiety which reveals itself in the actions of Americans."[28] "He who has con-stricted his heart to the sole quest for the goods of this world is always in a hurry"; "the recollection of the brevity of life goads him on continu-ally"; "apart from the goods he already possesses, he imagines at every moment a thousand others that death will prevent him from enjoying, if he doesn't hurry." Yet the passion for physical pleasure is by nature easily discouraged: since the goal is enjoyment, the means must be pretty prompt and easy or they contradict the goal. As a consequence, in mod-ern democracy "most of the souls are at one and the same time ardent and soft, violent and enervated." To this must be added the peculiarly depressing effects of the equality of opportunity. For this equality arouses in the imagination the ultimately delusive prospect of a boundless,

---

27 Quotations in this paragraph are from ibid., 2.2.17, "How in Times of Equality and Doubt it is Important to Distance the Goal of Human Actions."

28 Quotations in this paragraph are from ibid., 2.2.13, "Why the Americans Show Themselves to be so Anxious in the Midst of their Well-Being."

preeminent success, if only one works hard enough and has a bit of luck; but in fact, "when men are more or less equal and following the same course, it is very difficult for any of them to move quickly and get through the uniform crowd surrounding and hemming them in." The equality democratic citizens find among themselves is then never quite the equality they seek; it is always disappointing. They always think themselves on the verge of being in a social station where they wish to be: they never find a station in which they can be content. "It is to these causes," Tocqueville says in summation, "that it is necessary to attribute the singular melancholy which the inhabitants of democratic countries often exhibit in the midst of their abundance."

THE REMEDY OF RELIGION

The preceding résumé does not by any means exhaust Tocqueville's diagnosis, but it circumscribes some of the most important ills of modern democracy to which religious belief and authority may provide remedies.

Religion counteracts in manifold ways the "secret anxiety" to which democratic man is prey. "Most religions," Tocqueville submits, "are only general, simple, and practical means for teaching to men the immortality of the soul."[29] This is "the greatest advantage that a democratic people draws from the faiths, and one which makes those faiths more necessary to such a people than to all the others." In worship that inspires and is inspired by belief in the immortality of one's soul, the inhabitant of democracy is momentarily liberated "from the petty passions which agitate his life and from the evanescent interests which preoccupy it." "Religions instill a general habit of behaving with the future in view"; "in this respect," Tocqueville adds, "they work as much in favor of happiness in this world as of felicity in the next."[30]

Besides, no human being can avoid some obsession with the question of man's fate after death. Drawing on his studies of, and firsthand experiences in, the successive French Revolutions, Tocqueville argues that in the absence of authoritative religious answers to metaphysical questions, the anxiety which is in any case endemic in democracy grows to the point of a paralyzing enervation that prepares a people for bondage. Worried and exhausted by the "perpetual agitation of things," by the total mutability of the spiritual world, "they wish, at least, that every-

---

29 This and the preceding quotations in this paragraph are from ibid., 2.2.15, "How Religious Faiths from Time to Time Turn the Soul of Americans Toward Spiritual Enjoyments."

30 Ibid., 2.2.17.

thing would be firm and stable in the material realm, and, not being able to recover their old beliefs, they give themselves a master."[31]

Religion does not only counter in a direct way the anxiety peculiar to democratic man; it goes to the root causes of that anxiety, by opposing both materialism and individualism. It is this, Tocqueville judges, that is "the greatest advantage of religions" for democracy:

> There is no religion that does not place the goal of the desires of the human being beyond and above earthly goods, and that does not naturally elevate his soul toward regions far superior to those of the senses. Nor is there any that does not impose on each certain duties toward the human species, or in common with it, and that does not thus draw one, from time to time, away from the contemplation of oneself.
>
> Religious peoples are then naturally strong precisely where democratic peoples are weak; this shows clearly how important it is that men preserve their religion in becoming equal.[32]

One of Tocqueville's great themes is the way in which Americans combat the effects of individualism through "the doctrine of self-interest rightly understood" (*la doctrine de l'intérêt bien entendu*). This enlightened utilitarianism or egoism "does not inspire great sacrifices, but every day it prompts some small ones; by itself it cannot make a man virtuous, but its discipline shapes a lot of orderly, temperate, moderate, careful, and self-controlled citizens."[33] But if this doctrine "had in view this world only, it would be far from sufficient; because there are a great number of sacrifices which cannot find their recompense except in the other world."[34] Religion provides this crucial additional dimension to the doctrine.

Still, Tocqueville cannot avoid drawing attention to a grave difficulty. It is, to say the least, far from clear that Christianity, or perhaps any refined religion, maintains itself as a matter of calculation of future rewards. Christianity teaches, Tocqueville reminds us, that "one ought to do good to one's fellows out of love of God." Christianity at its purest teaches the "magnificent" doctrine that a human being can "enter, through his intelligence, the divine thought," and, "in sacrificing his individual interests to that admirable order of all things, awaits no other recompense except the pleasure of contemplation." Tocqueville thus leaves his readers in some doubt as to whether he believes, in the final

---

31 Ibid.

32 Ibid., 2.1.5.

33 Ibid., 2.2.8.

34 This and the following quotations are from ibid., 2.2.9, "How the Americans Apply the Doctrine of Self-Interest Rightly Understood as Regards Religion."

analysis, that Christianity, or any religion of truly sublime power, is altogether compatible with the central moral doctrine of modern democracy. In this very chapter, Tocqueville reminds us that for him *the* guide and model for Christian faith at its peak is Pascal; and in an earlier chapter Tocqueville "confessed" that he could "hardly believe" that passions such as are exhibited in Pascal "can emerge and develop as easily in the midst of democratic societies as they can in the bosom of aristocracies."[35]

Yet if truly profound religious faith is at some tension with modern democratic morality, Tocqueville insists that religion is to a much more massive degree supportive of and even essential to the morality democracy needs. Precisely because the private sphere assumes such importance in the lives of modern democrats, it is crucial, Tocqueville argues, that in their domestic lives Americans experience an oasis of order, tranquility, love, decency, and trust. The role of women in America—their piety, chastity, and fidelity, their voluntary submission to the non-despotic authority of their husbands, their often nigh heroic devotion to the nurture and education of their children—Tocqueville regards as perhaps the single most important factor in the success of the democratic experiment in America, as contrasted with France or Europe more generally. "In Europe, almost all the disorders of society are born around the domestic hearth and not far from the nuptial bed." In America, "religion reigns supreme over the soul of woman, and it is woman who makes the mores." Piety at once expresses and strengthens the mores and influence on mores of American women. It is at the hearth and in the home, under the influence of mothers and wives, that Americans learn to surmount selfishness, appreciate order and stability, control sensual appetites, and enjoy pleasures that cannot be purchased.[36]

This means to say that American women, largely through and because of their piety, decisively influence political life. The Americans' religion, though it does not directly intervene in politics, must nevertheless "be considered as the first of their political institutions."[37] The various denominations and priesthoods make no claim to participate in earthly legislation, but they remind citizens of supramundane limits that the citizens, even when gathered together in the majority, are obliged to heed, in thought as well as in action. "Thus the human spirit never sees an unlimited field before itself; however great its audacity, it feels from

---

35 Ibid., 2.1.10, pp. 461–62.

36 Quotations are from ibid., 1.2.9, "On the Principal Causes Which Tend to Maintain the Democratic Republic in the United States," subsection entitled, "Indirect Influence Which Religious Faiths Exercise on Political Society in the United States"; for Tocqueville's analysis of the role of women, see also ibid., 2.3.8–12.

37 Quotations in this paragraph are from ibid., 1.2.9, pp. 292–94.

time to time that it must arrest itself before insurmountable barriers."
"Up until now," Tocqueville adds with some caution, "no one has ever
been found, in the United States, who has dared to advance this maxim:
that everything is permitted in the interests of society—an impious
maxim, which seems to have been invented in a century of liberty in
order to legitimate all the tyrants to come." For "what can be done with
a people that is master of itself, if it is not subject to God?"

The philosophic method popularized by the eighteenth-century philosophers does not reign unchallenged in America, as it does in France,
principally because Christianity has "preserved a great empire over the
spirit of the Americans, and—this is the point I wish to emphasize—it
does not at all reign only as a philosophy adopted after examination, but
as a religion that is believed without discussion."[38] The Christian
religion, with its authoritative and unquestioned dogmas, thus provides
a powerful counterweight to that sway of public opinion that, combined
with the inescapable need for authoritative guidance, is the outcome of
the dogmatic distrust of all authority.

On the strictly political level, Tocqueville helps us to appreciate the
advantages derived from the fact that the churches or religious denominations in modern democracy, and especially the Roman Catholic Church,
are institutions whose authority and structure are neither dictated by, nor
intermingled with, nor simply subordinate to, the constituted political
authorities. The churches do not directly compete with democratic political authority, but they do stand apart, reminding all citizens of a higher
law and a higher legal authority.

Tocqueville argues fervently and repeatedly that the strict but friend-
ly separation of church and state in American democracy, so far from
representing a compromise of religion's influence and strength, in fact
creates the condition under which religion's true strength and influence
can flourish. "Considering religions from a purely human point of view,"
their real strength lies in the overwhelming natural human desire for
immortality. When a religion founds itself on this, "it can aspire to
universality"; "it can draw to itself the heart of the human species." But
when it allies itself to political powers or governments, religion mort-
gages its universal and permanent appeal to the limited and temporary
prop of a specific regime. "It augments its strength over some but forfeits
the hope of reigning over all." In addition, "it is sometimes constrained
to defend allies who are such from interest rather than love; and it has
to repulse as adversaries men who still love religion, although they are
fighting religion's allies." In the long run, religion allied with any specific
political authority is compelled to share in some measure the mortality
and ultimate fragility of any such specific regime. These general

---

38 Ibid., 2.1.1.

considerations take on heightened significance in democracy, where the struggle of parties, factions, and individuals produces a natural agitation and restless instability in political life.[39]

Moreover, since "in times of enlightenment and of equality, the human spirit is loath to receive dogmatic beliefs, and senses vividly the need for them only in religion," it follows that "in these centuries, religions ought to restrict themselves more discretely than in other ages to the limits which are proper to them"; "for, in wishing to extend their power beyond religious matters, they risk not being believed in any matter."[40]

THE DIFFICULTIES IN TOCQUEVILLE'S PRESENTATION

Tocqueville's argument for the essential harmony between religion and modern democracy is not free from ambiguities and even grave problems. He admits, nay, he calls attention to, the implication that the Catholic religion and modern democracy are incompatible.[41] Reminding us that he speaks "as a practising Catholic," Tocqueville further concedes that, in the case of Roman Catholicism, the at first sight felicitous situation of religion in America is paradoxical; he confesses, indeed, that this situation is contrary to the historical practice and, what is more, the traditional spirit of Roman Catholicism. But "I think," he wavers, with uncustomary hesitation, that the experience of American Catholicism shows that "one is mistaken in regarding the Catholic religion as a natural enemy of democracy."[42]

To be sure, "every religion has some political opinion linked to it by affinity"; the human spirit "seeks, I daresay, to *harmonize* earth with heaven"; and "Catholicism is like an absolute monarchy": "among Catholics, religious society is composed of just two elements—the priest and the people." This means that Catholicism is eminently compatible with equality, though less so with liberty or independence: "Catholicism places all intelligence on the same level," and "in applying to each human being the same measure, it loves to confound all the classes of society at the foot of the same altar." So how exactly does such a religion sympathize with democracy? Catholicism "disposes the faithful to obedience"; but does it dispose them to active private enterprise and republican

---

39 The preceding quotations are from ibid., 1.2.9, subsection entitled, "On the Principal Causes that Render Religion Powerful in America."

40 Ibid., 2.1.5.

41 Ibid., 2.1.5, p. 445.

42 Quotations in this paragraph are from ibid., 1.2.9, subsection entitled, "On Religion Considered as a Political Institution, How it Powerfully Contributes to Maintaining the Democratic Republic Among the Americans."

citizenship? If American Catholics "are not strongly drawn by the nature of their beliefs toward democratic and republican opinions, at least they aren't naturally opposed, and their social position, as well as their being in a minority, make it a law for them to embrace those opinions." In America, Catholics, because they tend to be poor and few in number, "are led, perhaps in spite of themselves, toward political doctrines which, perhaps, they would adopt with less zeal were they rich and predominant."

The deep roots of the fruitful American partnership between religion and politics lie in the anti-Catholic New England Protestantism that is the fertile soil of the American experiment: "most of English America was peopled by men who, having shaken off the pope's authority, submitted to no other supremacy in religion; they thus carried into the New World a Christianity which I cannot describe better than in calling it democratic and republican: this fact singularly favored the establishment of the republic and of democracy in the conduct of business"; Protestantism "directs men much less towards equality than towards independence."[43] The Protestantism of New England saw "in civil liberty a noble exercise of the human faculties, the world of politics being a field opened up by the Creator to the efforts of intelligence."[44]

But Tocqueville's detailed study of New England Protestantism does not confirm the purported symbiosis between even this religion and modern democracy. The founders of New England were "ardent sectarians."[45] They were "held within the narrowest bounds by certain religious beliefs"; not merely in the religious, but "in the moral world, everything was classified, coordinated, foreseen, and decided in advance." Their moral rigidity was balanced, however, by their political flexibility: "In the world of politics," everything was "in turmoil, contested, and uncertain." "In the one case obedience is passive, though voluntary; in the other there is independence, contempt of experience, and jealousy of all authority."

Tocqueville insists that "far from harming each other, these two apparently opposed tendencies work in harmony and seem to lend mutual support." Religion, he contends, "being free and powerful within its own sphere and content with the position reserved for it, realizes that its sway is all the better established because it relies only on its own powers and rules men's hearts without external support."

Yet Tocqueville is compelled to take note of the fact that Puritanism "was almost as much a political theory as a religious doctrine." The

---

43 Ibid., 1.2.9, p. 288.

44 Ibid., 1.1.2, p. 47.

45 Quotations in this paragraph are from ibid., 1.1.2, "On the Point of Departure of the Anglo-Americans and its Importance for their Future."

framers of the early New England penal laws "were especially concerned with the maintenance of good behavior and sound mores in society, so they constantly invaded the sphere of conscience, and there was hardly a sin not subject to the magistrate's censure." They took their inspiration from the Bible, and "conceived," as Tocqueville puts it, "the strange idea of borrowing their provisions from the text of the Holy Writ." Tocqueville deplores the "ridiculous and tyrannical laws" which resulted, although he stresses that "we must not forget" that these laws "were not imposed from outside—they were voted by the free agreement of all the interested parties themselves." He adds a reminder that Puritan "mores were even more austere and puritanical than their laws." In short, Tocqueville has to admit that the democratic spirit of the New England Protestants was neither modern nor liberal, but at best a contradictory, uneasy, and untenable compromise between pre-modern and modern, between closed and open, conceptions of society.

It may be doubted whether Tocqueville succeeds in sustaining his thesis that the steady progress of a more liberal outlook strengthens or even in the long run maintains religious faith and authority of a healthy sort. He concedes that "the spirit of individual independence" is religion's "most dangerous enemy," even while insisting that "religion succeeds in struggling successfully" against this spirit, by "respecting all democratic instincts which are not contrary to religion and making use of many of them."[46]

On the very next page he remarks that men who live in democratic centuries "are strongly inclined to shake off all religious authority."[47] When they do submit to such authority, he continues, "they want it at least to be single and uniform," because the democratic spirit is one which gives men "the taste for and the idea of a power in society that is unique, simple, and the same for all." The prospects for Protestantism, and the support it provides for a spirit of independence, are therefore not sanguine: "our contemporaries are naturally little disposed to belief, but once they have a religion, they encounter immediately within themselves a hidden instinct which unconsciously urges them toward Catholicism." This "instinct" draws strength from the fact that it is not illogical:

> One of the most familiar weaknesses of the human intelligence is to want to reconcile contrary principles and to purchase peace at the price of logic. There have therefore always been and always will be men who, after having submitted in some of their religious beliefs to an authority, still seek to exempt some of their other religious beliefs, and allow their spirits to float at random between obedience and liberty. But I am led to

---

46 Ibid., 2.1.5, p. 449.
47 Ibid., 2.1.6, p. 450.

believe that the number of these types will be smaller in democratic centuries than in other centuries, and that our grandchildren will tend more and more to divide themselves between those who abandon Christianity completely and others who enter into the bosom of the Church of Rome.[48]

Even more disturbing than this prediction of the inanition of Protestantism is Tocqueville's warning about the future vigor and effects of Pantheistic religious beliefs. The strength of Pantheism is the predictable outcome of the fact that "as conditions become more equal, each individual becomes more like his fellows, weaker, and smaller, and the habit grows of ceasing to think about the citizens and considering only the people; individuals are forgotten, and the species alone counts." In this democratic age, "the concept of unity becomes an obsession for the human spirit; it searches for unity everywhere." Precisely because pantheism "destroys human individuality," it will "have secret charms for the men who inhabit democracy": "it fosters the pride and soothes the laziness of their minds." "It is against this that all those who still appreciate the true grandeur of man ought to unite and fight."[49]

All of these observations, Tocqueville notes, are perfectly compatible with the further observation that Americans are and will increasingly be given to feverish outbreaks of short-lived religious enthusiasms and madnesses of all sorts, manipulated by wild or cunning preachers "hawking the word of God from place to place": "if ever the thoughts of the great majority of mankind came to be concentrated solely on the search for material goods, one can anticipate that there would be a colossal reaction in the souls of some; they would distractedly launch out into the world of spirits."[50]

At the bottom of Tocqueville's richly ambiguous and thought-provoking reflection on the place of religion in American democracy, one discerns the following fundamental difficulty. The spirit of Tocqueville's analysis is that of an enlightened and prudent supporter of modern democracy. Religion, properly conceived in terms of this spirit, is valued not for its truth, but for its usefulness in remedying or limiting the secular ills of a secular society. But the overwhelming stress on the utility of religion does not establish, and indeed it may contribute to undermining, its credibility. To esteem religion above all for its usefulness in serving worldly ends entails denying what is, from the religious point of

---

48 Ibid., 2.1.6.

49 Quotations in this paragraph are from ibid., 2.1.7, "What it is that Inclines the Spirit of Democratic Peoples Toward Pantheism."

50 Ibid., 2.2.12.

view, the necessarily supreme value of the essentially otherworldly ends of religion itself.

As Tocqueville repeatedly remarks, he is viewing religion "from a purely human point of view," and in that perspective, "what is most important for society is not that all citizens should profess the true religion but that they should prove religion."[51] "The main business of religion is to purify, to regulate and to restrain the overly ardent and too excessive taste for well-being that is felt by men in ages of equality."[52] Insofar as the democratic citizenry come more and more to share this perspective, Tocqueville argues, "religion is loved, supported, and honored, and only by looking into the depths of men's souls will one see what wounds it has suffered."[53]

But what if anything can heal or even staunch these wounds? "I do not know," confesses Tocqueville, "what is to be done to give back to European Christianity the energy of youth: God alone could do that."[54] Yet Tocqueville cannot shirk the duty of attempting to discern how government might foster religious faith without violating religious liberty. "I think that the only effective means which governments can use to make the doctrine of the immortality of the soul respected is daily to act as if they believed it themselves. I think that it is only by conforming scrupulously to religious morality in great affairs that they can flatter themselves that they are teaching the citizens to understand it and to love and respect it in little matters."[55]

Tocqueville knows that this is not enough. "Governments must study means to give men back that interest in the future which neither religion nor social conditions any longer inspire"; "in accustoming the citizens to think of the future in this world, they will gradually be led without noticing it themselves toward religious beliefs. Thus the same means that, up to a certain point, enable men to manage without religion are perhaps after all the only means we still possess for bringing mankind back, by a long and roundabout path, to a state of faith."[56]

It is hard to believe that this thought satisfied Tocqueville. Tocqueville's defense of religious liberty and the separation of church and state, and his defense of modern democracy as resting essentially, for its stability as well as its dignity, on such liberty and separation, is not as

---

51 Ibid., p. 290.

52 Ibid., p. 448.

53 Ibid., p. 300.

54 Ibid., p. 301.

55 Ibid., 2.2.15, end.

56 Ibid., 2.2.17, end.

reassuring as one might hope. If Tocqueville is largely correct in his analysis, then our situation and our difficulties are grave indeed.

Returning to the comparative considerations with which we introduced this Tocquevillian reflection on the role of religion in modern democracy, we may close with the following observations. If or to the extent that we decide Tocqueville is right in his analysis of the specific ways religion—especially organized religion—can contribute to saving modern democracy from some of its worst proclivities, we will be inclined to prefer the more moderate Canadian constitutional approach to the establishment of religion. We will surely be led to recommend that Canadian jurists think twice before rushing to incorporate into Canadian constitutional law any approximation to the recent American (and original Madisonian) view of the radical constitutional separation of church and state, especially at the levels of provincial and local government, and in the administration of the nation's schools.

The Robe and the Cloth:
The Supreme Court and Religion
in the United States

J. Woodford Howard, Jr.

Mark Twain once addressed freedom of expression in the United States with what he called "the calm confidence of a Christian with four aces." "It is by the goodness of God," he said, "that in our country we have those three unspeakably precious things: freedom of speech, freedom of Conscience, and the prudence never to practise either of them."[1]

Speakers on religion and the state today keep an eye on the nearest exit. A glance around the world shows that this subject is among the most volatile in human affairs. Religious warfare plagues India, Ireland, the Middle East, and the former Soviet empire. In Poland students demonstrate to *return* crucifixes to their classrooms. American religious diversity and toleration are among the wonders of the world, but our polity is hardly immune from religious strife. Bomb threats against synagogues recently occurred in New York City. While Justice William J. Brennan, Jr., received an honorary degree in Los Angeles, a plane flew over with a large banner: "Pray for the death of baby killer Brennan."[2] Protesters in some cities blocked showing of the controversial film, *The Last Temptation of Christ*, ensuring a box-office bonanza elsewhere.

The purpose of this essay is to assess the role of the U.S. Supreme Court in resolving disputes over religious freedom and church-state relations in the United States. It speaks volumes that Americans rely heavily on constitutions and courts for this purpose. Because the subject is complex, and because we tend to invoke both God and Constitution for support in political controversies, my goal is to take stock of American experience in order to clarify constitutional choices in protecting freedom for, and from, religion. The argument is divided into four parts, which in the end may resolve into one.

---

1 As quoted in Joseph Wood Krutch, "The Kremlin Claims Mark Twain," *New York Times Magazine*, 6 March 1960, 69. Hereafter cited as *NYT*.

2 *National Law Journal*, 16 June 1986, 14; *Los Angeles Times*, 23 July 1990, B5.

1. The United States Constitution speaks with a dual and uncertain voice on this subject.
2. The two religious guarantees of the First Amendment—the free exercise and establishment clauses—collide, especially as interpreted in the last five decades.
3. A newly conservative, but divided Supreme Court still searches for standards to resolve this conflict.
4. Judicial remedies are limited. Though Supreme Court leadership has contributed substantially to religious freedom in the United States, the tribunal plays an auxiliary rather than a primary role in protecting these constitutional values.

A DUAL AND UNCERTAIN VOICE

The U.S. Constitution, unlike the *Canadian Charter of Rights and Freedoms,* invokes neither "the supremacy of God" nor "the rule of law."[3] It speaks with a double and ambiguous voice about religion. The original Constitution forbids religious qualifications for federal public office and allows "affirmation" in lieu of oaths.[4] The central commands are in the First Amendment, which declares: "Congress shall make no law respecting an establishment of religion, or prohibiting the free exercise thereof."[5] In light of current controversies, note what is *not* said. The Constitution does not divorce religion and politics. It does not forbid Congress from making laws affecting religion. It does not prohibit a "national religion," as the House floor leader, James Madison, initially proposed. It says nothing about states, though Madison attempted and failed to extend freedoms of conscience against the states as well.[6] The Amendment precludes laws *"respecting an establishment of religion, or prohibiting the free exercise* thereof" (my emphasis). What do these words mean?

Madison once advised that to comprehend a constitution, one should examine the evils to be remedied and the benefits to be secured.[7] The apparent objectives of these dual safeguards were to protect religious liberty of individuals from government and government from religious factions. The clauses were written against a backdrop of centuries of religious warfare, persecution, and intolerance abroad, not to mention their offshoots in the colonies. The clauses reflect suspicion of strong

---

3 Albert P. Blaustein and Gisbert H. Flanz, eds., *Constitutions of the Countries of the World* (Dobbs Ferry, N.Y.: Oceana Publ., 1987), 3:97.

4 U.S. Constitution, Art. VI, cl. 3; Art. I, s. 3, cl. 6; Art. II, s. 1, cl. 8.

5 U.S. Constitution, Amend. I.

6 *Annals of the Congress of the United States, 1789–1824,* 42 vols. (Washington, D.C. Gales and Seaton, 1834–56), 1:451–52 (hereinafter *Annals of Congress*).

7 Edward S. Corwin, *National Supremacy: Treaty Power vs. State Power* (New York: Henry Holt and Co., 1913), 21.

central government as well as rapidly changing American attitudes and public policies toward religion resulting from the Enlightenment, growing religious diversity, and intense Protestant evangelism after the Great Awakening. It should be stressed that from the Revolution through framing of the Constitution and the Bill of Rights, this whole subject was in considerable flux.

Thoughtful scholars identify three main sources of the religion clauses: voluntarism, separatism, and federalism.[8] *Voluntarism*, expressed in the free exercise clause, is the principle that religion is a private choice, a relation solely between God and the individual. It grew from traditions of religious toleration in the middle colonies, especially Quakers in Pennsylvania and Roman Catholics in Maryland, and spread rapidly with Protestant evangelism before and during the Revolution. Despite disagreements over its reach, then and now, the principle of government noninterference with personal religious faith is a fundamental human right, copied over the globe. Mrs. Raisa Gorbachev affirmed the principle succinctly at the Reykjavik summit conference. Expressing respect for all faiths, though herself an atheist, she said: "It is, after all, a personal matter."[9]

Separatism, expressed in the establishment clause, is the principle of dividing state and religious affairs into public and private spheres. This tradition grew from both religious and rationalist sectors in American thought. Roger Williams in the seventeenth century, as well as Baptists and Quakers in the eighteenth, called for a "wall of separation" between the garden of God and the wilderness of the world in order to insulate the purity of religion from temporal control and corruption.[10] Virginia statesmen in the eighteenth century—notably George Mason, Thomas Jefferson, and James Madison—also sought separation to insulate the peace of the state from religious conflict. Weaving both strands into his great *Memorial and Remonstrance against Religious Assessments* in 1785, Madison argued that separating sacred and secular affairs would benefit both realms.[11] Judges sometimes call this principle "nonentanglement."

---

8 William Van Alstyne, "Trends in the Supreme Court: Mr. Jefferson's Crumbling Wall— A Comment on *Lynch v. Donnelly*," *Duke Law Journal* (1984), 770 at 772–79.

9 *NYT*, 13 October 1986, A10.

10 Mark De Wolfe Howe, *The Garden and the Wilderness* (Chicago: University of Chicago Press, 1965), 6.

11 See Walter Berns, *The First Amendment and the Future of American Democracy* (New York: Basic Books, 1976), 1–32; Sanford H. Cobb, *The Rise of Religious Liberty in America* (New York: Cooper Square Publishing, 1968), 491–93; Thomas J. Curry, *The First Freedoms: Church and State in America to the Passage of the First Amendment* (New York: Oxford University Press, 1986); and Michael W. McConnell, "The Origins and Historical Understanding of the Free Exercise of Religion," *Harvard Law Review* 103 (1990), 1409, 1421–80. For Madison's Remonstrance, see Robert A. Rutland and William M. E. Rachal, eds., *The*

Federalism, expressed by addressing Congress only, is the principle of state autonomy in religious affairs. In 1791, when the federal Bill of Rights was framed, six states still supported churches financially.[12] Federalism in this context was widely understood to mean national non-interference with state religious policies. Under the framers' constitutional theory of enumerated powers, Congress lacked authority over religion and the First Amendment did not apply to states. As Justice Joseph Story stated the understanding, "the whole power over the subject of religion is left exclusively to the state governments."[13]

The opaque language, "respecting an establishment of religion," thus was more than a clumsy way to forbid a national church. This phrasing enabled the drafters of the First Amendment to blend potentially incompatible principles of voluntarism, separatism, and federalism into a working consensus regarding constitutional limitations on the new national government. These principles were: (1) Congress, and by implication all federal officials, cannot interfere with peaceful exercise of private religion; (2) Congress cannot establish a national religion; (3) Congress cannot prefer one or more religions over other religions, though states could; and (4) Congress must keep hands off state establishments.

Truth to tell, few thought these "milk-and-water" provisions amounted to much. Protecting individual rights was considered largely the province of states until after the Civil War. The First Amendment, redundant against nation and irrelevant to states, was basically a symbolic and declaratory act to calm fears of skittish people. As Congressman Samuel Livermore observed, these amendments were worth "no more than a pinch of snuff; they went to secure rights never in danger."[14]

The central problem is determining what restraints the religion clauses impose on governments 150 years later when judges extend First Amendment guarantees to states and localities through the Fourteenth Amendment. Are they the same, more, or less? Answers turn largely on interpretation of "free exercise," "establishment," and "religion." Judges and scholars look to text, history, and original intentions for light,

---

Papers of James Madison (Chicago: University of Chicago Press, 1973), 8:298–306.

12 Connecticut, Georgia, Massachusetts, New Hampshire, South Carolina, and Vermont had multiple establishments providing nonpreferential aid to Christian denominations in each state. The Maryland constitution authorized public support which the legislature did not provide. See Leonard W. Levy, *The Establishment Clause: Religion and the First Amendment* (New York: Macmillan, 1986), 40–49, 60–61.

13 Herbert Storing, "The Constitution and the Bill of Rights," in M. Judd Harmon, ed., *Essays on the Constitution of the United States* (Port Washington, N.Y.: Kennikat Press, 1978), 36–37; quote, Joseph Story, *Commentaries on the Constitution of the United States* (1833), 3:731. So the Supreme Court ruled in *Permoli* v. *First Municipality of New Orleans*, 44 U.S. (3 How.) 589 at 609 (1845).

14 *Annals of Congress*, 1:805.

assuming that constraints on national action now extend to all public officials. The framers rejected this assumption, to be sure, but the answers
are critical because states are where most conflicts arise.

Generally speaking, two traditions have developed, with many
shades between, on the meaning of each religion clause. Moreover, the
Supreme Court has developed conflicting lines of precedent for both.
Contemporary Justices, like their predecessors, engage in selective history
as the high tribunal revamps constitutional doctrine to reflect the values
of their appointive constituencies.

The free exercise guarantee is widely understood to forbid government interference with religious belief or peaceful worship. The main
questions are whether, and how far, the Constitution also shelters religiously motivated conduct.[15] These issues form concretely in claimed religious exemptions from generally applicable laws, such as compulsory
education, flag salutes, military service, and taxation. The Justices have
seldom anchored free exercise decisions in extensive historical analysis,
perhaps because the federal evidence is so spare; but the basic options
show substantial continuity over time. Differences between Jefferson and
Madison over the scope of exemptions are a useful starting point.[16]

Jefferson, following John Locke, favored restricting Virginia's free
exercise guarantee to religious belief, not behavior. Accenting equal
toleration of secular and religious opinions, and the government's perspective of shielding civil society from sectarian conflict, he opposed
religious exemptions as conferring special privileges on individuals to
worship as they please. Jefferson construed the two religion clauses of the
First Amendment as "building a wall of separation between church and
State."[17] Just as government lacked power to prohibit, penalize, prefer,

---

15 For support of free exercise exemptions, see McConnell, "Free Exercise of Religion,"
1421–73; and Michael W. McConnell, "Free Exercise Revisionism and the *Smith* Decision," *University of Chicago Law Review* 57 (1990), 1109 at 1129–51. For critiques of free
exercise exemptions, see, e.g., Berns, *First Amendment*, 1–24; Michael J. Malbin, *Religion
and Politics: The Intentions of the Authors of the First Amendment* (Washington: American
Enterprise Institute, 1978); William P. Marshall, "The Case Against the Constitutionally
Compelled Free Exercise Exemption," *Case Western Reserve Law Review* 40 (1989–90), 357;
Mark Tushnet, "Of Church and State and the Supreme Court: Kurland Revisited,"
Supreme Court Review (1989), 373; and note 68 below.

16 A notable exception is Justice Souter's historical analysis in *Lee* v. *Weisman*, 112 S. Ct.
2649 at 2668 (1992). For contrasting interpretations of Jefferson's and Madison's views
of free exercise, see McConnell, "Free Exercise of Religion," 1449–55; and Malbin,
Religion and Politics, 27–37.

17 Thomas Jefferson, "Notes on the State of Virginia: Religion," in Merrill D. Peterson, ed.,
Writings (New York: Hill and Wang, 1984), 123; and quote, letter to Danbury Baptist
Association of Connecticut, 1 January 1802, ibid., 510. Also see "A Bill for Establishing
Religious Freedom" (1779), in Philip B. Kurland and Ralph Lerner, eds., *The Founders'
Constitution* (Chicago: University of Chicago Press, 1987), 5:77.

or compel religious faith, he argued, so religious rights did not relieve individuals from social duties. His sharp line between opinion and action thus left the scope of permissible conduct based on religion to the judgment of public officials.

Madison, by contrast, favored immunity for action dictated by religious conscience that did not trespass on rights of others or public peace. Sensitive to his evangelical constituents, and the believer's perspective of the primacy of religious duty, he proposed to exempt Quakers and other religious objectors from compulsory militia service, though not on secular, moral, or philosophical grounds. Even though religious exceptions rubbed against the nonestablishment principle, which Madison also championed, this proposal was accepted in the House but failed in the Senate.[18]

It is difficult to say how representative Jefferson's and Madison's views were of the general understanding, because Congress and state ratifying conventions left incomplete records of their proceedings. Projecting debates from prior state battles onto the framing of the national Bill of Rights, a common surrogate by scholars, has obvious risks. No one knows why the Senate rejected the House's conscientious objector provision or, more importantly, whether it dropped the House's proposal to protect both "rights of conscience" and "free exercise of religion" for stylistic or substantive reasons. Still, the activist ring of "free exercise," the Amendment's specific protection of religion instead of broader rights of conscience, the pervasive religiosity of American political culture at the time, all lend weight to Michael W. McConnell's conclusion that Madison was closer to the popular pulse than Jefferson's rational secularism. The Father of the Constitution seemed to want it both ways.[19] So did followers of republican political theory. Prominent leaders, including George Washington, thought that government should encourage religion and morality to bolster civic virtue and a fragile republican experiment.[20]

---

18 *Annals of Congress*, 1:451. See McConnell, "Free Exercise of Religion," 1452–55.

19 McConnell, "Free Exercise of Religion," 1480–1503. Cf. Levy, *Establishment Clause*, 91–119; Malbin, *Religion and Politics*, 25–39; Van Alstyne, "Trends in the Supreme Court," 776; and Thomas Lindsay, "James Madison on Religion and Politics: Rhetoric and Reality," *American Political Science Review* 85 (1991), 1321–37. For close connections between religious and political thought of the Founders, see, e.g., Thomas Pangle, *The Spirit of Modern Republicanism* (Chicago: University of Chicago Press, 1988); John P. Diggins, *Lost Soul of American Politics* (New York: Basic Books, 1984); James Reichley, *Religion in American Life* (Washington, D.C.: The Brookings Institution, 1985); and Jack Fruchtman, Jr., *Thomas Paine and the Religion of Nature* (Baltimore: Johns Hopkins University Press, 1993).

20 Washington, *Farewell Address* (19 September 1796), in Kurland and Lerner, eds., *The Founders' Constitution*, 1:681, 684; Gordon S. Wood, *The Creation of the American Republic 1776–1787* (Chapel Hill, N.C.: University of North Carolina Press, 1969), 426–29.

Since adoption of the Bill of Rights, the Supreme Court has alternated between no-exemption and exemption standards for religiously motivated conduct. When approving national bans on Mormon polygamy in 1879, for example, the Court explicitly endorsed Jefferson's theory that the First Amendment built a wall of separation between church and state but restricted free exercise to religious belief.[21] To exempt Mormon polygamists from the crime of bigamy, Chief Justice Waite declared, would "make the professed doctrines of religious belief superior to the law of the land, and in effect . . . permit every citizen to become a law unto himself."[22] The Court reversed field in the 1940s, recognized that conscience compels action, elevated religious expression into a "preferred freedom," and exempted Jehovah's Witnesses from compulsory flag salutes and taxes on religious pamphlets.[23] The leading modern precedent is *Sherbert* v. *Verner* (1963), which invalidated a state requirement that a Seventh Day Adventist must work on her Sabbath to be eligible for unemployment benefits.[24] The high tribunal expanded potential religious exemptions by heightening judicial scrutiny to insure that generally applicable laws do not unduly burden free exercise of religion, including religiously grounded conduct.

This doctrine, as we shall see, is now in jeopardy. After 1972, the Court not only rejected every claim to extend free exercise exemptions beyond the field of unemployment benefits, but substantially narrowed *Sherbert*'s scope in recent cases involving religious practices of native American Indians.[25] Refusing to constitutionalize sacramental peyote use in an Oregon unemployment benefits case, Justice Antonin Scalia's majority opinion revived the Jefferson-Waite principle that free exercise rights shelter opinions only, undercut the preferred freedom concept, and restored balancing of incidental burdens on religious activity to the political process. The pendulum of constitutional interpretation is swinging back to nonexemption.

The meaning of the establishment clause is even more problematic. Here again, opposing theories of church-state relations have spawned conflicting judicial doctrines. Separatists like Jefferson and Madison, accenting civil peace and minority rights, construe the establishment

---

21 *Reynolds* v. *United States*, 98 U.S. 145 (1879).

22 Ibid., 163.

23 *Cantwell* v. *Connecticut*, 310 U.S. 296 at 303 (1940); *Murdock* v. *Pennsylvania*, 319 U.S. 105 at 115 (1943); *West Virginia State Board of Education* v. *Barnette*, 319 U.S. 624 (1943); *Follett* v. *McCormick*, 321 U.S. 573 (1944).

24 374 U.S. 398 (1963).

25 *Employment Division, Oregon Department of Human Resources* v. *Smith*, 485 U.S. 660 (1988); 494 U.S. 872 (1990). See also *Lyng* v. *Northwest Indian Cemetery Protective Ass'n.*, 485 U.S. 439 (1988).

clause broadly in order to segregate private religion and public authority into autonomous spheres. Government must be neutral between religion and nonreligion. The subject is depoliticized. Religion is privatized. Hence, the Constitution forbids more than a national church, favoritism, or financial aid to the cloth. It displaces all government power over religion.[26]

Accommodationists, accenting voluntarism as the paramount value, construe the establishment clause narrowly in order to encourage free exercise of religion and public morality. Justice Story gave this view an honorable pedigree in his pioneering *Commentaries on the Constitution*:

> The general, if not the universal, sentiment in America was, that Christianity ought to receive encouragement from the state so far as was not incompatible with the private rights of conscience, and the freedom of religious worship. An attempt to level all religions, and to make it a matter of state policy to hold all in utter indifference, would have created universal disapprobation, if not universal indignation.[27]

This heritage is an important baseline for modern champions of nondiscriminatory state aid to religion, such as historian Robert L. Cord, former Attorney General Edwin W. Meese 3d, and Chief Justice William H. Rehnquist.[28] These so-called nonpreferentialists view the establishment clause as essentially a home-rule and antidiscrimination statute. Accordingly, public authorities may aid religion in order to accommodate the local majority's freedom of worship and to foster public morals, provided these acts do not invade private conscience, create an official church, or discriminate among denominations.

Complexity arises because practice in the early republic supports both positions. Few Americans felt the need to develop complete theories of

---

26 Van Alstyne, "Trends in the Supreme Court," 773–74; and Levy, *Establishment Clause*, 75–89.

27 *Commentaries* (1833), 3:726. Distinguishing between supporting and forcing religion, Story added: "The real object of the amendment was, not to countenance, much less to advance, Mahometanism, or Judaism, or infidelity, by prostrating Christianity; but to exclude all rivalry among Christian sects, and to prevent any national ecclesiastical establishment, which should give to an hierarchy the exclusive patronage of the national government. It thus cut off the means of religious persecution, (the vice and pest of former ages) and of the subversion of the rights of conscience in matters of religion, which had been trampled upon almost from the days of the Apostles to the present age." Ibid., 728.

28 Reichley, *Religion in American Life*, 52–114; also Reichley, "Religion and the Constitution," *This Constitution* 18 (Spring-Summer 1988), 46; Robert L. Cord, *Separation of Church and State: Historical Fact and Current Fiction* (New York: Lambeth Press, 1982), 5 at 15; (for Meese) Levy, *Establishment Clause*, 92; and Rehnquist J., dissenting in *Wallace v. Jaffree*, 472 U.S. 38 at 91 (1985).

church-state relations in an overwhelmingly Christian and Protestant society. Practice also contradicted theory at both national and state levels. The national government, for example, initially approximated Jefferson's ideal of a secular republic, neutral toward the diverse religions of its parts. The nation's motto—*E Pluribus Unum*—omitted God. Slogans on federal coins did not proclaim "In God We Trust," as they do now. They admonished: "Mind Your Business." God replaced Mammon on coins in the cauldron of Civil War.[29] On the other hand, melding of sacred and patriotic symbols in national observances started early. The first Congress itself called for a day of thanksgiving and prayer after drafting the Bill of Rights.[30]

A key issue is what to make of diverse state practices in the Union's formative years. One cannot assume that all states disestablished their churches during or soon after the Revolution. This complex development was partial, pluralistic, localistic—very American in form. Eight of fourteen states had severed official church ties when the Bill of Rights was ratified. Four New England states waited until much later: Vermont in 1807, Connecticut in 1818, and New Hampshire in 1819. Massachusetts tarried until 1833, two generations after framing of the First Amendment. Assuming that these states supported a single church as in England or colonial Virginia, accommodationists from Story to Rehnquist conclude that the target of disestablishment was merely preference, not government neutrality between religion and irreligion.[31]

But is the premise sound that "establishment" meant only one official church? In an important study of disestablishment state-by-state, the separatist legal historian, Leonard W. Levy, shows that no state in 1791 supported an exclusive religion. Instead, six states authorized public financial support for several Protestant denominations on a nonpreferential basis. A common practice during this transitional period was taxation to support the church of the freeholder's choice. In some states dissenting individuals, congregations, and entire localities (such as diverse Boston) were exempt. Levy concludes that current state practices were what the framers meant by establishment: public support of religion on a nondiscriminatory basis. He thus flunks Chief Justice Rehnquist and Justice

---

29 Van Alstyne, "Trends in the Supreme Court," 774–78.

30 Levy, *Establishment Clause*, 172–73; Chester J. Antieau, Arthur T. Downey, and Edward C. Roberts, *Freedom from Federal Establishment: Formation and Early History of the First Amendment's Religion Clauses* (Milwaukee: Bruce Publishing Co., 1964), 163.

31 See, e.g., Levy, *Establishment Clause*, 26–46; Berns, *First Amendment*, 7; and Edward S. Corwin, "The Supreme Court as National School Board," *Law and Contemporary Problems* 14 (1949), 3, 20.

Byron R. White in history and flips nonpreferentialism on its head. To outlaw establishment is to outlaw any public aid.[32]

Language further compounds the puzzle. Levy's student, Thomas J. Curry, counters in another important study that the framers' words had not adjusted to changing ways. Statesmen then did not distinguish between single and multiple establishments. They still used "establishment" to mean exclusivity and opposed it as an invasion of free conscience. While intending to ban all national support of religion, they used words of preference to mean no aid. Supporters of multiple establishments, in turn, did not regard their system as an establishment at all.[33]

The vagaries of law and language at the First Amendment's birth illustrates how treacherous it is to project the understandings of one age to solve the problems of another. In truth, most framers of the Bill of Rights had unclear intentions about the main problem vexing us today—the scope of federal constitutional limits on state and local action affecting religion—except that the subject was none of the central government's business. Especially is this so for religion in public education, perhaps the prime issue in both the U. S. and Canada. Public schools did not exist in 1790. Who knows what compromises might have resulted had the framers attempted to interpose national power over religious policies in their home states? Had they tried, there probably would have been no First Amendment.

So let us ring down the first curtain with the Constitution's dual but uncertain trumpets on religion and the states. Standard materials of interpretation—text, intention, history—do not settle the meaning of the religion clauses where the action was and still remains. Witnesses, historians, and jurists divide. While the bedrock consensus expressed in the First Amendment protected religious freedom far more than in any other nation in 1791, there was no golden age from which we regress. Ambiguity has prevailed from the start. And ambiguity, as every judge knows, invites choice.[34]

THE RELIGION CLAUSES COLLIDE

It usually comes as a surprise to learn that the free exercise and non-establishment guarantees of the First Amendment can clash. By virtue of home rule in the states, tension between voluntarism and separatism hardly arose in the Supreme Court until passage of the Civil War Amendments and, in particular, the last fifty years. Meanwhile, develop-

---

32 Levy, *Establishment Clause*, 49, 60–61; 155.

33 Curry, *First Freedoms*, 133, 191–92, 208–212.

34 See White J., in *Committee for Public Education* v. *Nyquist*, 413 U.S. 756 at 820 (1973).

ments in the nineteenth and early twentieth centuries had complicated the problem. Free immigration greatly enriched religious diversity—and potential conflicts. Religious groups engaged in political action over slavery, public education, and prohibition, while Jefferson's separatist principles increasingly attracted pluralistic and secular elites. Except for Mormon polygamy, however, few religious issues reached the Supreme Court until World War II.[35] Two critical developments in the "living" Constitution revolutionized the role of the judiciary as an arbiter of religious disputes.

First is nationalization of the federal Bill of Rights. Starting with property in the 1880s and speech in 1925, the Supreme Court gradually extended most of the first eight amendments to state action through the word "liberty" in the due process clause of the Fourteenth Amendment. Free exercise was absorbed in 1940, the establishment clause in 1947.[36] These were fateful steps in American religious history, because judges assumed jurisdiction over rights and disputes the framers had left to state law and politics. Federal hands off was now judicial hands on a vastly more complex church-state environment covering potentially every creed and community in the country.

The second major development, also starting in the 1940s, is separate, libertarian interpretation of each religion clause, which has accentuated their latent tension up to the present. In the midst of World War II, the Supreme Court declared that First Amendment rights of expression were "preferred freedoms," entitled to stronger judicial protection than property and other constitutional interests.[37] In one of the most dramatic reversals in modern times, the tribunal struck down compulsory flag salutes by public school students for invading freedoms of worship, speech, and thought. Government lacked power to compel affirmation of belief; free expression presupposed silence.[38] Recognizing that religious conscience commands action, moreover, the Justices exempted religious pamphlets

---

35 Levy, *Establishment Clause*, 170. The first major free exercise case was *Reynolds* v. *United States*, 98 U.S. 145 at 166 (1879). Cf. *Bradfield* v. *Roberts*, 175 U.S. 291 (1899); and *Quick Bear* v. *Leupp*, 210 U.S. 50 (1908).

36 *Cantwell* v. *Connecticut*, 310 U.S. 296 (1940); *Everson* v. *Board of Education*, 330 U.S. 1 (1947). For criticism of absorbing the establishment clause against the states, see "Note, Rethinking the Incorporation of the Establishment Clause: A Federalist View," *Harvard Law Review* 105 (1992), 1700.

37 *Murdock* v. *Pennsylvania*, 319 U.S. 105 at 115 (1943).

38 *West Virginia State Board of Education* v. *Barnette*, 319 U.S. 624 (1943), overruling *Minersville School District* v. *Gobitis*, 310 U.S. 585 (1940).

from local vendor taxes and expanded access of religious evangelists to public streets, parks, and doorbells of private homes.[39]

Free exercise of religion was in the vanguard of a momentous shift in the judiciary's role after the New Deal of protecting constitutional rights of individuals and "insular and discrete" minorities who lack power to protect themselves politically.[40] As Justice Robert H. Jackson declared for the Court in the second flag salute case, "the very purpose of a Bill of Rights was to withdraw certain subjects from the vicissitudes of political controversy, to place them beyond the reach of majorities and officials and to establish them as legal principles to be applied by the courts." Fundamental rights "may not be submitted to vote; they depend on the outcome of no elections."[41] From these seeds developed current concepts that judges are "peculiar guardians" of minority rights and free exchange of ideas.[42]

For the establishment clause, the Supreme Court adopted Jefferson's theory of strict separation between church and state. The seminal case, *Everson* v. *Board of Education*, challenged government reimbursement of bus fares to parents of parochial school students, mostly Roman Catholic, on an equal basis with parents of public school students.[43] The Justices, working on a clean slate, unanimously extended the establishment clause to the states, endorsed the separatist principle of government neutrality toward religion, and condemned public aid to religious schools. The real problem was application of these principles. Justice Hugo L. Black declared for the Court:

> The "establishment of religion" clause of the First Amendment means at least this: Neither a state nor the Federal Government can set up a church. Neither can pass laws which aid one religion, aid all religions, or prefer one religion over another. Neither can force nor influence a person to go to or to remain away from church against his will or force him to profess a belief or disbelief in any religion. No person can be punished for entertaining or professing religious beliefs or disbeliefs, for church attendance or non-attendance. No tax in any amount, large or small, can be levied to support any religious activities or institutions, whatever they may be called, or whatever form they may adopt to teach or practise religion. Neither a state nor the Federal Government can, openly or secretly, participate in the affairs of any religious organizations

---

39 *Cantwell* v. *Connecticut*, 310 U.S. 296 at 303 (1940); *Jones* v. *Opelika*, 319 U.S. 103 (1943); *Kunz* v. *New York*, 340 U.S. 290 (1951); *Niemetko* v. *Maryland*, 340 U.S. 268 (1951); *Martin* v. *Struthers*, 319 U.S. 141 (1943). Cf. *Reynolds* v. *United States*, 98 U.S. 145 at 166 (1878).

40 *United States* v. *Carolene Products Co.*, 304 U.S. 144 at 154, n. 4 (1938).

41 *West Virginia State Board of Education* v. *Barnette*, 319 U.S. 624 at 638 (1943).

42 Madison's phrase, *Annals of Congress*, 1:457.

43 330 U.S. 1 at 3 (1947).

or groups and vice versa. In the words of Jefferson, the clause against establishment of religion by law was intended to erect a "wall of separation between Church and State."[44]

No sooner said than the Court compromised the strict-separation principle in application. A 5–4 majority upheld the refund on the theory that New Jersey benefitted children primarily and churches only incidentally. The dissenters, virtual absolutists, protested that this lawyer-like splitting of hairs breached the "high and impregnable" wall at the first crack. Justice Wiley B. Rutledge, in a powerful opinion, charged that the decision would beget more pressure for state subsidies of parochial education and the very thing Jefferson and Madison guarded against, embroiling the state in the sectarian struggles over shares in the public till. Justice Jackson, a Protestant who sent his children to Catholic schools, struck with the stiletto of wit. The most fitting precedent, he said, was Byron's report of Julia who, "whispering, 'I will ne'er consent'—consented."[45]

Tension between free exercise of religion and strict separation thus appeared in the first case applying the establishment clause to the states. By tipping the scales in favor of individual worship and the public purpose of education, the Justices of the 1940s, like other statesmen fore and aft, preached separation but practised accommodation. In their élan to declare libertarian principles for both clauses, the jurists of the Roosevelt Court did not fully perceive the pitfalls of separate development of each. The uproar over two "release-time" cases affecting religious instruction in forty-six states soon indicated that they had a tiger by the tail: minority vs. majority rights to worship.

In *Illinois ex rel. McCollum* v. *Board of Education*, the Justices struck down a parentally requested release of public school students for religious instruction during regular hours in school buildings.[46] In *Zorach* v. *Clauson*, four years later, they upheld release of such students for devotionals in premises outside. "We are a religious people whose institutions presuppose a Supreme Being," Justice William O. Douglas declared in an attempted accommodation at the school-house door.[47] The Court has

---

44 Ibid., 15–16.

45 Ibid., 53–54, quote 19. According to Justice Frank Murphy's conference notes, Justice Rutledge would have prohibited government aid to all private schools. No other Justice would go that far. Justice Douglas apparently stressed government endorsement of religion as the primary evil. Conference note, *Everson* v. *New Jersey*, October Term 1946, Frank Murphy Papers, Bentley Historical Collections, University of Michigan, Ann Arbor. For debates within the Court, see the author's *Mr. Justice Murphy: A Political Biography* (Princeton, N.J.: Princeton University Press, 1968), 449.

46 333 U.S. 203 (1948).

47 343 U.S. 306 at 313 (1952).

never reconciled the two decisions satisfactorily. Public school officials assisted both programs. Analysts widely assumed that the Justices, having pushed separatism too far ahead of public opinion, sacrificed the neutrality principle to majority will and political necessity.[48]

Whatever the reasons for the tribunal's retreat to a flexible wall of separation, the *Everson* and *Zorach* cases were sobering lessons regarding popular limits on judicial power. Defeated at the threshold was an absolutist approach, championed by Justices Jackson and Rutledge, that the Court should relax neither religious guarantee but remove both from political control. Jackson was a tough-minded "lawyer's lawyer," keenly aware that absolute rights in law are "certainly rare."[49] After strict separation lost in *Zorach*, he rendered a remarkably prescient lament that is well worth pondering for both the political calculus underlying absolutism and the dilemmas of the Court's balancing approach. To fellow separatist Justice Felix Frankfurter, he wrote:

> The battle for *separation* of Church and School is lost. From here on it is only a question of how far the intermixture will go. The doctrine of separation never had a chance against pressure groups, except that this Court should unwaveringly apply it as an absolute, or as near an absolute as anything can be in law. As an absolute it was an American doctrine—just as American as the red Indian. If once this Court wavered, began debating fine distinctions, tolerated little evasions, it was then lost.
>
> The wavering came in *Everson*. Black, in all good faith, believed that strong words about separation of Church and State would be acceptable to its enemies if it were seasoned with bus fare refunds. What he overlooked was that the enemies of separation were at once given an incentive to further aggressions and the dialectics to support it. His argument about policemen, firemen and due process apply just as well to providing shelter, lunches or teachers of secular subjects for those who attend parochial schools.
>
> In the *McCollum* case, I doubted whether the Court should take over so big a field, for I distrusted its constancy. But once engaged in it, it had no choice except to become the school board of the Nation by passing on petty distinctions and separating one from another, or to take a firm stand against any intermixture of religion and education. Monday's decision means that separation is not an absolute separation but such an intermingling as from time to time strikes this Court as not too bad. This is the very thing that makes us the school board of the Nation.
>
> As a legal doctrine, separation is gone. It may still be argued in the political sphere or in every school district in the country. The schools are

---

48 See Note, "The 'Released Time' Cases Revisited: A Study of Group Decisionmaking by the Supreme Court," *Yale Law Journal* 83 (1974), 1202 at 1228–33.

49 *United States* v. *Willow River Power Co.*, 324 U.S. 499 at 510 (1945).

in religion and religion is in the school meetings, because the different sects will now find it important to control the school programs.

Reactions in the press shattered hopes that "these appeasements" were a temporary deviation, Jackson concluded. Complete failure to grasp the importance of not wavering and the significance of picking up each little distinction as a constitutional problem for this Court means, to me, that the cause not only is lost in this Court but with and for the public. I think we can charge it off as a lost cause.[50]

Debates in these seminal decisions merit attention in any nation that attempts to protect religious liberty or to defuse church-state conflicts by constitutional adjudication. Justice Black's summary of legal principles in *Everson* and Justice Jackson's critique of judicial balancing after *Zorach* still set the parameters of the problem. For now, let us draw essential conclusions about the modern threshold.

1. By nationalizing the First Amendment's religion clauses and choosing independent, libertarian standards for each, the Supreme Court in the 1940s made momentous gains for freedom and tolerance of religious minorities in the United States.

2. The role of the Court, by like token, shifted from bystander to policeman of public policies affecting religion in the states and localities, where disputes over religious freedoms concentrate. If it is ironic that Jefferson's wall was erected by the judicial review he detested, these developments illustrate the revolutionary implications of the Civil War Amendments for individual rights and the judicial function under the living Constitution. Judges have been immersed ever since in issues of voluntarism and separatism which federalism had permitted the framers and succeeding statesmen to sidestep for 150 years.

3. By separately interpreting the free exercise clause as a preferred freedom and the establishment clause as a high wall separating church and state, the Supreme Court accentuated latent conflict between the First Amendment's dual commands, which the framers perhaps saw as one.

The Court's operating principle is government neutrality—neither encouragement of nor hostility toward religion. Its practice since *Everson* and *Zorach* is balancing interests, and necessarily so. Both clauses declare rights. The establishment clause limits government aid to religion; the free exercise clause prevents total separation of church and state. Just as the Court became a special guardian of politically impotent minorities, so it recognized that majorities, too, have rights to free worship. How to reconcile these colliding values is among the most sensitive constitutional and political problems of our time.

---

50 Robert H. Jackson to Felix Frankfurter, 30 April 1952, Box 19, Frankfurter Papers, Manuscripts Division, Library of Congress.

THE SEARCH FOR STANDARDS

Broadly speaking, during the last three decades, the Warren and Burger Courts vigorously pursued both libertarian goals of free worship and strict separation. They also aggravated tension between the two principles by interpreting each clause as independent rather than integral branches of First Amendment jurisprudence. The apparent reason is inability to agree whether voluntarism or separatism takes priority when both values come into play. The disagreement reflects changes in American life and conceptions of the judicial function that inexorably magnify points of conflict and political pressures on the judiciary. Consequently, Justices still struggle to develop coherent standards for the First Amendment. Critics commonly complain that constitutional doctrine is in disarray, especially in expanding grey areas where both principles overlap.[51] These conditions are likely to continue as the reconstituted Rehnquist Court, reflecting turnover in personnel, reconstructs what the religion clauses mean.

For free exercise claims, the Court developed relatively coherent guidelines—and recently retreated from them. Public compulsion of religious faith is presumed invalid under the *Cantwell* principle that freedom of thought is absolute.[52] According to doctrines of *Sherbert* v. *Verner*, religious activity is exempt from discriminatory or burdensome regulation, unless officials show a compelling public purpose and choose least restrictive means.[53] This so-called "strict scrutiny" test, which generally governs regulation of free expression based on content of ideas, ostensibly balances the interests of government and individuals. It is heavily weighted toward personal freedom and accommodation of minority religious practice. A high point of this principle is the Burger Court's decision in *Wisconsin* v. *Yoder*, which exempted the Amish from an ordinary duty of citizenship—compulsory school-attendance beyond the age of sixteen.[54]

---

51 See Note, "Developments in the Law—Religion and the State," *Harvard Law Review* 100 (1987), 1606, 1631, 1712; Michael W. McConnell, "Religious Freedom at a Crossroads," *University of Chicago Law Review* 59 (1992), 115.

52 *Cantwell* v. *Connecticut*, 310 U.S. 296 (1940).

53 374 U.S. 398 (1963); and *Thomas* v. *Review Board of Indiana Employment Security Division*, 450 U.S. 707 (1981).

54 406 U.S. 205 (1972).

At first glance, this audacious decision greatly expanded the scope of potential religious exemptions.[55] In retrospect, however, *Yoder* marks the turning point of consolidation and retreat. Consolidating *Sherbert* doctrine, the Court consistently invalidated civil regulations forcing religious objectors to choose between working on their Sabbaths and losing unemployment benefits.[56] Indeed, in the *Frazee* case, the Justices unanimously extended this exemption to sincerely religious individuals unconnected to an organized religious sect, a limitation Chief Justice Burger had imposed in *Yoder* to keep educational exceptions in bounds.[57]

Since *Yoder*, on the other hand, the Justices conducted a three-stage retreat from the strict judicial scrutiny of free exercise claims. First, they restricted free exercise exemptions to the field of employment compensation. While purporting to apply strict scrutiny standards, they refused to exempt religious organizations from sales tax, minimum wage, social security, or racial discrimination laws.[58] Next, they lowered the standards in other contexts. *Goldman* v. *Weinberger*, for instance, upheld Air Force punishment of an Orthodox Jewish psychologist for wearing a yarmulke while on duty indoors in violation of uniform dress regulations.[59] Chief Justice Rehnquist ruled for the Court that judicial review is far more deferential toward military than civilian regulations. The lowest standard of judicial scrutiny—rational relationship—governs sincere worship in prisons.[60] This minimum standard of judicial scrutiny requires only a showing of rational means to a legitimate end.

Finally, in major decisions involving native American Indians, the Court gutted the system of free exercise exemptions by converting strict scrutiny into the exception and the rational relationship test into the rule. This switch began with Chief Justice Burger's suggestion in *Bowen* v. *Roy* that "compelling interest" standards should apply only to direct or intentional government coercion of individual conduct contrary to religious be-

---

55 Practical problems remained of how to determine sincere religious motivations, incidental burdens, and the reach of special treatment for religions. See John T. Noonan, Jr., "How Sincere Do You Have To Be To Be Religious?" *University of Illinois Law Review* (1988), 713; Ira C. Lupu, "Where Rights Begin: The Problem of Burdens on the Free Exercise of Religion," *Harvard Law Review* 100 (1989), 933.

56 *Thomas* v. *Review Board*, 450 U.S. 707 (1981); *Hobbie* v. *Unemployment Compensation Commission of Florida*, 480 U. S. 136 (1987).

57 *Frazee* v. *Illinois Department of Employment Security*, 489 U.S. 829 (1989); 406 U.S. 205 at 215–16.

58 *Jimmy Swaggart Ministries* v. *California Board of Equalization*, 493 U.S. 378 (1990); *Tony and Susan Alamo Foundation* v. *Secretary of Labor*, 471 U.S. 290 (1985); *United States* v. *Lee*, 455 U.S. 252 (1982); and *Bob Jones University* v. *United States*, 461 U.S. 574 (1983).

59 475 U.S. 503 (1986).

60 *O'Lone* v. *Shabazz*, 482 U.S. 342 (1987).

lief, not to incidental or unintended effects on religion from neutral laws of uniform applicability.[61] Building on this distinction, a 5–3 majority in *Lyng* v. *Northwest Indian Cemetery Protective Association* refused to block the U.S. Forest Service from building a road for purposes of logging and tourism through a national forest in California that would destroy sacred worship sites of several Indian tribes.[62] While conceding that the road could have "devastating effects on traditional Indian religious practices," Justice O'Connor held for the Court that "compelling interest" justification applies only to direct government penalties or discrimination against religiously motivated conduct, not to even-handed, federal land use policies that merely prevent acts of worship commanded by particular religious beliefs. Otherwise, she argued, diverse religious objectors in a pluralistic society could veto a host of government programs. "Whatever rights the Indians may have to the use of the area," she wrote, "those rights do not divest the Government of its rights to use what is, after all, *its* land."[63]

The *Lyng* decision illustrates the practical differences between the strict and minimum scrutiny tests. Under compelling interest, least-means analysis, the government might well have had to build a costlier road around the site. Under minimum scrutiny, such claims are unlikely to prevail if the question is debatable. To avoid the "cruelly surreal result" of destroying the religious practice of 5,000 Indians for sake of a marginally beneficial road, the dissenters led by Justice Brennan proposed a compromise: objectors must show some central religious belief at stake before the government must demonstrate a compelling purpose.[64] Balancing such interests, O'Connor countered, was for Congress.[65]

Retreat turned into rout in the Oregon peyote case of 1990, *Employment Division, Department of Human Resources of Oregon* v. *Smith*.[66] After lengthy litigation, a 5–4 majority abandoned the *Sherbert* test for free exercise exemptions from general criminal laws. The claimants were two native American counsellors in a private drug rehabilitation center who

---

61 476 U.S. 693 at 707–708 (1986). In *Bowen*, an 8–1 majority sustained a federal food stamp program requiring beneficiaries to produce social security numbers despite religious objections.

62 485 U.S. 439 (1988).

63 Ibid., 449–51, quote 453.

64 Ibid., 472–74.

65 Ibid., 457–58. For discussion, see Lupu, "Where Rights Begin"; Note, "Conduct and Belief in the Free Exercise Clause: Developments and Derivations in *Lyng* v. *Northwest Indian Cemetery Protective Association*," *Cornell Law Review*, 76 (1990), 268. Congress overturned this decision (Pub. L. 101–612, 101st Cong., 2d Sess., 16 November 1990; 104 Stat. 3209 at 3212) by placing the area under protection of the Wilderness Act (16 U.S.C. § 1131) and federal regulations forbidding commercial enterprises and permanent roads in wilderness units (50 C.F.R. c. 1, § 35.5, 10–1–90).

66 485 U.S. 660 (1988); 494 U.S. 872 (1990).

were fired, and subsequently denied unemployment benefits for work-related misconduct, after using peyote during religious ceremonies. Rather than constitutionalize exemptions for sacramental use of peyote, or reverse on the facts, the majority drastically narrowed the range of incidental government burdens subject to strict scrutiny. Justice Scalia stated the Court's "sounder approach": "generally applicable, religion-neutral laws that have the effect of burdening a particular religious practice need not be justified by a compelling government interest."[67]

Even though the outcome was expected, the Court's activism, going far beyond what was necessary to decide the case, shocked the civil liberties community.[68] Justice Scalia's majority opinion revived Jefferson and viscerated the concept of religiously motivated conduct as an independent preferred freedom. Calling private rights to ignore generally applicable laws a "constitutional anomaly," Scalia contended that the criminal-conduct exemptions in *Cantwell*, *Barnette*, and *Yoder* were based on a hybrid of expressive and parental rights, not the free exercise clause alone.[69] Free exercise exceptions to general laws are now ancillary rights; and exacting judicial scrutiny is limited to religious belief, worship, communication, child rearing, workers' compensation, and hostile government attacks on religious groups.

To justify this contraction, Scalia quoted *Reynolds* with approval, rejected the minority's proposed centrality inquiry as "utterly un-workable," and stressed the dilemmas of special privileges and uneven

---

67 494 U.S. 872 at 886, n. 3. For Justice Scalia's criticism of judicial balancing as requiring excessive discretion, see Antonin Scalia, "The Rule of Law as a Law of Rules," *University of Chicago Law Review* 56 (1989), 1175.

68 The majority not only spurned the Oregon Supreme Court's repeated view that the criminality of peyote was immaterial to eligibility for state unemployment compensation, but decided a hypothetical question and interjected the issue of reconsidering the compelling interest standard without a request by either party or oral argument. McConnell, "Free Exercise Revisionism," 1112–13. Oregon subsequently exempted sacramental use of peyote. *NYT*, 9 July 1991, A14. For other criticism, see *NYT*, 11 May 1990, A16; 29 February 1992, A10; Michael W. McConnell, "Accommodation of Religion: An Update and a Response to Critics," *George Washington Law Review* 60 (1992), 685; Jesse Choper, "The Rise and Decline of the Constitutional Protection of Religious Liberty," *Nebraska Law Review* 70 (1991), 651, and the proposed Religious Freedom Restoration Act of 1991, which would restore strict scrutiny standards by statute, H.R. 2797, 102d Cong., 1st Sess., *Cong. Rec.*, 137, No. 100, H5210, 26 June 1991. Cf. William P. Marshall, "In Defense of Smith and Free Exercise Revisionism," *University of Chicago Law Review* 58 (1991), 308; and Ira C. Lupu, "Reconstructing the Establishment Clause: The Case Against Discretionary Accommodation of Religion," *University of Pennsylvania Law Review* 140 (1991), 555.

69 494 U.S. 872 at 886. For a sharp critique of Justice Scalia's use of precedents ("bordering on the shocking"), see McConnell, "Free Exercise Revisionism," 1120–27.

judicial application of strict scrutiny standards.[70] Noting that several states and the federal government had exempted sacramental use of peyote from their drug laws, he referred such balancing to the political process. Disadvantaged though unorthodox religious minorities might be in the fray, he declared, this unavoidable consequence of democratic government was preferable to systems in which "each conscience is a law unto itself" or "judges weigh the social importance of all laws against the centrality of all religious beliefs."[71]

Small wonder that Justices Blackmun, Brennan, and Marshall protested the decision as "a wholesale overturning of settled law."[72] Even Justice O'Connor, who found Oregon's interest compelling in the case, balked at the majority's reformulation of exemption doctrine. Given the free exercise clause's express guarantee of liberty from overweening majorities, and the indistinct line between belief and action, she argued, conduct grounded in sincere religion at least should be presumptively protected so that unpopular religious minorities may have their day in court.[73]

A valid distinction exists between what governments cannot compel individuals to do and what individuals cannot compel governments to do under the free exercise clause. Justice Scalia is correct that the Court's application of compelling interest standards has been more discretionary in religion cases than in other fields such as equal protection. The *Smith* decision, nonetheless, is a radical retreat toward Jefferson's view of free exercise exemptions. In cases where cultures clash regarding sacred versus secular use of public land and its fruits, the high tribunal converted exceptions from strict judicial scrutiny into a general rule of nonexemption. Decisions since *Smith*, moreover, appear to extend this principle to civil as well as criminal cases.[74] An unexpected outcome of conservative Court-packing is a sharp break from the New Deal philosophy of special judicial protection of politically impotent minorities in a field that gave it birth. The postwar Court's major contribution to free exercise jurisprudence and its method of protecting minority religions are in serious jeopardy. Their fate will depend increasingly on state laws and politics.[75]

---

70 494 U.S. 872 at 888.

71 Ibid., 890.

72 Ibid., 908.

73 Ibid., 890, 902–903, 895.

74 See, e.g., *Committee to Oppose Sale* v. *Rector of St. Bartholomew's*, 914 F. 2d 348 (2d Cir. 1990), cert. denied, 111 S. Ct. 1003 (1991); *First Covenant Church* v. *City of Seattle*, 114 Wash. 2d 392, 787 P. 2d 1352 (1990), vacated and remanded, 113 S. Ct. 1097 (1991); *McDonald* v. *Oklahoma*, 787 P. 2d 466 (1989), cert. denied, 111 S. Ct. 60 (1990); and *Yang* v. *Sturner*, 750 F. Supp. 558 (D.R.I. 1990). See *Washington Post*, 9 March 1991, A1.

75 See *Minnesota* v. *Herschberger*, 495 U.S. 901 (1990); 462 N.W. 2d 393 (1990).

For the establishment clause, in contrast, the Court's rather muddled guidelines are hanging in the balance. The basic principle since *Everson* is government neutrality toward religion. The state must neither be for nor against it, nor favor one sect over another. But what is neutral? Must neutral be secular? To guide decision makers, the Burger Court offered a "three-prong test" in *Lemon* v. *Kurtzman*.[76] This categorical test presumably has balanced interests in advance. To satisfy the establishment clause a statute or government activity must: (1) reflect a secular purpose, (2) have a primary effect that neither advances nor inhibits religion, and (3) avoid excessive government entanglement with religious organizations.

History pulsates in these categorical commands, but applying them consistently proved to be very troublesome. Logically, *Lemon* contradicts *Sherbert* on its face. Government accommodation of religion, by definition, violates the secular purpose prong. Different methodologies of balancing interests and categorical commands are uneasily meshed when both clauses apply. How a claim is classified may substantially affect the outcome.[77]

Beyond lawyerly problems are controversial results. Separatists were upset when the Justices, facing practical considerations of money, competing policies, and popular tolerances, made pragmatic adjustments that smacked of ad hoc balancing. For example, they approved Sunday closing laws, tax exemptions for religious institutions, and public aid to some parochial schools under some conditions.[78] The latter came largely under two exceptions: the child-benefit theory of *Everson* and the distinction between university and elementary schools, whose pupils are considered more vulnerable to religious indoctrination and attend under state compulsion.[79] These distinctions have enduring impact on educational

---

76 403 U.S. 602 at 612 (1971). The purpose and effect prongs originated in *Abington School District* v. *Schempp*, 374 U.S. 203 (1963); the entanglement prong in *Walz* v. *Tax Commission*, 397 U.S. 664 at 669 (1970). For neutrality, see *NYT*, 19 September 1983, A18.

77 "Developments—Religion and the State," note 51 above, 1633, 1717, 1723. For penetrating discussion, see Brief for the U.S. as *amicus curiae*, *Thornton* v. *Caldor*, No. 83–1158, filed 5 June 1984, 27; Jesse H. Choper, "The Religion Clauses of the First Amendment: Reconciling the Conflict," *University of Pittsburgh Law Review* 41 (1980), 673; Douglas Laycock, "Towards a General Theory of the Religion Clauses: The Case of Church Labor Relations and the Right of Church Autonomy," *Columbia Law Review* 81 (1981), 1380; and Phillip E. Johnson, "Concepts and Compromise in First Amendment Religious Doctrine," *California Law Review* 72 (1984), 817.

78 *McGowan* v. *Maryland*, 366 U.S. 420 (1961); *Walz* v. *Tax Commission*, 397 U.S. 664 (1970).

79 See, e.g., *Board of Education* v. *Allen*, 392 U.S. 236 (1968); *Committee for Public Education and Religious Liberty* v. *Regan*, 444 U.S. 646 (1980); *Tilton* v. *Richardson*, 403 U.S. 672 at 685 (1971); *Roemer* v. *Public Works Board of Maryland*, 426 U.S. 736 (1976); and *Lee* v. *Weisman*, 112 S. Ct. 2649 (1992).

finance and, as Justice Jackson predicted, the Court's role as a national school board.

Accommodationists protested decisions removing religion from government activities. The most emotionally wrenching nullified officially sponsored prayers and Bible-reading for purposes of worship in public schools.[80] To protect freedom of conscience for the few, the Warren Court uprooted customary devotionals of the many—and provoked a storm. "The Supreme Court," exclaimed Senator Sam J. Ervin, Jr., "has made God unconstitutional."[81]

It is no accident that the Burger Court decided most of the establishment clause cases in our history. During the 1970s and 1980s, the tribunal came under heavy pressure to relax strict separation in favor of more accommodation with freedom of worship. Substantial segments of the population believe that an activist judiciary has converted separatism into hostility toward religion. This feeling may be strongest among evangelical and fundamentalist groups but is hardly limited to them. A majority of American adults in public opinion polls persistently favor organized prayer in public schools.[82] The high court's abortion decisions, based on unwritten rights of privacy, sear the religious consciences of millions of Americans.[83] The result is a powerful political counter-reaction that impinges on the judiciary. Proposals to overturn these decisions by constitutional amendment or appointing sympathetic Justices are staples in Republican Party platforms.

Professional commentators, in turn, criticize the incoherence and unpredictability of the tribunal's decisions. Everyone has a favorite list of anomalies. For example, tax exemptions and tax deductions for parents of parochial school students are permissible; tax credits and direct grants are not.[84] Would economists perceive constitutional differences in these subsidies? Public schools may not offer religious instruction, nor may public

---

80 *Engel* v. *Vitale*, 370 U.S. 421 (1962); *Abington School District* v. *Schempp*, 374 U.S. 203 (1963).

81 Leo Pfeffer, *Church, State, and Freedom*, rev. ed. (Boston: Beacon Press, 1967), 466.

82 For reactions to school prayer decisions, see, e.g., "Developments—Religion and the State," note 51 above, 1660; S.J. Res. 37 and H.J. Res. 161, 100th Cong., 1st Sess. (1987). Also see Herbert McClosky and Alida Brill, *Dimensions of Tolerance: What Americans Believe About Civil Liberties* (New York: Russell Sage Foundation, 1983), 133; *NYT*, 16 August 1984, 16.

83 *Roe* v. *Wade*, 410 U.S. 113 (1973).

84 *Walz* v. *Tax Commission*, 397 U.S. 664 (1970); *Mueller* v. *Allen*, 463 U.S. 388 (1983); *Committee for Public Education* v. *Nyquist*, 413 U.S. 756 (1973). See Rehnquist J., in *Wallace* v. *Jaffree*, 472 U.S. 38 at 91 (1985).

employees teach secular subjects in sectarian schools.[85] Yet, public schools may release students for religious instruction elsewhere and supervise the transfers under truancy laws, while nonworshippers remain in school.[86] States may subsidize transportation of students to parochial schools, though not field trips to study secular subjects.[87] States may lend geography texts containing maps of the U.S. to parochial school students, not maps to their geography teachers, who might take better care of them.[88]

The Justices themselves engaged in self-criticism. Chief Justice Warren E. Burger observed in *Lemon* that the wall of separation is "a blurred, indistinct, and variable barrier," depending on the particulars of each case.[89] Justice Rehnquist concluded in 1985 that the precedents are irreconcilable and unprincipled.[90] "This is an area," Justice Blackmun conceded, "where we have not done well."[91]

Erosion and refinement of the *Lemon* test contributed to the confusion. Chief Justice Burger, author of *Lemon* and champion of "benevolent neutrality," attempted to relax strict separation in order to accommodate free exercise of religion in public life.[92] A few decisions drifted in that direction. The tribunal upheld public pay for Nebraska's sole legislative chaplain on the basis of historic practice, ignoring *Lemon* altogether.[93] In *Widmar* v. *Vincent* the Court sustained the rights of University of Missouri students to meet in campus buildings for voluntary worship equally with other student groups.[94] Administrators had denied access solely to religious groups for fear of violating the establishment clause. Accepting the students' free exercise and free speech claims, the Justices extended the open forum principle to public colleges and universities. Congress

85 *McCollum* v. *Board of Education*, 333 U.S. 203 (1948); *Grand Rapids School District* v. *Ball*, 473 U.S. 373 (1985); *Aquilar* v. *Felton*, 473 U.S. 402 (1985).

86 *Zorach* v. *Clauson*, 343 U.S. 306 (1952).

87 *Everson* v. *Board of Education*, 330 U.S. 1 (1947); *Wolman* v. *Walter*, 433 U.S. 229 at 252 (1977).

88 *Board of Education* v. *Allen*, 392 U.S. 236 (1968); *Meek* v. *Pettinger*, 421 U.S. 349 (1975).

89 403 U.S. 602 at 614 (1971).

90 *Wallace* v. *Jaffree*, 472 U.S. 38 at 107 (1985).

91 *NYT*, 25 September 1986, B10.

92 *Walz* v. *Tax Commission*, 397 U.S. 664 at 669 (1970).

93 *Marsh* v. *Chambers*, 463 U.S. 783 (1983). Also see *Larson* v. *Valente*, 466 U.S. 228 (1982).

94 454 U. S. 263 (1981).

extended these rights to secondary public schools in 1984, and judges now grapple with varying applications in high schools across the land.[95]

Then in *Lynch* v. *Donnelly*, a well-publicized Pawtucket, Rhode Island, crèche case, a 5–4 majority sustained a nativity scene that mixed sacred and secular symbols—Jesus Christ, Santa's house, teddy bears, and a wishing well—at public expense in a nonprofit park.[96] Chief Justice Burger paid lip service to the high wall as a "useful figure of speech," but undercut it by accenting historic custom and reinterpreting the First Amendment: "It affirmatively mandates accommodation, not merely tolerance, of all religion, and forbids hostility" toward any.[97] Religion's special status in the Constitution obliged government to foster the majority's freedom of worship. Holiday displays thereafter became a fertile source of litigation and doctrinal struggle.

Courtwatchers expected a showdown between separatists and accommodationists in the 1985 term when the Justices heard an unusual number of cases challenging each prong of the *Lemon* test. The Reagan Administration entered the fray to champion its abandonment. The Solicitor General proposed an alternative test: public aid to religion is constitutional that does not coerce, discriminate, or intrude on church governance. Jefferson's side of the high wall—shielding government from sectarian conflicts—went unheeded.[98]

The outcome was defeat for accommodationists. Shifting coalitions under Justice Brennan's leadership held fast to the *Lemon* test, warts and all, and refined it significantly. Invigorating the purpose prong, the Court struck down Alabama's minute of silence for "meditation or voluntary prayer" in public schools for want of secular motives.[99] Purpose was the defect as well in Louisiana's law requiring public science teachers to give balanced treatment to supernatural theories of creation whenever they teach evolution.[100] Brennan dismissed the official purpose of promoting academic freedom as a "sham" on its face.[101]

To woo Justice O'Connor's support, the Court absorbed endorsement of religion into both the purpose and effects prongs and added religious

---

95 Equal Access Act, 20 U.S.C. § 4071 (1984), sustained in *Board of Education* v. *Mergens*, 496 U.S. 226 (1990). See, e.g., *Centennial School District* v. *Gregoire*, 907 F. 2d 1366 (3d Cir. 1990), cert. denied, 111 S. Ct. 253 (1990).

96 465 U.S. 668 (1984).

97 Ibid., 672–73.

98 *NYT*, 6 August 1984, A16, and 21 October 1984, E2; *National Law Journal*, 10 September 1984, 1, 28.

99 *Wallace* v. *Jaffree*, 472 U.S. 38 (1985).

100 *Edwards* v. *Aguillard*, 482 U.S. 578 (1987).

101 Ibid., 586–89. Cf. Justice Scalia's biting dissent at 610.

symbolism to them.[102] The most far-reaching decisions in social consequence invalidated publicly funded programs of remedial education in
secular subjects taught by public school teachers to disadvantaged pupils
in neighborhood parochial schools. Grand Rapids' program, the Court
ruled, was an "impermissible symbolic union of government and religion."[103] A New York City program ran afoul of the entanglement
prong. Judges reluctantly concluded that procedures to prevent religious
influences excessively meshed church and state bureaucracies.[104] The
decision illustrates why critics view the effect-entanglement combination
as a Catch-22. This widely praised program, secular in purpose and effect,
was a model in funnelling $3.2 billion in federal funds for remedial
education of disadvantaged children over the country. Having tried other
methods, New York found that neighborhood schools worked best. What's
more, the city's subsequent steps spawned new litigation over free
exercise rights of Hasidic Jews.[105]

Churning best describes recent doctrinal struggles over the establishment clause. Several alternatives vie for support. Chief Justice Rehnquist,
attacking the high-wall metaphor for having "little use," would abandon
Everson's wall, *Lemon's* test, and neutrality for sake of minimalism: no
national church, no discrimination among sects, and deference to state
policies.[106] So far, he has one solid vote for that. Justice John Paul
Stevens, at the opposite pole, would rebuild *Everson's* "high and impregnable" wall.[107] In between, Justice Scalia, joined by Chief Justice
Rehnquist, challenges the Court's selective emphasis on legislative purpose and neglect of historical traditions.[108] Justice O'Connor, though
sharing Justice White's worry that the effect and entanglement combination creates a Catch-22, seeks to refine the purpose and effects standards

---

102 *Wallace v. Jaffree*, 472 U.S. 38 at 76 (1985); *Grand Rapids School District v. Ball*, 473 U.S. 373
(1985). Under the effects prong, the Court also condemned for advancing religion a
Connecticut statute that granted private employees an absolute right not to work on
their Sabbaths. See *Thornton v. Caldor, Inc.*, 472 U.S. 703 (1985). Cf. *Ansonia Board of Education v. Philbrook*, 479 U.S. 60 (1986); and *Corporation of Presiding Bishop of the Church of
Jesus Christ of Latter-Day Saints v. Amos*, 483 U.S. 327 (1987).

103 473 U.S. 373 at 392 (1985).

104 *Aguilar v. Felton*, 473 U.S. 402 (1985). Cf., *Witters v. Washington Department of Services for
the Blind*, 474 U.S. 481 (1986).

105 473 U.S. 373 at 383 (1985); *NYT*, 10 October 1984, A23; *Felton v. Secretary, U.S.
Department of Education*, 739 F. 2d 48 at 72 (2d Cir. 1984). See note 130 below.

106 *Wallace v. Jaffree*, 472 U.S. 38 at 112–13 (1985).

107 *Committee for Public Education and Religious Freedom v. Regan*, 444 U.S. 646 at 671 (1980).

108 *Wallace v. Jaffree*, 472 U.S. 38 at 108; *Edwards v. Aquillard*, 482 U.S. 578 at 613; and *Lee v.
Weisman*, 112 S. Ct. 2649 at 2678 (1992).

by accenting endorsement.[109] In influential opinions she proposes accommodation to lift burdens on free worship but not to endorse or confer benefits on religion, purposes which imply exclusion of non-believers from the political community.[110] A master coalition builder, Justice Brennan, absorbing this theme in the Grand Rapids case, managed to keep *Lemon* alive through pluralities thick and thin.

Conservative reinforcements promptly reshaped the battle lines. Just before Justice Brennan retired in 1989, a narrow majority reaffirmed the *Lemon*-endorsement test in *County of Allegheny* v. *American Civil Liberties Union*.[111] Declining the government's request to relax the rules in fact-sensitive cases from Pittsburgh, the Court struck down a nativity scene in the county courthouse but approved a large menorah next to a Christmas tree outside a city-county building on the theory that the display celebrated a secular theme of diversity. A dissenting quartet of Justice Anthony M. Kennedy, joined by Rehnquist, White, and Scalia, sharply attacked the endorsement standard as hostile toward religion, invited substantial revision of church-state doctrine, and offered a new approach to accommodate the central role of religion with the "pervasive public sector" in American life.[112] Emphasizing compulsion and official prosely-tizing as the central concerns, Kennedy proposed two principles to police the border between accommodation and establishment: Government may neither coerce religious exercise nor benefit religion "'in such a degree that it in fact establishes a religion or religious faith, or tends to do so.'"[113]

A showdown thus looms between two readings of the establishment clause—endorsement versus coercion—on the reconstituted Rehnquist Court. Having replaced staunch separatists, Brennan and Marshall, with

---

109　White J., in *Lemon* v. *Kurtzman*, 403 U.S. 602 at 668–70 (1971); O'Connor J., 692.

110　See O'Connor J., in *Lynch* v. *Donnelly*, 465 U.S. 668 at 687–89, 692; *Wallace* v. *Jaffree*, 472 U.S. 38 at 70; *Thornton* v. *Caldor*, 472 U.S. 703 at 711; *Corporation of the Presiding Bishop* v. *Amos*, 483 U.S. 327 at 346; *County of Allegheny* v. *American Civil Liberties Union*, 492 U.S. 573 at 625, 628 (1989); *Board of Education* v. *Mergens*, 496 U.S. 226 at 249 (1990). For critiques of the endorsement test, see Steven D. Smith, "Symbols, Perceptions and Doctrinal Illusions," *Michigan Law Review* 86 (1987), 266; Mark Tushnet, "Religion and Theories of Constitutional Interpretation," *Loyola Law Review* 33 (1987), 221 at 222–24; and McConnell, "Religious Freedom," 147–57.

111　492 U.S. 573 (1989). A foursome of O'Connor, Rehnquist, White, Blackmun—plus Marshall and Brennan implicitly—employed the Lemon framework in sustaining the Equal Access Act. See *Board of Education* v. *Mergens*, 496 U.S. 226 at 249 (1990). Also see *Bowen* v. *Kendrick*, 487 U.S. 588 at 593 (1989), in which Chief Justice Rehnquist applied the first two prongs while sustaining federal subsidies to religious organizations that counsel teenage chastity as an alternative to abortion.

112　Ibid., 678, 659 (1989).

113　Ibid., 659, quoting *Lynch* v. *Donnelly*, 465 U.S. 668, 678. See also Kennedy's similar statement, joined by Scalia J., in *Board of Education* v. *Mergens*, 496 U.S. 226 at 260 (1990).

Justices David H. Souter and Clarence Thomas, the Bush administration seized the opportunity to scuttle *Lemon* in *Lee* v. *Weisman*.[114] In this case lower federal courts held that the establishment clause forbad public school officials from arranging nonsectarian prayers at graduation exercises of a Providence middle school. Federal lawyers, intervening as amicus even before review was granted, asked the Court to replace the *Lemon*'s "rigid doctrinal framework" with Justice Kennedy's coercion test. While stopping short of supporting school prayers in compulsory classroom settings, Solicitor General Kenneth W. Starr argued that traditional acknowledgments of God in civic ceremonies are constitutional if they neither threaten to establish an official religion nor coerce participation in religious activities.[115] Many observers expected that a tribunal of six Reagan-Bush appointees would scrap *Lemon* and approve a greater role for religion at public events in keeping with popular customs, Republican promises, and the free exercise retreat in *Smith*.

In a stunning surprise, five Justices led by Kennedy himself declined to reconsider *Lemon* and extended the Warren Court's ban on state-sponsored prayers to graduation exercises in primary and secondary public schools. Rejecting as formalistic the contentions that participation was voluntary or minimally inconvenient, Kennedy concluded that pervasive government involvement in arranging the prayers put students in a coercive dilemma of participating or protesting. "The Constitution," he declared, "forbids the State to exact religious conformity from a student as the price of attending her own high school graduation."[116] The dissenters—Scalia, Rehnquist, White, and Thomas—angrily scored psychological jurisprudence in teenage minds and ignoring a "longstanding American tradition of nonsectarian prayer to God at public celebrations generally."[117] Justice Souter's careful concurrence demonstrated that historical intentions and practices cut both ways.

The *Weisman* decision not only rebuffed a long campaign to allow state-sponsored prayer in public schools; it signalled the rise of a "cautious center"—O'Connor, Kennedy, and Souter—who likewise curbed a Reaganite counterrevolution in habeas corpus and abortion.[118] Holding the balance of power in an unexpectedly splintered tribunal of conservatives, this centrist trio spurned aggressive advocacy and overruling of controversial precedents for fear of undermining the Supreme Court's

---

114 112 S. Ct. 2649 (1992).

115 Baltimore *Sun*, 11 March 1991, A16; *NYT*, 19 March 1991, A16; 60 L.W. 3351 (12 November 1991); *National Law Journal*, 11 November 1991.

116 112 S. Ct. 2649 at 2660.

117 Ibid., 2679.

118 *NYT*, 26 June 1992, A16. See especially *Planned Parenthood* v. *Casey*, 112 S. Ct. 2791 (1992); *Wright* v. *West*, 112 S. Ct. 2482 (1992).

legitimacy and popular faith in the rule of law. Incrementalism, they hinted, especially in the abortion case, is law's natural bent. Tantalizing seeds of *limited* constitutional change thus appear in the offing. The future of the establishment clause is "up for grabs."[119] Adding zip is a 4-1-1-3 cleavage. Four Justices—O'Connor, Blackmun, Stevens, Souter—support the *Lemon* endorsement test. Three others—Rehnquist, White, Scalia— would overrule it. Thomas remains uncommitted. Kennedy is perhaps the key player, just as his predecessor, Lewis F. Powell, Jr., was in 1985. Assuming personal *stare decisis*, *Lemon*'s future looks bleak. Kennedy merely postponed a showdown in *Weisman*. His majority opinion, ignoring *Lemon* and leaving the door open to future reconsideration, stressed coercion. Still, Souter's critique that a coercion standard for establishment adds nothing to free exercise guarantees and Kennedy's phrasing of noncoercion as a "minimum" command also leave room for rethinking and regrouping, which Kennedy did about abortion.[120]

What a difference a new Justice could make! Neither foursome seemed eager to fight on after *Weisman*.[121] Though only four votes are needed to accept a case, the Justices declined to hear several other establishment clause appeals, which ranged from religious symbols on municipal seals to Hawaii's declaration of Good Friday as a state holiday.[122] Significant issues regarding religion remain unresolved as a result. In public schools, for example, about half the states require or permit moments of silence for private meditation in classes and assemblies. Five Justices hinted in the Alabama prayer case that they would uphold a minute-of-silence law that had a plausible secular purpose, such as quieting students, or merely protected "every student's right to engage in voluntary prayer during an

---

119 *National Law Journal*, 6 July 1992, 1.

120 112 S. Ct. 2649, 2655–56, 2673. The coercion test has drawn two main criticisms: (1) redundancy with the coercion element of the free exercise clause might render the establishment clause a virtual nullity—see Souter J., ibid., 2673; and Douglas Laycock, "Nonpreferential Aid to Religion: A False Claim about Original Intent," *William and Mary Law Review* 27 (1986), 875 at 922; cf. Michael W. McConnell, "Coercion: The Lost Element of Establishment," *William and Mary Law Review* 27 (1986), 933; and (2) shifting the focus of establishment cases from government involvement in religion to its subjective effect on individuals—see Scalia J., 112 S. Ct. 2649 at 2681, and Ruti Teitel as quoted in *National Law Journal*, 11 November 1991. Also see McConnell, "Religious Freedom," 157–68. Cf. Douglas Laycock, "Summary and Synthesis: The Crisis in Religious Liberty," *George Washington Law Review* 60 (1992), 841 at 844.

121 The Court granted certiorari with an instruction for reconsideration in light of *Lee* v. *Weisman* in a case involving nonsectarian prayers by student volunteers at graduation exercises. See *Jones* v. *Clear Creek Independent School District*, 930 F. 2d 416 (5th Cir. 1991); No. 91–310. Supreme Court docket for pending cases.

122 *NYT*, 26 June 1992, A16; *Village of Crestwood* v. *Doe*, 917 F. 2d 1476 (7th Cir. 1990), cert. denied, 112 S. Ct. 3025 (1992); *Cammack* v. *Waihee*, 932 F. 2d 765 (9th Cir. 1991), cert. denied, 60 L.W. 3878 (29 June 1992).

appropriate moment of silence during the school day."[123] The question whether this practice is coercion or endorsement is likely to recur.

So are persistent attacks by Protestant fundamentalists on "secular humanism" and offensive books in public education. Some fundamentalists regard neutrality as antireligious. Thwarted in their goal of sponsored worship in public schools, they seek to purge secular humanism, which they define as an atheistic, human-centered religion, from public education as well. The Supreme Court recognized humanist groups as religious in 1961, but left several burning controversies during the bicentennial years to the regional Courts of Appeals.[124] Circuit judges overturned a ban on forty-four books, for instance, by a federal district judge who, after hearing expert testimony that modern textbooks neglect the role of religion in American history and culture, concluded that a Mobile, Alabama, reading program was hostile to theistic religions and established secular humanism.[125] Circuit judges also reversed a free exercise exemption of children in Tennessee from compulsory reading of books that offended their religious consciences.[126] The offensive material, used in thousands of U.S. school districts, included Alice Walker's prize-winning novel, *The Color Purple*, classic tales of witchcraft and magic like *Cinderella* and *The Wizard of Oz*, and the *Diary of Anne Frank*. The circuit court distinguished compulsory belief from compulsory exposure to diverse ideas.

The Supreme Court ruled in 1952 that "the state has no legitimate interest in protecting any or all religions from views distasteful to them."[127] It would be hard to accommodate religious sensibilities under that view. Most Americans and judges support competing goals of making room for minority religions as well as the assimilation mission of public schools and exposure of students to conflicting ideas.[128] Reconciling

---

123 *Wallace* v. *Jaffree*, 472 U.S. 38 at 59 (1985). See *Karcher* v. *May*, 484 U.S. 72 (1987); *NYT*, 19 September 1983, A18.

124 *Torasco* v. *Watkins*, 367 U.S. 488 at 495 n. 11 (1961).

125 *Smith* v. *Board of School Commissioners of Mobile County*, 655 F. Supp. 939 (S.D. Ala. 1987); 827 F. 2d 684 (11th Cir. 1987). See *NYT*, 13 October 1986, A14; 7 March 1987, 7; 2 July 1987, A16; and 21 October 1987, A25.

126 *Mozert* v. *Hawkins County Public Schools*, 765 F. 2d 75 (6th Cir. 1985); 647 F. Supp. 1194 (E.D. Tenn. 1986); 827 F. 2d 1058 (6th Cir. 1987). By contrast, an Oregon federal judge excused a high school sophomore from reading Gordon Park's novel, *The Learning Tree*, in which Jesus Christ is called "a poor white-trash God" and "a long-legged white son of a bitch"; but the circuit court declined her mother's request to ban the book after the daughter attended class anyway. *Grove* v. *Mead School District No. 354*, 753 F. 2d 1528 at 1540, 1547, 1549 (9th Cir. 1985), cert. denied, 106 S. Ct. 85 (1986).

127 *Joseph Burstyn, Inc.* v. *Wilson*, 343 U.S. 495 at 505 (1952).

128 *NYT*, 22 October 1986, A22. *Ambach* v. *Norwick*, 441 U.S. 68 at 76 (1979); *Bethel School District No. 403* v. *Fraser*, 106 S. Ct. 3159 (1986).

these objectives in a multicultural society might have given Jefferson and Madison pause. Intolerance can masquerade as tolerance. Fundamentalists are "discrete and insular" minorities, too. Most religions have them.

It is important to realize that these issues are not confined to the Bible Belt. Nor do the Constitution's text and the *Smith-Lemon* tests offer a litmus when preferred values collide. Which should prevail in bankruptcy courts: a debtor's free exercise claim to exempt religious tithes or a creditor's counterclaim that such exemptions establish religion? The Justices recently refused to review a decision favoring creditors.[129] In conflicts between sex discrimination and free exercise claims, a Brooklyn federal judge accepted the demands of Hasidic Jews to run a wall separating male and female students in a crowded public school; but a colleague rejected, as advancing religion, Hasidic claims that females cannot drive public school buses transporting Hasidic males to sectarian schools.[130] What's the difference?

The *Smith* decision hardly settles how sensitive governments must be to religious beliefs in implementing the public policies of a heterogeneous society. Should the *Yoder* exemption apply to over 1,200 organized religions in the United States? To Hare Krishnas who distribute beads for voluntary donations on the Mall of the nation's capital?[131] To polygamous Mormons after a revolution in sexual mores and family life?[132] To Laotian Hmongs for whom mandatory autopsies violate deep religious beliefs?[133] To religious sects that practise ritual animal sacrifice?[134] To ultimate protestants after *Frazee* who proclaim, as Justice Holmes did in solo dissent, "I flocked alone"?[135]

---

129 *Ivy* v. *Myers*, 111 S. Ct. 2825 (1991); cf. *In re Green*, HK 87–00354, *National Law Journal*, 22 June 1987, 7. Also see *Baltimore Sun*, 2 August 1987, C13; and 18 June 1991, A2.

130 *Parents' Association of P.S. 16* v. *Quinones*, 803 F. 2d 1235 (E.D.N.Y. 1986); *Bollenbach* v. *Monroe-Woodbury Central School District*, 659 F. Supp. 1450 (S.D.N.Y. 1987). Cf. *McLaurin* v. *Oklahoma*, 339 U.S. 637 (1950), which rejected racial segregation of students inside an Oklahoma law school. A New York state judge also struck down a special public school district for handicapped children in a Hasidic enclave: *Grumet* v. *Kiryas Joel Village School District*, 579 N.Y.S. 2d 1004 (1992). See *NYT*, 23 January 1992, B1.

131 *Baltimore Sun*, 8 May 1992, A8.

132 For debate, cf. Burger and Douglas JJ., in *Wisconsin* v. *Yoder*, 406 U.S. 205 at 216, 247 (1972).

133 *Yang* v. *Sturner*, 750 F. Supp. 558 (D.R.I. 1990).

134 *Church of the Lukumi Babalu Aye, Inc.* v. *Hialeah, Fla.*, No. 91-948, cert. granted, 60 L.W. 3058, 3652 (1992). For a proposed ordinance against killing animals at religious rituals in San Francisco, see *Baltimore Sun*, 27 July 1992.

135 489 U.S. 829 (1989); Letter, Oliver Wendell Holmes, Jr., to Morris R. Cohen, 9 April 1923, in Leonora D. Rosenfield, *Portrait of a Philosopher: Morris R. Cohen in Life and Letters* (New York: Harcourt, Brace and World, 1962), 340.

What is religion anyhow? Can judges and juries define it—or even sincere religious belief—without themselves violating the establishment clause? To dodge this dilemma courts traditionally decline to hear internal church disputes over religious doctrine.[136] In the last two decades, Justices have defined religion generously to widen statutory rights of individuals. For purposes of conscientious objection, the Court in Pete Seeger's case expanded Congress's requirement of belief in a Supreme Being to include sincere belief that "occupies a place in the life of its possessor parallel to that filled by the orthodox belief in God."[137] This functional, subjective view of religion extends beyond traditional theism to secular beliefs.[138] Two decisions in 1987 even permitted Jews and Moslems to take advantage of civil rights statutes against racial discrimination by treating them as ethnic groups, according to nineteenth century understandings of "race."[139] The recent retreats regarding sacred Indian sites and sacramental peyote, nonetheless, show how precarious such line-drawing can become when cultures clash over environmentalism and drugs.

The varied and free-floating concepts of religion in this global nation magnify the problem of colliding rights—and illuminate old wisdom. General propositions seldom decide concrete cases. Great principles of constitutional limitation are "not susceptible of comprehensive statement in an adjective."[140] Reasonable accommodation of competing demands without destroying them, Chief Justice Harlan F. Stone preached, is "where the judicial function comes in."[141] Retreats in free exercise and churnings about establishment complicate the goal.

Is the problem infidelity to the principle of neutrality or inability to say what neutral is? As we contemplate the future of the religion guarantees in a revamped conservative judiciary, it is helpful to remember the baselines. Fundamental is the tribunals' continuing commitment to principles of religious freedom and government neutrality. As Justice Kennedy recently stated the First Amendment's central meaning: "Religious beliefs

---

136 *Presbyterian Church* v. *Hull Church*, 393 U.S. 440 (1969); *Jones* v. *Wolf*, 443 U.S. 595 (1975). See *Ballard* v. *United States*, 329 U.S. 187 at 193–94 (1946); Noonan, "How Sincere?"; "Developments—Religion and the State," note 51 above, 1622–31, and sources cited.

137 *United States* v. *Seeger*, 380 U.S. 163 at 166 (1965).

138 See *Welsh* v. *United States*, 398 U.S. 333 (1970); and *Gillette* v. *United States*, 401 U.S. 437 (1971).

139 *Shaare Tefila Congregation* v. *Cobb*, 107 S. Ct. 2019 (1987); *St. Francis College* v. *Al-Khazraji*, 107 S. Ct. 2022 (1987).

140 Holmes J., in *Lochner* v. *New York*, 198 U.S. 45 at 76 (1908); and quote, Cardozo J., in *Carter* v. *Carter Coal Co.*, 298 U.S. 238 at 327 (1936).

141 Alpheus T. Mason, *Harlan Fiske Stone: Pillar of the Law* (New York: Viking Press, 1956), 535.

and religious expression are too precious to be either proscribed or prescribed by the State." "All creeds must be tolerated and none favored."[142] At the same time, the Rehnquist Court has sharply altered
what these principles mean in practice. The tribunal has reduced free
exercise exemptions to an auxiliary right, shielding individuals only from
laws that attack specific religious groups; and it appears ready to allow
greater accommodation of religion in public affairs. The divisive questions are how, who decides, and who benefits?

A continuing issue is whether tension between the two religion
clauses can be resolved by a unified approach. Which is the best way to
harmonize the First Amendment's great commands: (1) reduced free exercise exemptions; (2) principled exceptions to the high wall, such as the
child-benefit theory or the distinction between colleges and secondary
schools; (3) *ad hoc* balancing of interests, case by case, in hope that
general principles will evolve incrementally according to the vaunted
advantage of case-law systems; or (4) lowering the wall? A fifth alternative—interpreting the clauses together—has gone begging because the
Justices cannot resolve which value, free exercise or separation, takes
precedence.[143] Still another, sensitive to federalism, judicial restraint,
and majority rule is reducing both federal rights to noncoercion and
returning responsibility to states and politics.

These options have profound implications for the Supreme Court's
roles and religious constituencies in the governmental scheme. The
Sherbert-Lemon combination of the Brennan era heightened judicial review
under both religion clauses to protect religious minorities and non-
believers who presumably are unable to protect their rights politically.
Relaxation of judicial safeguards for religious minorities under both
guarantees, already effected for free exercise rights and likely to come for
establishment in some degree, favors mainstream religions and—as
Justice Jackson feared—leaves minorities to their fate in fifty-one political
spheres.

---

142 *Lee* v. *Weisman*, 112 S. Ct. 2649 at 2656, 2657 (1992).

143 Gerald Gunther, *Constitutional Law*, 12th ed. (Mineola, N.Y.: Foundation Press, Inc.,
1991), 1502; and "Developments—Religion and the State," note 51 above, 1683–1703. For
proposed attempts at reconciliation, see ibid., 1723–40, and especially Philip B.
Kurland's "Of Church and State and the Supreme Court," *University of Chicago Law Review* 29 (1961), 1 at 6. Kurland proposes religion-blind neutrality: government cannot
use religion as a standard of action "either to confer a benefit or to impose a burden."
Symptomatic of the difficulties in melding both religion guarantees is *Texas Monthly, Inc.*
v. *Bullock*, 489 U.S. 1 (1989), which held that exclusive exemption of religious periodicals
from state sales taxes violates the establishment clause. Attempts to reconcile exemptions commanded by the free exercise clause with exemptions forbidden by the establishment clause fractured the Court into mirror-imaged factions. Justice Blackmun opposed subordinating either constitutional value as a way to resolve the problem. Ibid.,
24, 26–29.

In sum, the Supreme Court, aggravating tension between the dual religion clauses of the First Amendment by developing separate standards for each, still searches for unifying doctrine governing the rights of religious worship and church-state relations in a pluralistic society. The struggle, some believe, puts the Court "up against the wall."[144] If this generation of judges, like its predecessors, commits inconsistencies in the changing tides of political appointment and public sentiment, perhaps the poet, Walt Whitman, had a comforting word: "Do I contradict myself? Very well, then, I contradict myself, (I am large, I contain multitudes.)"[145]

JUDICIAL REMEDIES ARE LIMITED

In religion, as in other human rights, the U.S. Supreme Court during the last half-century became a model on the world stage of constitutional adjudication as an instrument of reform.[146] For all its doctrinal difficulties, the tribunal made major contributions to religious liberty and tolerance in American society. Under the free exercise clause, as we have seen, heightened judicial scrutiny of public restraints on religious expression greatly enlarged individual rights to worship freely against forces of compulsion and conformity at all levels of government. Recognizing that belief compels action, the Court also expanded access of all persons to propagate their faith in public forums. The current issues are how far these principles extend—e.g., to minors and unorthodox faiths—without unduly crimping majority worship or favoring religion over other public interests such as education, equality, and separation of church and state, which officials are also obliged to promote.

Under the establishment clause, the Court drastically reduced religious activity in government operations. The prime targets are public schools. The movement to secularize public education, rooted in the nineteenth century, found a powerful judicial ally after World War II. By legitimating indirect public subsidies to private sectarian schools, however, the Court profoundly affected educational finance in the United States—and the judicial function. If policing church-state relations did not

---

144 A. E. Dick Howard, "Up Against the Wall: The Uneasy Separation of Church and State," in A. E. Dick Howard, John W. Baker, and Thomas S. Derr, *Church, State, and Politics*, Final Report of the 1981 Chief Justice Earl Warren Conference (Washington, D.C.: Roscoe Pound—American Trial Lawyers Foundation, 1981), 5.

145 Song of Myself, s. 51, *Collected Writings of Walt Whitman* (New York: New York University Press, 1965), 7:88.

146 Archibald Cox, *The Warren Court: Constitutional Decision as an Instrument of Reform* (Cambridge: Harvard University Press, 1969); and the author's "Constitution and Society in Comparative Perspective," *Judicature* 71 (1987), 111–13.

convert the Supreme Court into a national school board, as Justice Jackson feared, it clearly ensnared jurists in fine line-drawing across a broad spectrum of public policy issues as the two clauses and other constitutional values collide.

Judicial leadership in effect transformed judicial roles. Americans today by and large expect judges to be "peculiar guardians" of religious liberty and separation of church and state under a living Constitution. Courts do more than vindicate constitutional rights. They are agents of peaceful conflict resolution and nationalization of values. They play ancillary roles in educating and bargaining with other elites—and thereby increase their political risks.[147] Whatever one's view of particular decisions, policy making and controversy have become the judiciary's daily lot, and no end is in sight.

On entering the vale of religion in the 1940s, the Justices consciously faced ultimate questions of the judicial role in democratic government. The great debate then focused on the *legitimacy* of unelected judges restraining majority rule to protect minority rights. Debate today centers more on the *capacity* of courts to do the job.[148] Precisely because the Supreme Court has been so prominent in the postwar rights explosion, at the risk of flogging a straw man I close with words of caution: Judicial remedies are limited. Judges alone cannot preserve religious freedom, separate church and state, or harmonize the First Amendment's dual commands. Nor were they intended to in the constitutional scheme. The primary control on a free government, as Madison and Hamilton knew, is "dependence on the people." Judicial review is basically an "auxiliary precaution" against "ill humors" and oppressions until they give way to better information and sober reflection in the community.[149]

Those who trust judges more than politicians to defend religious liberty dislike hearing that the essential problems and solutions of religious freedom and church-state relations lie less in courthouses than in their own backyards. A few realities suggest why judicial power is limited.

---

147 For example, twenty years after he lambasted the Justices for "having driven God out" of the public schools, Senator Sam J. Ervin, Jr., vigorously opposed school prayer amendments in 1983. Leo Pfeffer, *Religion, State, and the Burger Court* (Buffalo: Prometheus Books, 1984), 83. For the Court's educational role, see William K. Muir, *Prayer in the Public Schools: Law and Attitude Change* (Chicago: University of Chicago Press, 1967); Richard Johnson, *The Dynamics of Compliance* (Evanston, Ill.: Northwestern University Press, 1967); and *NYT*, 11 March 1983, A1. Cf. McClosky and Brill, *Dimensions of Tolerance*, 133.

148 *Minersville School District* v. *Gobitis*, 310 U.S. 586 at 601 (1940); *West Virginia State Board of Education* v. *Barnette*, 319 U.S. 624 at 646 (1943). For capacity, see, e.g., Donald L. Horowitz, *The Courts and Social Policy* (Washington, D.C.: The Brookings Institution, 1977).

149 *The Federalist*, Nos. 51 and 78.

The most important factor is that American society has become too pluralistic, and power centers too diffuse, for unified direction or doctrinal formulas, even assuming them desirable. Flourishing religious activity, on one side, and government regulation affecting religions, on the other, inexorably multiply their contacts and potential conflicts. God is not dead in the United States. According to Gallup, 95 percent of adults profess belief in a supernatural being; about 40 percent say they attend religious services at least once a week.[150] The religious landscape is far more diverse than the framers' world of Christianity and *de minimis*. Roman Catholics are now the country's largest denomination. There are six million Jews, more Muslims than Episcopalians, and scores of sects from across the globe. In 1842, the City of Brotherly Love suffered fatal riots over which version of the Bible to recite in public schools.[151] Imagine the problem today in San Francisco for a student body containing atheists, Buddhists, Native Americans, Muslims, Shintoists, and Taoists, let alone splintering mainstream sects. Toleration is not a luxury but a necessity for social peace.

Then, too, the organizational dimension of modern church-state relations increasingly blurs the private-public distinction which separatism traditionally presumed. Organized religions today are interest groups, serving as intermediaries between government and individuals. They employ sophisticated techniques to influence public opinion and policy. They help administer government programs in education, health, and welfare. In turn, public regulations such as social security, minimum wage, and civil rights laws control the internal affairs of religious institutions.[152] In contemporary society, as the Justices recognized a decade ago, strict separation is impossible.[153]

Workload, in addition, severely restricts the high court's supervisory capacity. The tribunal currently accepts only about 125 cases from roughly 5,000 appeals reaching it annually. As these cover many subjects

---

150 See George Gallup, Jr., and Jim Castelli, *The People's Religion: American Faith in the 90s* (New York: Macmillan, 1984); Andrew Greeley, *Religious Change in America* (Cambridge, Mass.: Harvard University Press, 1989); and Garry Wills, *Under God: Religion and American Politics* (New York: Simon and Schuster, 1990).

151 Levy, *Establishment Clause*, 175, 170.

152 See, e.g., Allen D. Hertzke, "The Role of Religious Lobbies," in Charles W. Dunn, ed., *Religion in American Politics* (Washington, D.C.: Congressional Quarterly, Inc., 1989), 123; Paul J. Weber, "Religious Interest Groups, Policymaking, and the Constitution," in Stephen D. Johnson and Joseph B. Tanney, eds., *The Political Role of Religion in the United States* (Boulder, Colo.: Westview Press, 1986), 15–43. Also see *United States* v. *Lee*, 455 U.S. 252 (1982); *Bob Jones University* v. *United States*, 461 U.S. 574 (1983); *Church of Jesus Christ of Latter-Day Saints* v. *Amos*, 481 U.S. 1066 (1987).

153 *Roemer* v. *Public Works Board of Maryland*, 426 U.S. 736 at 745 (1976); *Lemon* v. *Kurtzman*, 403 U.S. 602 at 614 (1971).

from abortion to zoning, the Justices' span of attention to a single field is limited.

Political acceptability is another key factor. Tension between doctrinal coherence and popular tolerances conditions judicial authority.[154] Disagreements between absolutists and balancers since *Everson* reflect different strategic assessments of the Court's power to enforce its rulings. Though the tribunal's decisions formally bind the whole nation, resistance has been sharp in the field of religion. Students still pray, sing hymns, and recite Bible verses in public schools, despite decisions made twenty-five years ago.[155] Recently a public schoolgirl who flocked alone in Miami was ostracized by her teacher and classmates for refusing to salute the American flag. Her constitutional right against compulsory affirmation of belief was established in 1943. Even George Bush made hay in the 1988 presidential campaign by proposing that "public school teachers be required to lead our children in the pledge of allegiance" to the United States, a pledge that includes the phrase "under God." Any constitutional questions he referred to the Supreme Court.[156]

Justices, to be sure, serve to vindicate and define legal rights. Their rulings generate administrative remedies as well. But courts lack a self-starter. Mobilizing lawsuits costs time, effort, and money. In reality, as Archibald Cox observed, the Supreme Court is largely "helpless to enforce its own commands." "The effectiveness of all law in a free society, depends for the most part on voluntary compliance."[157]

Finally, protecting religious freedom should be placed in a wider contest over intellectual freedom in American society. Pressures to censor what is said, read, and heard appear throughout the Union, especially in public schools and libraries. Religion is only part of this problem, as parents and puritans seek to influence education in controversial subjects such as communism, drugs, science, and sex. Though we hardly face a wave of intolerance, watchdog groups report a 168 percent increase in

---

154 Richard E. Morgan, *The Supreme Court and Religion* (New York: The Free Press, 1972), 1.

155 "Developments—Religion and the State," note 51 above, 1661 n. 105; *NYT*, 26 December 1980, A20; 11 March 1984, A1; and 2 September 1989, A1. See generally Jesse H. Choper, "Consequences of Supreme Court Decisions Upholding Individual Constitutional Rights," *Michigan Law Review* 83 (1984), 1 at 78–82, 179–83; Kenneth M. Dolbeare and Phillip E. Hammond, *The School Prayer Decisions: From Court Policy to Local Practice* (Chicago: University of Chicago Press, 1971); Charles A. Johnson and Bradley Canon, *Judicial Policies: Implementation and Impact* (Washington, D.C.: Congressional Quarterly, Inc., 1984), 65–68, 89–90, 145–47, 160, 178–79, 196–97, 236. Frank Sorauf, *The Wall of Separation: The Constitutional Politics of Church and State* (Princeton, N.J.: Princeton University Press, 1976), 277–337; Stephen L. Wasby, *The Supreme Court in the Federal Judicial System*, 3d ed. (Chicago: Nelson-Hall Publishers, 1988), 349, 373–76.

156 *NYT*, 19 August 1988, A14; and 25 August 1988, A1, B15.

157 Archibald Cox, *The Court and the Constitution* (Boston: Houghton-Mifflin, 1987), 13–14.

attempts at censorship since 1982. Educators worry about their ability to offer broad-based education in public schools. Chilling effects occur as commercial publishers reduce texts to the least offensive pablum. Slighting the role of religion in Mobile is the twin of expunging sex scenes from Shakespeare's *Romeo and Juliet* in Virginia.[158] What can—or should—judges do about all this?

Safeguarding religious freedom is an unending task. Courts lack the capacity to handle the job alone. Pressures on free exercise and anti-establishment values today are simply too big for removal from the vicissitudes of politics and public finance in a governmental system where losers in one arena may continue the battle in another. The attitude—leave it to judges—courts danger. Losing a claim in the high tribunal can nationalize defeat. Depoliticizing religion risks politicizing the judiciary. Constitutionalizing petty distinctions trivializes the great charter, if not the Court itself. The judiciary was never intended to be the primary protector of individual rights in the American system. Its role is to supplement the spirit of tolerance and the dictates of religious diversity on which we ordinarily rely against religious oppressions until the community's "sober second thought" prevails.[159] Should the people's faith in freedom be lost, as Justice Jackson reminded us, "five or nine men in Washington could not long supply its want."[160]

After all, the Supreme Court does not function in a vacuum. Traditional remedies are available when new judicial coalitions consolidate and retreat. Congress and the President extended equal access rights to students of public high schools before the Justices acted.[161] National legislation overturned the *Goldman* yarmulke decision and preserved sacred wilderness sites after *Lyng*.[162] Efforts continue in Congress to restore by statute the strict scrutiny standards for free-exercise exemptions undercut in *Smith*.[163] Oregon's subsequent exemption of sacramental use of peyote illustrates the capacity of fifty state governments to take independent paths.[164]

In sum, the United States is one nation with many robes and cloths. If you feel "in fog" over how to strike a fair balance between freedom for and from religion in a highly diverse polity, that is natural. The problem

---

158 *NYT*, 1 September 1988, A21; 14 September 1988, B9, and 16 September 1986, C1.

159 Chief Justice Stone as quoted in Mason, *Stone*, 785. This concept of the Court's supplemental role resembles Hamilton's in *The Federalist*, No. 78.

160 *Douglas* v. *Jeannette*, 319 U.S. 157 at 182 (1943).

161 20 U.S.C. § 4071 (1984); *Board of Education* v. *Mergens*, 496 U.S. 226 (1990).

162 See 10 U.S.C. § 774 (1989), and note 65 above.

163 See note 68 above.

164 *NYT*, 9 July 1991, A14.

has been around a long time. (1) Customary tools of constitutional inter-pretation—text, intention, history—do not solve it. The framers side-stepped it. The Constitution embraces it. (2) The two religion clauses of the First Amendment collide, especially in the last four decades, as the Supreme Court has applied separate, libertarian standards of preferred freedoms and strict separation against state as well as national action. (3) For all its travail in supervising church-state relations, Supreme Court leadership has contributed substantially to religious freedom and toler-ation. Judges play vital roles as special guardians of religious rights when political checks and cultural pluralism falter. (4) Judicial remedies, however, are limited. While I hardly advocate a judicial retreat from this field, beware of false hopes. In the ebb and flow of appointment and opinion, judges are likely to mirror divisions in the society. It is unrealistic to expect jurists to provide easy answers for conflicts that so divide the people. Preaching separation while practising accommodation is a longstanding continuity in American life.

In the final analysis, safeguarding freedom for and from religion is everyone's responsibility. It is one thing for the Supreme Court to declare the law, another for public officials to comply.[165] The scope of religious toleration among American multitudes, and entwined relations among civil and religious institutions, depend far more on daily decisions of ordinary individuals in homes, classrooms, school boards, PTAs, budget hearings, and polling booths across the land than in courtrooms. That is how civil liberties are implemented. If current pressures on religious liberty are troubling, the Madisonian answer is to roll up sleeves and get busy. This was Mark Twain's real moral, I suspect, in ridiculing Amer-ican freedom to conform—and the way it should be in republican govern-ment. That is why our four points may resolve into one: When we view the Constitution of the United States, we see ourselves.

---

165 ACLU president, Nadine Strossen, *NYT*, 28 January 1991, A14.

II

Federalism in Canada
and the United States

Canadian Confederation and the Influence of American Federalism

Jennifer Smith

What was the impact of United States federalism on the deliberations of the Fathers of Canadian Confederation? What lessons did the Canadian founders suppose that they had drawn from the U.S. example, and how did they apply them to the constitutional provisions that they drafted at the Quebec Conference in the fall of 1864 and that were adopted, with minor changes, in the *Constitution Act, 1867*? Why did they not profit from these lessons quite as they had hoped?

Students of the Confederation period agree that the delegates from the British North American colonies attending the Quebec Conference were highly critical of American federalism. However, they do not agree on what the delegates understood by federalism, as is indicated in the first section of this essay, in which I review the contending interpretations that Canadian historians and political scientists have developed from their reading of the delegates' pronouncements. One promising way of systematically determining the delegates' views is to measure them against James Madison's analysis of the federalism of the Constitution drafted at the Philadelphia Convention in 1787, as set out in the thirty-ninth paper of *The Federalist*. Madison's analysis, described briefly in the second section, is an account of the concept itself as well as an examination of its role in U.S. constitutional arrangements. Accordingly, in the sections that follow, it is used to help identify the delegates' understanding of American federalism, their criticisms of it, and the ways in which they sought to correct its excesses and thereby produce a better constitution for Canada. Of course it is a commonplace of the history of Canadian federalism that the delegates' intentions were confounded, at least to some extent. In the concluding section of the article, I consider whether they seriously misunderstood American federalism and, if they did, the extent to which that misunderstanding undermined their efforts.

THE FEDERAL PRINCIPLE

For the colonists living in British North America in the mid-nineteenth century, the rarefied concept of federalism was defined by its greatest example to hand. Federalism meant American federalism, and it was a notably unpopular identification. The historian P.B. Waite is emphatic about the aversion to federalism: "No understanding of Confederation is possible unless it be recognized that its founders, many of its supporters, and as many of its opponents, were all animated by a powerful antipathy to the whole federal principle."[1] Since their referent was the American version, how did they understand it? Waite refers to the connection many drew between federalism and the Civil War, a connection often expressed in causal terms. Federalism seemed a suspect principle, an arrangement that encouraged dissension, not unity.[2] As for the principle itself, he suggests that those who grasped it at all saw it less in the distribution of legislative powers between Congress and the state legislatures than in the compromise on representation that had been worked out between the two houses of Congress, that is, population-based representation in the House of Representatives and equal state representation in the Senate. This was the understanding that was brought to the Confederation proposal. For the founders, Waite argues, the federal principle was reflected largely in the different bases for representation in the House of Commons and the Senate. The question of the distribution of legislative powers, while not unimportant, was not the central *federal* question.[3]

Recently students of Canadian government have shown considerable interest in the federal dimensions of national institutions, and for them Waite's view that the composition of the second chamber was central to the nineteenth-century understanding of federalism is both encouraging and suggestive. The competing view asserts the centrality of the division of powers concept. Thus, Frank Scott, a keen student of the Confederation debates as well as a noted authority on constitutional law, stressed the extent to which the theory of federalism embodied in the Quebec Resolutions differed from the theory of American federalism, and his argument centred on the relationship between the two levels of government. According to Scott, the chief feature and chief flaw of American federalism in the eyes of the Quebec delegates originated in the fact that at the time of the union the American states were independent and sovereign.

---

1 P.B. Waite, *The Life and Times of Confederation, 1864–1867* (Toronto: University of Toronto Press, 1962), 33.

2 Ibid., 34, 113.

3 Ibid., 111, 115.

This meant that sovereign authority flowed from the states to the central government, with the regrettable consequence, prescribed by the feared states' rights doctrine, that what flowed upwards could return with a vengeance, as it did when the Confederate States seceded from the union. Moreover, this initial problem of sovereignty was compounded by constitutional provisions assigning specific powers to the Congress and the remaining or residual powers to the states.[4] The result was a federation without a sufficiently strong, unifying central government, a federation that, temporarily at least, was overwhelmed by its parts. As Scott indicates, the delegates to the Quebec Conference, especially John A. Macdonald, harped constantly on the sovereignty problem, and their answer was a central legislature equipped with an extensive array of legislative powers conferred on it by the British Parliament, not delegated to it by colonial legislatures.

In a recent commentary on the views of federalism of leading members of the governing coalition formed in 1864 in the largest of the British North American colonies, the Province of Canada, Robert Vipond, like Scott, focuses on the relationship between central and local governments. He argues that for Macdonald the test of a federal system was the exclusivity of local jurisdiction, and even the highly centralized system that he favored could be considered federal so long as local legislatures, however limited their concerns, possessed exclusive legislative competence in relation to them, just as the central legislature possessed exclusive competence in relation to its general concerns. In this sense, according to Vipond, Macdonald followed the theory of federalism that Madison set out and defended in *The Federalist* and that is reflected in the American Constitution, the same theory that forms the basis of our modern understanding of federalism.[5] Vipond's commentary appears in his article on the constitutional doctrine developed by the provincial rights movement in the generation following Confederation, a doctrine, he argues, that centred on the notion of legislative exclusivity. But Madison's test of federalism extends beyond that to encompass the object of Waite's concern as well.

MADISON'S FEDERAL TEST

To judge from the Articles of Confederation, the first constitution of the independent American states, a federation was conceived as a voluntary alliance of states based upon a thoroughgoing principle of state equality.

---

4 F.R. Scott, *Essays on the Constitution* (Toronto: University of Toronto Press, 1977), 25–26, 41.

5 Robert C. Vipond, "Constitutional Politics and the Legacy of the Provincial Rights Movement in Canada," *Canadian Journal of Political Science* 18 (1985), 271–72.

Under the Articles, most legislative matters were handled independently by the states themselves. The central governing body, the Congress, in which member states were represented equally by delegates they appointed, addressed a limited number of concerns and relied entirely on the states to carry out its decisions. It could not itself legislate on citizens and therefore could neither levy taxes nor regulate commerce. Any changes in the terms of the Articles required the unanimous consent of the states. Such was the arrangement Gouverneur Morris had in mind when, speaking to fellow delegates at the Philadelphia Convention, he distinguished federal from national governments: "the former being a mere compact resting on the good faith of the parties; the latter having a compleat and *compulsive* operation."[6] The successor constitution drafted at Philadelphia did not outline a "mere compact." Yet one of its ablest defenders, James Madison, was not about to abandon a federal claim on its behalf. In No. 39 of *The Federalist*, in an attempt to show that opponents of the proposed constitution were wrong when they charged that it did not preserve the federal principle, he devised a "federal test" that covered five points: the basis of consent on which the proposed constitution was to stand, the sources of the new central government's ordinary powers, the operation and extent of those powers and, finally, the constitutional amending power. Assessing the constitution on each point in turn, he produced an interesting and mixed review.

On the first item, consent, federalism triumphed. According to Madison, ratification of the constitution was a federal procedure, not a national one, because it required the approval of each of the state constitutional conventions as opposed to the consent of the people as citizens of one nation: "Each state, in ratifying the Constitution, is considered as a sovereign body, independent of all others, and only to be bound by its own voluntary act." On the fifth item, constitutional amendment, he argued that the results were "neither wholly *national* nor wholly *federal*."[7] A national procedure required a national majority of voters, a federal one the consent of each state. The procedure recommended seemed to fall somewhere in between, using states over citizens and requiring the agreement of more than a majority of them, but not unanimous agreement.

The second test concerned the sources of the central government's executive and legislative powers, and Madison judged them to be federal and national. In the legislative branch, the House of Representatives was national because it derived its electoral mandate from the people and

---

6 W.U. Solberg, ed., *The Federal Convention and the Formation of the Union of the American States* (New York: Bobbs-Merrill, 1958), 81.

7 Alexander Hamilton, John Jay and James Madison, *The Federalist* (New York: Modern Library, 1937), 247, 249 (emphasis in original).

represented them on a population basis. The Senate, by contrast, was federal because its members were appointed by the state legislatures, each appointing two senators. The executive power, he continued, was based on a "very compound source," that is, the more complicated mix of federal and national features combined in the presidential selection process. The process began with the states "in their political character" because the number of electors per state was determined by the total of its representatives and senators. Yet that total itself reflected the states "partly as distinct and co-equal societies, partly as unequal members of the same society." If the electors were unable to produce a candidate with a majority, the election would revert to the national House of Representatives which, for this purpose, would form itself into state delegations, each with one vote. The executive power, Madison concluded, combined "at least as many *federal* as *national* features."

In his account of the third test, the operation of the ordinary powers of government, Madison began by supposing that in federal governments the central authorities could operate only on the member states, whereas in national governments they reached the citizens of the nation. In the light of this supposition he found the proposed central government national. However, on the fourth test, the extent of its powers, it could not be considered national because its jurisdiction extended only to enumerated matters, while the states retained a "residual and inviolable sovereignty" over the rest. Madison identified the concept of legislative exclusivity that has since become a benchmark of our understanding of divided jurisdiction: "The local municipal authorities form distinct and independent portions of the [legislative] supremacy, no more subject, within their respective spheres, to the general authority than the general authority is subject to them, within its own sphere."[8]

Madison concluded that the proposed constitution was "in strictness, neither a national nor a federal Constitution, but a composition of both." It was a remarkably harmonious composition in which the two elements were interwoven and balanced throughout. Only the tests on ratification and the operation of the central government's powers revealed whether one or the other was to prevail, the federal element in the former, the national in the latter. The other three revealed combinations. The central government itself was a "composition," the fine balance of which reflected the balance in the constitution as a whole.

From the perspective of Canadian federalism, a noteworthy aspect of the complexity of the balance was the wide-ranging use of the federal element in the design of political institutions and in procedures such as ratification and amendment, as well as in the matter of jurisdiction. The jurisdictional question was only one of five used to test the presence or

---

8 Ibid., 249.

absence of federalism. Had it alone tested positive, it would hardly have been enough to permit Madison to present the constitution as federal, at least not at that time. On the other hand, it was equally important that the constitution proposed a strong national government in place of the Congress of the Articles of Confederation; that is, a government empowered, among other things, to raise and collect taxes, to frame laws and enforce them in its own courts, although not to disallow state laws in violation of the constitution or treaties with other nations, as Madison had urged at the Philadelphia Convention.[9] There, too, Alexander Hamilton had argued the desirability of a "compleat sovereignty" such that the passions supporting governments, like the love of power, could be made to work in favor of the central government at the expense of state governments.[10] In the event, the powers agreed upon, while less than complete, proved sufficient for the purpose.

CONFEDERATION AND THE FEDERAL TEST

The Quebec delegates, too, thought in terms of a composite. This time the two opposing models were legislative union and federal union, and neither term conveyed quite the same meaning as the U.S. concepts, national and federal. By legislative union, Macdonald meant one government, almost certainly a parliamentary one like Britain's, and termed it "the best, the cheapest, the most vigorous, and the strongest system of government we could adopt."[11] His colleague Alexander Galt, Minister of Finance in the coalition government of the Province of Canada, described it as a "more complete union" that enabled "more direct action and control of the government" over the interests of the citizens, or "unity of action."[12] It never occurred to either of them to revert to such rudimentary considerations as that contained in Madison's third test—the power to legislate on individuals and therefore impose and collect taxes—when discussing the advantages of legislative union. Assuming these powers to prevail, they were concerned to convey a sense of the strength and vigor they supposed such a government to possess. But it was an impracticable model in the circumstances, unless it could be moderated somehow, and this brought them up against the federal alternative and the experience of the United States.

---

9 Solberg, *The Federal Convention*, 116.

10 Ibid., 142–43.

11 P.B. Waite, ed., *The Confederation Debates in the Province of Canada/1865* (Toronto: McClelland and Stewart, 1963), 40.

12 *Speech on the Proposed Union of the British North American Provinces* (Montreal, 1864), 4.

The Fourth Test

Early in the proceedings at the Quebec Conference, Macdonald defined the federal question in terms of an American error. The alleged error was to have permitted sovereign states to delegate specified powers to a national government, reserving the unspecified remainder to themselves. Subsequently the issue emerged as a critical point of difference between partisans of the local legislatures and those who regarded them as an administrative necessity to be tolerated but contained, and they joined issue when Oliver Mowat, another member of the coalition ministry representing Canada at the conference, introduced motions defining the powers of local legislatures. E.B. Chandler of New Brunswick objected that this was the mark of a legislative, not a federal union, and urged instead that their powers be unspecified and include all those not assigned to the central government. In Chandler's opinion, the issue was decisive as to whether the union could be regarded as federal or legislative. In response, Charles Tupper, premier of Nova Scotia, recalled the understanding reached earlier at the Charlottetown Conference that, contrary to the American system, the powers not assigned to the local legislatures be reserved to the central legislature. It was, he said, a "fundamental principle" held by delegates from the Province of Canada, and if it pointed in the direction of legislative union, so much the better.[13] Macdonald, who intervened to say that Chandler was proposing to make the same mistake as the Americans had, added that the effect of what he termed the "decentralization" of the United States was a lack of patriotic feeling. In a contest between the interests of a person's state and those of the union, the state won out. Since the British North American colonies, like the American states, had very different economic interests and therefore different tariff requirements, it was essential to avoid institutional arrangements that enhanced rather than moderated local attachments.[14]

Later, when Macdonald defended publicly the resolutions drafted at the conference, it was clear that his views on the issue remained unchanged. In his speech in the debate on the resolutions in the Legislative Assembly of the Province of Canada, he referred to the U.S. Constitution with the understanding air of an admirer who knows what has gone wrong. It was, he suggested, an adaptation of the British constitution, and "perhaps the only practicable system that could have been

---

13 G.P. Browne, ed., *Documents on the Confederation of British North America* (Toronto: McClelland and Stewart, 1969), 122.

14 Ibid., 124.

adopted under the circumstances existing at the time of its formation."[15] But time and events had revealed grave defects, chief among them the relationship between the national and state governments. Macdonald was preoccupied with two aspects of that relationship, state sovereignty and the residual power: "They declared by their Constitution that each state was a sovereignty in itself, and that all the powers incident to a sovereignty belonged to each state, except those powers which, by the Constitution, were conferred upon the General Government and Congress."[16] He objected to the assignment of the residual power to the states because it reflected and gave impetus to the notion of state sovereignty, and he identified state sovereignty as the weak link of the constitution and ultimately the source of the Civil War. Galt, in distinguishing for his constituents the federalism of the Quebec scheme from American federalism on the ground of the source of sovereignty, made much the same point. The American states, he declared, entered the union as sovereign states, and delegated express powers to the national government, reserving the remainder to themselves. The result was the states' rights doctrine so fatal to the stability of a federal union, and it was essential to avoid it.[17] But how to avoid it?

Macdonald, Galt and Tupper, legislative unionists at heart, were fond of emphasizing and elaborating the decision to assign the "great subjects of legislation" to the general legislature. The Americans, however, had done that too, and clearly it was not enough. Hence the emphasis on rectifying the problems of state sovereignty and residual power. On the residual power, Macdonald touted the provision that reserved to the new parliament "all matters of a general character, not specially and exclusively reserved for the Local Governments and Legislatures."[18] At one stroke, he declared, the authors of the Quebec scheme had rectified the American error and true cause of the Republic's misfortunes. He did not point out that they had also included a reserve power clause for the provinces that covered, of course, unspecified matters of a "private or local nature."[19] He seems not to have been troubled by the possibility that there might be disagreement on what was general and what was local. On the contrary, he predicted that the sheer weight of power on the national government's side was sufficient to preclude it. On the

---

15 Waite, *Confederation Debates*, 44.

16 Ibid.

17 *Speech on the Proposed Union*, 4.

18 *Parliamentary Debates on the Subject of the Confederation of the British North American Provinces* (Quebec: Parliamentary Printers, 1865), 33.

19 Browne, *Documents*, 161. Section 43 assigns 18 subjects to the local legislatures, the last of which reads: "And generally all matters of a private or local nature, not assigned to the General Parliament."

sovereignty problem, as Galt explained, a solution was at hand in the form of the British colonial system, because the British Parliament, not the colonial legislatures of the provinces joining the union, would establish the powers of the general and local governments in a statute embodying the terms of the Quebec scheme.[20] Thomas D'Arcy McGee, another of the Canadian delegates and a fervent monarchist, speaking in the debate on the scheme in the Canadian parliament, said of it: "this is not an ordinary parliamentary measure. We do not legislate upon it. . . . It is for the Imperial Parliament to act upon it."[21]

Two other features of the scheme borrowed from colonial practice signalled the subordinate status of provincial governments. One was the mechanism of reservation and disallowance placed at the disposal of the general government in relation to bills passed by the local legislatures. It was a colonial institution replicating the same powers as were held by the British government in relation to the bills of colonial legislatures. Disallowance, or the veto, as it was often called, was unpopular in some constituencies, especially French-speaking ones. Thus the politic Macdonald declined to mention it at all, while his close colleague from Montreal East, George Étienne Cartier, only alluded to it when seeking to placate the fears of the British minority in Canada East that the French-speaking majority in the local assembly would injure it through laws adversely affecting the rights of property. He referred vaguely to a "remedy," but did not elaborate.[22] Galt, whose constituency was this very minority, did not hesitate to elaborate. Even when a lieutenant-governor had assented to provincial legislation, he pointed out, it was still subject to disallowance by the general government for a period of one year. There was no need to rely wholly on the lieutenant-governor's discretionary power to reserve provincial bills for consideration.[23] And yet there was every reason to do just that because appointment to the office of lieutenant-governor was in the hands of the general government.

In his own discussion of this point, Macdonald explained that subordinate legislatures required subordinate executives: "As this is to be one united province, with the local governments and legislatures subordinate to the General Government and Legislature, it is obvious that the chief executive officer in each of the provinces must be subordinate as well."[24] He described the relationship between these local executives and the general government as colonial, modelled after the relationship between

---

20 *Speech on the Proposed Union*, 8.

21 *Parliamentary Debates on the Subject of Confederation*, 136.

22 Ibid., 61.

23 *Speech on the Proposed Union*, 16.

24 *Parliamentary Debates on the Subject of Confederation*, 42.

colonial governors and the British government. Galt observed that one effect of the model was to put an end to direct relations between the provinces and the British government, and that this was intentional. Since the provinces were confined to local matters, he argued, they had no need to deal with Britain and any attempt to do so would only arouse "very great mischief." Moreover, the lieutenant-governors would serve as the general government's most important "links of connection" with the provincial governments, the conduits through which it could resolve difficulties arising between itself and them. Galt recognized the conflict between the obligation of these officials to act on the advice of their provincial ministers, and their obligation to the government that appointed them, and he sided with the latter: "all action beginning with the people and proceeding through the Local Legislature, would, therefore, before it became law, come under the revisions of the Lieutenant Governor, who would be responsible for his actions and be obliged to make his report to the superior authority."[25]

From the point of view of the Quebec delegates, therefore, the U.S. example first and foremost illustrated the problems associated with the fourth test of federalism, the extent of powers available to the central government. And the British colonial system provided solutions that Madison would have regarded as strong injections of the national element. What aspect of the federal element, then, did the delegates retain in this matter? Was it exclusivity of jurisdiction in relation to those matters assigned to the local legislatures, as Vipond suggests? Since Macdonald, in particular, was less attached to the federal principle than others, it is important for Vipond to show that Macdonald ultimately accepted the exclusivity doctrine. Certainly the future prime minister of the new federation supposed there to be a clear distinction between general and local matters and therefore that local legislatures had a role to play. Each province, he said, would have the "power and means of developing its own resources and aiding its own progress after its own fashion and in its own way." But not entirely in its own way. The general government's arsenal of intrusive powers included more than the formidable combination of reservation and disallowance. For example, it might declare any local work, although situated wholly within a province, to be for the general advantage, and bring it within its jurisdiction. As for the criminal law, Macdonald could not resist pointing out that under the terms of the Quebec scheme it was assigned to the general parliament, whereas the American Constitution unwisely permitted each state its own criminal code: "I think this is one of the most marked instances in which

---

25 *Speech on the Proposed Union*, 14.

we take advantage of the experience derived from our observations of the defects in the Constitution of the neighbouring Republic."[26]

There was also a provision enabling the general parliament to legislate uniformity in the laws on property and civil rights and in procedure in the courts, but only in the common law provinces that agreed to it. Except in Canada East, where the Code Civil prevailed, Macdonald explained, the laws of the provinces, diverse in superficial ways, were based on the same principles. Accordingly, the first general administration would pursue the project of assimilation. Uniformity in the criminal law provided the standard which, he hoped, the civil law of the common law provinces might one day meet.[27] And yet there is another side to this provision. In its final form, as s. 94 of the *Constitution Act, 1867*, it essentially established a procedure for transferring jurisdiction over property and civil rights from the provinces of Ontario, New Brunswick and Nova Scotia to the federal parliament.[28] But the procedure required their consent and in that way, as Samuel LaSelva argues, it could be understood to have signalled the sovereignty of the provinces in relation to their jurisdiction. Section 94 was the closest the 1867 Act came to anything resembling an amending formula, and it affirmed the provinces' jurisdictional control.[29] The federal government, through such devices as the disallowance power, could interfere unilaterally in provincial lawmaking, but it could not alter the distribution of legislative powers itself. To this extent the Confederation agreement formally satisfied the requirements of a federal principle now understood to mean security of jurisdiction at the local level.

To understand the political significance of security of local jurisdiction it is necessary to turn to those of the delegates for whom it was important. For the leaders of the French-speaking community in the eastern section of the Province of Canada, it was the non-negotiable condition in return for which they were prepared to concede the principle of representation by population in the lower house of the new parliament, a principle that would institutionalize their minority position within the new nation. Sir Étienne-Pascal Taché, premier of the coalition government

---

26 *Parliamentary Debates on the Subject of Confederation*, 41.

27 Ibid.

28 Browne, *Documents*, 159. Section 33 of the Quebec Resolutions opens with the words: "Rendering uniform all or any of the laws relative to property and civil rights in Upper Canada, Nova Scotia, New Brunswick, Newfoundland and Prince Edward Island," and adds a clause on the requirement of the agreement of the provincial legislatures. Section 94 of the *Constitution Act, 1867* contains a major substantive addition enabling Parliament, in the event of the passage of uniformity legislation, "to make Laws in relation to any Matter comprised in any such Act."

29 Samuel V. LaSelva, "Federalism and Unanimity: The Supreme Court and Constitutional Amendment," *Canadian Journal of Political Science* 16 (1983), 761.

in the Province of Canada, who opened the debate on the scheme in the Legislative Council, emphasized in both languages his view that it was "tantamount to a separation of the provinces" and that "Lower Canada would thereby preserve its autonomy together with all the institutions it held so dear, and over which they could exercise them unimpaired."[30] Tache's real object was to persuade the worried English-speaking minority in Canada East that it had no reason to fear the French-speaking majority that would dominate the assembly in the new province, and he had a good deal to say about goodwill, forbearance and trust as well as the federal structure of the scheme. While Tache looked inward, Cartier looked to the promise of national politics. But he too relied on a federal structure that would separate local from national matters and establish different levels of government to deal with them. His object was to persuade French-speaking members that they need not fear the prospect of forming a minority in the national legislature because that body was not charged with matters related to the rights and privileges of nationalities. The provincial legislatures were. The national agenda, by contrast, was constituted by the "large questions of general interest in which the differences of race or religion had no place," for example, by commercial questions.[31] Cartier was hopeful that the federal structure would banish tiresome questions of nationality to the local level, thus freeing men of both nationalities to deliberate constructively at the national level on questions of commercial policy. This they could do if, as he supposed, commerce transcended nationality.

George Brown, leader of the Reform party in Canada West and member of the coalition ministry, took a position rather like Cartier's in the end. A defender of strong central government, nonetheless he was interested in the role of local governments in the scheme he supported because, among other things, it promised to release his beleaguered Canada West from the ordeal of its existing union with Canada East. The people of Canada West (subsequently Ontario), he exulted, would be free to spend money for local purposes, dispense local patronage and pursue land and settlement policies in their own community without having to seek the agreement of other communities, particularly Canada East. While Tache spoke about the freedom to guard cherished institutions, Brown was anticipating impatiently his province's freedom to pursue its commercial and political life. However, Brown was also interested in the substance of a national politics, and like Cartier he supposed that it could be purified if purged of local considerations. "If we look back on our doings of the last fifteen years," he said, "I think it will be acknowledged

---

30 Waite, *Confederation Debates*, 22.

31 *Parliamentary Debates*, 55–61.

that the greatest jobs perpetrated were of a local character—that our fiercest contests were about local matters that stirred up sectional jealousies and indignation to its deepest depth."[32] Members who were compelled to champion their own section in disputes over local matters, he argued, invariably found themselves unpopular elsewhere. However, if they could participate in a national politics unencumbered by local considerations, they could appeal to voters everywhere. They could aspire to national popularity and reputation without having to sacrifice local loyalties.[33] It is hard not to conclude that Brown's vision of a rational politics at the national level—rational because it excluded the affectionate attachments that always interfere with consideration of issues on the merits—was the politics of Canada West itself, writ large.

The Second Test

The Quebec delegates liked to talk about the great projects that the new central government would pursue and they were determined to equip it with the powers such projects would require. This meant adjusting the relationship between national and local governments in ways that favored the former to a greater extent than they thought the American relationship did. They were anxious to avoid the threat of upstart local governments, but having guarded against that, they were prepared for political and administrative reasons to secure jurisdiction on purely local matters to local authorities. As Madison's federal criteria demonstrated, however, there were other areas in which to consider the mix of national and federal elements, such as the design of central government institutions, a matter covered in his second test.

The Canadian and Maritime delegates favored the British parliamentary model for the central government, a decidedly national choice in Madison's terms. The Canadians, anxious to escape the federal-like conventions that had come to hobble governments in the Province of Canada, were determined to follow the model as closely as possible. Still, the Senate posed something of a problem for them. At the Quebec Conference, the composition of the Senate, often referred to there as the Legislative Council or upper house, was the first specific question delegates addressed. Macdonald moved the initial motion, and it included two vital proposals on representation, namely that the provinces be formed into three sections and that each section be represented equally.[34] The two Canadas of the Province of Canada, which were to

---

32 Ibid., 94.

33 Ibid., 96.

34 Browne, *Documents*, 64–65.

become the provinces of Ontario and Quebec in the event of union, would each constitute a section, the four Maritime provinces represented at the conference making up the third.

The sketchy records of the debate that followed on this and related motions and amendments indicate that Maritime delegates were prepared to accept equal regional as opposed to equal provincial representation, but not in the way Macdonald proposed. For instance, they successfully resisted the idea of the third section including four provinces, instead paring it to the three Maritime provinces, with Newfoundland assigned four additional representatives. The numbers finally arrived at were twenty-four members per section, the third section consisting of ten each for Nova Scotia and New Brunswick, and four for Prince Edward Island. Later, however, when it became clear to Island delegates that George Brown's population-based formula for the lower house would yield them a meagre five seats, they became increasingly unhappy. Edward Whelan announced that he had thought four members in the upper house unfair, although he had given way on it at the time. The idea of five members in the lower house was altogether unsatisfactory.[35] His Island colleagues agreed and chose to press for additional members in the lower house. Only A.A. Macdonald, an Island delegate, made a case for equal provincial representation in the upper house, citing the U.S. Senate as an example. He argued that the small provinces ought to be well represented in a body that was to guard their rights and privileges and that, as the constitutional equals of the large provinces, they were entitled to equal representation.[36]

The lack of interest in this line of reasoning was one indication that in general delegates were inclined to view the upper house more as a parliamentary institution like the British House of Lords than a federal one like the American Senate. Another was the decision that its members be appointed by the central government, and hold office for life. It was taken unanimously and, unlike the decision on the numbers, took little time to reach, possibly because the issue of election versus nomination had been discussed extensively at the meetings in Charlottetown that took place prior to the conference in Quebec.[37] The same was true of the decision to impose a high real property qualification on candidates.[38] In

---

35 Ibid., 110.

36 Ibid., 138.

37 Ibid., 44–49. In his letter to Edward Cardwell, the British colonial secretary, Lieutenant-Governor Gordon of New Brunswick reported that the composition and the method of selection of members of the federal upper house was one of two subjects "debated at some length in more elaborately prepared speeches" at the Charlottetown meetings (ibid., 45).

38 Ibid., 68.

his opening speech to the conference, John A. Macdonald had indicated that he knew that some delegates favored election over appointment and that his own mind was open on the subject. At the same time, he preferred appointment because he thought it best to "return to the original principle and in the words of Governor Simcoe endeavour to make ours 'an image and transcript of the British Constitution'." He also recommended a high property qualification for members of an upper house that was partly intended to protect property. "The rights of the minority must be protected," he reminded delegates, "and the rich are always fewer in number than the poor."[39] The closest he came to articulating a federal purpose in that speech was a reference to the need for an equality of representation in the upper house against population in the lower one in order to avoid "local jealousies" and generally keep things "conciliatory." For Macdonald, the House of Lords was the governing model that delegates would adapt to their purposes.

In the debate on the Quebec Resolutions, the Canadian delegates never attempted to develop much in the way of a federal rationale for the upper house. They talked generally about the protection of sectional interests, but declined to explain how an institution, the members of which were chosen for life by the Crown on the recommendation of the central government, could possibly serve that function. Instead they concentrated on defending what they obviously perceived to be the weak point of the upper house in the eyes of a Canadian public accustomed to electing legislative councillors since 1856, namely, the return to nomination. Macdonald defended the nominative principle as a return to the right practice of parliamentary government, or a near return, the heredity aspect of the House of Lords being unsuited to Canadian society. Thus his main concern was to explain why the marginally federal feature of fixed and equal sectional representation would not produce an independent-minded upper house in continual deadlock with the lower house.[40] Equal sectional representation was simply the price of representation by population in the lower house, and not a high one as it turned out. Many of the scheme's opponents suspected as much, especially those for whom the American Senate invariably served as the standard of a proper second chamber in a federal union.

In the Legislative Assembly of the Province of Canada, Christopher Dunkin, independent member from Brome County in Canada East and perhaps the shrewdest critic of the scheme, regarded the upper house as the "merest sham" of a federal institution. The American Senate, he pointed out, possessed important executive as well as legislative powers, and its members were chosen by the state legislatures themselves. It was

39 Ibid., 98.

40 *Parliamentary Debates*, 36–38.

a powerful political institution, a real "federal check." By contrast, the Canadian version—"a very near approach to the worst system which could be devised in legislation"—was essentially a legislative review body with the inappropriately vast and negative power of veto. It was not an integral part of the central government. Nor did it represent any public opinion, least of all local opinion. And yet, Dunkin argued, the Quebec scheme as a whole did contemplate a federation. As a result, local governments, not content to pursue their interests at the local level alone, would demand a voice at the national level. Unable to find effective expression in the upper house, they would turn to the cabinet. But the cabinet was a parliamentary institution shaped by conventions that caused it to act as a unit in the interests of the nation as a whole, not as a coalition of individuals visibly championing local interests. It was an inappropriate vehicle for the expression of local interests.[41]

Maritime anti-Confederates, disappointed with Maritime weight in the central government generally and in the upper house in particular, continually appealed to the American example. In New Brunswick, A.J. Smith, whose government had been defeated by Leonard Tilley's pro-union party in a second election on the Confederation issue, argued that the upper house did not provide the provinces with an effective check on the central government and that this was a more serious problem here, where the lower house could bring down an administration, than in the United States, where the House of Representatives could not. "Give us, at least," he wrote, "the guard which they have in the United States, although we ought to have more, because, here, the popular branch is all-powerful."[42] In Nova Scotia, Joseph Howe repeatedly warned readers of his *Botheration Letters* that Canadians would dominate the central government unless the small Maritime provinces held out for the American solution of equal representation in the upper house. He also explained to them that the American Senate, because it shared in the powers of the executive branch, was a far more weighty body than the typically parliamentary chamber of "sober second thought," and he concluded: "The Senate is therefore, in the American system, the body in which largely resides not merely the dignity but the real substantial power of the Government; and thus to the smaller States is secured a fair share of influence over the administration, that we, by no provision which the Quebec scheme includes, can ever hope to obtain."[43] Maritime anti-Confederates, worried about the fate of their provinces in the proposed union, were much more concerned about the central government

41 Ibid., 494–500.

42 *Morning Freeman*, Saint John, 30 June 1866.

43 *Morning Chronicle*, Halifax, 11 January 1865.

and the absence of federal features in it than they were about division of powers questions.

The First and Fifth Tests

As noted earlier, Madison had included ratification and amendment in his assessment of the Philadelphia Convention's work, finding the first federal and the latter a mix of federal and national elements. On both tests, the Confederation agreement resists much comparison because of the colonial circumstances of its birth and the role of the British Parliament in legislating the agreement and subsequent amendments to it. As far as ratification and amendment procedures were concerned, the real question in both instances was the consent required domestically before the British Parliament could be requested to act.

In the case of ratification, the Quebec delegates decided that a favorable vote on the Quebec Resolutions in the colonial legislatures was sufficient. No amendments to the Resolutions were permitted. Opponents often pressed for a more popular procedure, especially if they were from communities hostile to union, and occasionally cited American practice, as did the Rouge member of the Legislative Assembly of the Province of Canada, J.B.E. Dorion, who suggested that American *amendment* procedures offered a more appropriate course.[44]

In Nova Scotia, where the consent issue was debated hotly, anti-Confederates urged the parliamentary route of a general election.[45] They had good reason to press for an election. When the Nova Scotian delegates returned from the Quebec Conference, it soon became apparent to them that there was serious opposition to the Resolutions in the province. As a result, Tupper's government never did risk a vote in the legislature. What he did manage to get, in April 1866, was a motion authorizing the Lieutenant-Governor to appoint delegates to attend the London Conference and there, with the Imperial government and delegates from the other British North American colonies, arrange a new scheme of union ensuring "just provision for the rights and interests of Nova Scotia."[46] It was as close as the province came to giving formal sanction to Confederation.

In New Brunswick, two elections were fought on the issue against a backdrop of strong British pressure in favor of the Quebec scheme, and in the end Tilley's government secured a motion from the legislature with wording similar to that of Nova Scotia's. Only the legislature of the

---

44 *Parliamentary Debates*, 858.

45 J.G. Marshall, *An Examination of the Proposed Union of the North American Provinces* (Halifax, 1865), 65.

46 Nova Scotia, Legislative Assembly, *Journals*, 10 April 1866, 10.

Province of Canada voted in support of the scheme. In Prince Edward Island the legislature voted it down, and the Island waited six years before joining the union. Newfoundland, not prepared to deal seriously with the idea, waited many more years.

On the amendment question, the American example was even less relevant, mostly because the Quebec scheme did not include a comprehensive amending formula.[47] Amendment does not appear to have been discussed at the Quebec Conference, nor was it much pursued subsequently by opponents and advocates of the scheme. A notable exception among opponents appeared in a published *Letter to Lord Carnarvon*, under the heading "Federal Safeguards," in which Joseph Howe, William Annand and Hugh McDonald described the omission of a formula as a "radical defect." They pointed approvingly to the American Constitution and commented that although it was democratic in origin and character, it was "wisely protected from the hazard of rash innovation" by the explicit and strict requirements of its amending formula.[48] The three Nova Scotians, convinced that the "Canadians" were using the British government to impose upon the Maritime provinces a constitution, the terms of which their legislatures had not approved, saw in the American system a way of ensuring that there be widespread consent to constitutional change. In the event, Canadians did not acquire a comprehensive amending formula for many years, and until they did, they relied on developing precedents to govern domestic consent procedures.[49] Of these, one of the earliest and most enduring was the requirement of the favorable vote of legislatures, as opposed to that of special conventions or referenda. More controversial was the appearance of the unanimity rule for changes affecting provincial governments. Be that as it may, it was the developing logic of Canadian federalism, and not the example of American federalism, that mattered.

CONCLUSION

The American framers understood federalism as a governmental arrangement in its own right, and the constitution outlined by the Articles of Confederation was the example at hand. The Quebec delegates, on the other hand, knew federalism in terms of the constitution that *replaced* the Articles, that is, the constitution that Madison analyzed as a combination

---

47 Jennifer Smith, "Origins of the Canadian Amendment Dilemma," *Dalhousie Review* 61 (1981), 292–301.

48 *Letter Addressed to the Earl of Carnarvon by Mr. Joseph Howe, Mr. William Annand, and Mr. Hugh McDonald, Stating their Objections to the proposed scheme of union of the British North American Provinces* (London, 1867), 13–14.

49 The new amending formula is contained in Part V of the *Constitution Act, 1982*.

of national and federal elements. They were preoccupied with two features of it, state sovereignty and the residual power, and they were convinced that by reversing U.S. practice in relation to them, they could avoid the disintegrative pressures to which federal arrangements appeared vulnerable. In assigning the general residual power to the central government and in adhering to the colonial practice according to which the British Parliament, not the provinces, delegated power, they were lessening the weight of the federal element in Madison's fourth test, legislative jurisdiction. In choosing to follow as closely as possible the British parliamentary model, they came near to eliminating the federal element altogether from the subject of Madison's second test, the institutions of the central government. One result was a new combination of federal and national elements, or, in Galt's terms, the principle of union and the federal principle, and it was quite different from the one Madison had described. Not only did it feature fewer federal elements, it concentrated them at the local level.

In the Quebec delegates' account of the guide they used on jurisdictional matters, that is, the distinction between general and local matters, the connection between the federal and the local is quite clear. Galt explained that the Quebec scheme weakened the federal principle by giving effect to it at the local level only, and as much as possible removing it from the national government. This, he argued, marked a great improvement over the constitution of the Province of Canada, which suffered from an internal contradiction. On the one hand, it gave the two sections of the province equal representation in both houses of the legislature. On the other, members from both sections were expected to deal "as one" with all matters, general and local, much as a parliament of a legislative union. In the end, the federal element proved overwhelming, paralyzing government. The Quebec scheme, Galt continued, remedied this by modifying the federal element of the new national government so that it no longer interfered with unity of action. The half-hearted federal mechanism of sectional representation in the upper house, diluted further by the selection principle of central government nomination, was no match for the population-based representation in the lower house. Thus the scheme partook of the federal character only in relation to local matters, that is, matters of "private right and sectional interest," while preserving the union on matters common to all.[50] It relegated federalism to the parts.

As the history of Canadian federalism has demonstrated, Galt's confidence in the unfettered unity principle animating the central government was to prove misplaced, but not because of unexpected federal strength in the Senate. The trouble was in the parts themselves, in the provincial

---

50 *Speech on the Proposed Union*, 4.

governments which soon showed signs of resisting Galt's idea that they were no more than glorified municipal governments. If the Confederation agreement has failed at times to preserve the union principle on matters common to all, it is because powerful provincial governments have managed to lay claim to them, either by expanding the "local" to include arguably national matters or by demanding and acquiring a role in the determination of national policy. How have they done this? What has enabled them to confound the intentions of the founders? Students of Canadian politics have long considered the problem and offered various and compelling explanations, among them the strength and persistence of the autonomist tradition in Quebec, the internal dynamic of the political and bureaucratic institutions that comprise and sustain modern provincial administrations, and the role of the Judicial Committee of the Privy Council in developing constitutional doctrines favorable to provincial claims.

Recently political scientists have looked hard at Galt's unity principle in the central government and concluded, in effect, that he was wrong. They argue that the decision to deny serious institutional expression to local concerns within the central government has served to weaken rather than strengthen it. They point to the various institutional ways in which the Washington government gives effective representation to local interests, and argue that these have contributed to the importance and authority of the Congress and the executive branch and at the same time deprived state governments of a monopoly on the task of local representation. "Effective territorial representation," writes Roger Gibbins, "has been combined with, and indeed has helped to produce, a strong and relatively centralized national government."[51] He suggests several ways in which Canadians might follow the U.S. example, including the election of senators who, armed with a popular mandate, could compete with provincial premiers in the role of provincial spokesmen.

Gibbins's suggestion was an alternative open to the Quebec delegates. There was some support for an elected upper house, principally from two of the reform-minded members of the Canadian delegation, William McDougall and Oliver Mowat.[52] And, as indicated earlier, the issue was discussed at length at the meetings in Charlottetown. If Gibbins' reasoning is applicable, then the delegates helped defeat their own purposes by favoring a parliamentary over a federal model for the upper house, a decision arising in part out of a mistaken analysis of the American Constitution. They ought to have paid less attention to problems such as

---

51 Roger Gibbins, *Regionalism: Territorial Politics in Canada and the United States* (Toronto: Butterworths, 1982), 77.

52 Waite, *Confederation Debates*, 82.

state sovereignty and the residual power and more to the composition of the central government.

Moreover, they compounded the error by deciding to adopt the parliamentary model in the organization of the provincial governments as well as in the national government. The historian W.L. Morton considered this decision to be of the greatest importance because it established the ground of provincial sovereignty. It paved the way "for the continuation and development in the provinces of all the powers and pretensions of responsible and parliamentary government."[53] In the event, the "powers and pretensions" of what the Nova Scotia delegate Jonathan McCully called "miniature responsible Governments," have proven formidable. As Morton pointed out, the long-established Maritime governments lost some powers but, retaining their character, otherwise carried on as before, while the governments of the central provinces emerged stronger and "more self-governing" than their predecessors in the old provinces of Upper and Lower Canada prior to 1840.[54]

It is not possible to say whether the provincial governments would have been sufficiently powerful from the start to have resisted the nationalizing effects of an elected upper house, had the delegates opted for one. However, if the current constitutional talks underway in Canada are successful, these alleged effects may well be put to the test. The daunting array of issues under consideration includes Senate reform, and some of the provinces are pursuing it vigorously, not because they wish to strengthen the central government but because they are seeking to offset the perceived clout of the larger provinces in that government. Thus they propose to institutionalize the concept of the equality of the provinces in a classically designed federal upper house that would balance the House of Commons, the representation principle of which so clearly favors the larger, more populous provinces. The latter group, understandably, is less than enthusiastic about a Senate in which the provinces are represented equally. But neither is the federal government. Should equal provincial representation carry the day, it would be an irony, indeed, if the long-term beneficiary turned out to be the federal government.

---

53 W.L. Morton, *The Critical Years: The Union of British North America, 1857–1873* (Toronto: McClelland and Stewart, 1964), 210. As Morton points out, the alternative was the municipal government model, with the office of governor replaced by that of a superintendent, possibly an elected superintendent.

54 Ibid., 210–11, 199.

Federalism in a North American Context: The Contribution of the Supreme Courts of Canada, the United States and Mexico

Kenneth M. Holland

On 17 December 1992, the heads of government of the United States, Canada and Mexico signed a North American Free Trade Agreement (NAFTA). This historic step raises the prospect of the political as well as the economic integration of North America, a prospect suggested by the evolution since 1957 of the European Community from a common market toward political and military union. Any movement toward a North American confederation, however, must take account of the federal nature of each of the North American democracies. Although only one of the twelve EC members, Germany, is a federation, the constitutions of all three North American polities eschew the unitary political model of their mother countries—Great Britain, France and Spain. Efforts to integrate the economies and policies of North America will be shaped in large part by this federal reality. A study of the history of federalism in Canada, the United States and Mexico reveals, however, a variety of ways in which North Americans have conceived the relationship between levels of government. Some conceptions pose fewer obstacles to continental integration than others. One of the richest sources of federalist models is the judiciary, for the North American peoples have delegated to their federal supreme courts primary responsibility for resolving conflicts between the states and provinces, on the one hand, and the center on the other. The purpose of this paper is to summarize the various conceptions of the federal arrangement articulated by the supreme courts of Canada, the United States and Mexico and to reflect on the extent to which their contemporary jurisprudence might inhibit or facilitate the realization of the continental vision.

FEDERALISM IN THE UNITED STATES

The fundamental theoretical division at the Constitutional Convention of 1787 was between those delegates who accepted Montesquieu's teaching that liberty was safe only in small republics and those inspired by James

Madison's conviction that only a large commercial republic under a strong national government could safeguard individual freedom. Federalism emerged as the product of compromise between these two groups— neither of which sought it. As Madison later explained, the Constitution embodied a system "partly federal and partly national," a novel experiment which the world had never seen before.[1] The Supreme Court played a key role in giving shape to this experiment. The task has not been an easy one; in fact the Court has struggled to define the relationship between the states and federal government. We can identify at least six distinct understandings of the federal principle, each dominant at a particular historical period.

1. *The Constitution as Nation-Building Instrument (1801–35).* The chief justiceship of John Marshall was marked by the assertion of federal power over the states. The key principle was that the federal Congress's powers as granted by Art. I, s. 8, were supreme over those of the states. The powers reserved to the states by the Tenth Amendment (1791) did not restrict the national government. It was but a tautology, neither granting nor restraining powers. The only restrictions came from explicit prohibitions on the national government, such as the First Amendment's prohibition on laws abridging freedom of speech, and from the fact that the legislative powers of the national government were enumerated. Marshall, however, limited the scope of the doctrine of enumerated powers in *McCulloch* v. *Maryland* (1819),[2] where he stated that Congress enjoys not only the powers explicitly granted but those that could reasonably be implied therefrom. Animating the Marshall Court's generous view of the scope of federal power was the assumption, shared by members of the Federalist Party, that the single greatest threat to the public interest and the rights of minorities, especially the rights of property holders, was the state legislatures.

2. *Federalism as a Weapon in Class Conflict (1836–64).* Chief Justice Roger Taney, a Jacksonian Democrat, took a very different view of the constitutional division of authority. Beginning with the assumption that the federal government was overly sensitive to the demands of the wealthy, the Taney Court resolved many conflicts between state and federal power in favor of the former. The contrast with Marshall's approach is clearest in decisions concerning the scope of the states' power to make regulations affecting commerce among the states, a power which the Marshall Court denied to the states on the ground that interstate com-

---

1 James Madison, Alexander Hamilton and John Jay, *The Federalist Papers* (London: Penguin Books, 1987 [1788]), No. 39, 259. In 1788, the words "federal" and "confederal" were synonyms. There was no single word to describe the system devised at the Constitutional Convention.

2 17 U.S. (4 Wheat.) 316 (1819).

mercial regulation was a monopoly of the U. S. Congress under Art. I. By contrast, the Taney Court held that the states could, in the absence of federal law, regulate interstate and foreign commerce, either as a state regulation of commerce or as an exercise of police power, the power to protect the health, safety, welfare and morals of the people. Taney, also, in sharp contrast with Marshall, took a narrow view of Art. I, s. 10's prohibition against state laws impairing the obligation of contracts.[3] Decisions of the Taney Court, thus, had the effect of legitimating state government intervention in the market in the name of equal opportunity for all classes.

   3. *Dual Federalism (1865–1937).* In *Hammer* v. *Dagenhart* (1918),[4] the Supreme Court invalidated a congressional statute that restricted the transportation in interstate commerce of goods produced by child labor, even though Congress was explicitly granted the power in Art. I, s. 8, to regulate commerce among the states. The Court held that "the local power always existing and carefully reserved to the States in the Tenth Amendment" was a positive restriction on the otherwise valid powers of Congress. The Tenth Amendment thus became analogous to the First Amendment, and was read by the Court as saying: "Congress shall make no law destroying powers the states exercised before ratification of the Constitution." This principle became known as the doctrine of dual federalism, according to which the federal government could not intrude on powers reserved to the states and the state governments could not encroach on powers delegated by the Constitution to the federal government.

   4. *The States' Failure to Protect the Disadvantaged (1938–75).* As a result of President Franklin Roosevelt's attempt to pack the Supreme Court with justices supporting the New Deal, the Court, admitting defeat, abandoned its defense of state sovereignty and returned to the Marshall approach. In the words of Justice Harlan Stone in *United States* v. *Darby Lumber* (1941),[5] the Tenth Amendment "states but a truism that all is retained which has not been surrendered." The Court announced that the states were no longer part of its special constituency, because through their participation in the affairs of the federal government, such as the election of U. S. Senators, they were perfectly capable of protecting their own interests. Groups excluded from the political process, on the other hand, such as racial minorities, the poor, and political dissidents, were in need of judicial protection. The decisions of the Warren Court (1954–69) reveal that the justices assumed that the states were far greater threats to justice

---

3 See Taney's opinion for the Court in *Charles River Bridge* v. *Warren Bridge*, 36 U.S. (11 Pet.) 419 (1837).

4 247 U.S. 251 (1918).

5 312 U.S. 100 (1941).

and the interests of the "underdogs" of American society than was the federal government. Through the nationalization of the Bill of Rights during this period, the state legislatures came under comprehensive federal judicial control.

5. *The "New Federalism" of the Nixon Court (1976–84)*. The election of Republican Richard Nixon in 1968, due in part to popular reaction against the hostile attitude of the Warren Court to states' rights, led to the appointment by the president of a number of politically conservative justices. Under the intellectual leadership of William Rehnquist, the Court reversed direction on the state/federal issue in *National League of Cities* v. *Usery* (1976).[6] The Court invalidated a congressional attempt to apply minimum-wage and maximum-hours legislation to state governments and their political subdivisions because of the threat it posed to federalism. The law, said Rehnquist, threatened the states' "separate and independent existence," which he treated as a check on the power of Congress analogous to the First Amendment's ban on acts abridging freedom of speech. Significantly, Rehnquist did not rely on the Tenth Amendment but on "the total structure created by the Constitution" as the basis of this restriction. States were thus freed to set wage levels for state employees as they saw fit, thus enjoying a privilege that the private sector under the Fair Labor Standards Act did not.

6. *The Return to Judicial Restraint in State-Federal Conflicts (1985–Present)*. The Rehnquist doctrine did not long endure. In *Garcia* v. *San Antonio Metropolitan Transit Authority* (1985),[7] the Court overruled *National League of Cities*. The majority held that the "traditional governmental functions" test for the scope of federal power over the states was unworkable and inconsistent with the true meaning of Art. I and the Tenth Amendment. The Fair Labor Standards Act, said Justice Harry Blackmun for the Court, did not violate any specific constitutional provision. The states must rely on the political process, not the Constitution or the Supreme Court, to preserve their historic role in the federal system. Justice Rehnquist dissented.

This posture of the Supreme Court is not likely to change in spite of the fact that the Court since 1985 has acquired a solid conservative majority, for developments in the 1980s and 1990s have worked to reduce the interest of conservatives in preserving the rights of the states. While the Republican party has maintained its control over the executive branch of the federal government, many municipalities and states have come under the control of liberal Democrats and even, in a few jurisdictions, social-

6 426 U.S. 833 (1976).

7 469 U.S. 528 (1985).

ists.[8] Charles Fried, President Reagan's Solicitor General during his second term, typifies the conservative nationalists, who advocate "severe federal restrictions" on such "Luddite and leveling impositions" as rent-control schemes, affirmative-action policies and racial set-aside ordinances.[9]

Indicative of the declining salience of states' rights to conservatives is the Supreme Court's decision in *South Dakota* v. *Dole* (1987),[10] in which it upheld the constitutionality of a 1984 federal statute that forced the states to adopt a uniform twenty-one-year-old drinking age on pain of losing federal highway construction funds. Chief Justice Rehnquist wrote the opinion for the Court, holding that under the Constitution the federal government may induce policy changes by the states by attaching strings to its grants-in-aid. Justice William Brennan, the most liberal justice on the court, dissented, echoing Rehnquist's argument in *National League of Cities* that Congress may not intrude on the powers reserved to the states by the Tenth Amendment.

FEDERALISM AND THE SUPREME COURT OF CANADA

The architects of the Canadian confederation could not agree on a coherent conception of federalism.[11] English-speaking Canadians from Ontario preferred the British unitary system of government to the American federal arrangement.[12] Like nationalists James Madison and Alexander Hamilton at the Constitutional Convention of 1787 in the United States, the centralists compromised their vision in order to win the acquiescence of Quebec and the Maritimes. The Canadian constitution of 1867, in the end, established a federal system with a much more powerful central government than the American Federalists had succeeded in gaining in 1787. Since their founding, however, the two systems have evolved in roughly opposite directions. As the federal government in the United States has tamed and gained ever greater policy and fiscal dominance over the states, the government in Ottawa has conceded ever more powers to the provinces. The judiciary in Britain and Canada played a leading role in this evolutionary process.

---

8 Burlington, Vermont, for example, under the mayorship of socialist Bernard Sanders.

9 Charles Fried, *Order and Law: Arguing the Reagan Revolution—A Firsthand Account* (New York: Simon and Schuster, 1991), 186–87.

10 483 U.S. 203 (1987).

11 The various understandings held by the founders are described in P. B. Waite, *The Life and Times of Confederation, 1864–1867* (Toronto: University of Toronto Press, 1962), c. 8.

12 Peter H. Russell, *The Judiciary in Canada: The Third Branch of Government* (Toronto: McGraw-Hill Ryerson, 1987), 54.

1. *Equal Sovereignty (1880–1945)*. During the decades when the Judicial Committee of the Privy Council in London served as the final court of appeal for Canada the provinces made significant constitutional gains at the expense of the center. The Committee's doctrine was strikingly similar to the "dual federalism" conception which reigned supreme in the U. S. Supreme Court during roughly this same period.[13] The Judicial Committee held that the provinces were as sovereign within their spheres of power as was the federal government in its own.[14] The Committee interpreted the enumeration of powers granted to the provinces in s. 92 of the *British North America Act* broadly to include intraprovincial commerce and labor relations.[15] As a result of a series of decisions by the law lords of the Judicial Committee, by the 1930s the *B.N.A. Act* no longer matched the reality of powerful provincial governments and a federal government considerably weaker than that evolving in the United States and Mexico.

2. *Unilateral Federalism (1945–60)*.[16] Quebec did not welcome the abolition of appeals to the Privy Council in 1949. It launched immediately a campaign, that continues today, to check by means of changes in the appointment process what it feared would be Supreme Court decisions in favor of federal power. As Jacques-Yvan Morin put it, the Supreme Court assumed its new duties in 1949 "with all the hopes of English Canada hanging around the necks of its judges."[17] In fact, during this period the Canadian courts developed a very centralist conception of Confederation. The Supreme Court's tendency was to support the federal government's claims, especially in disputes with the provinces over labor law, trade and commerce, taxation, criminal law, and economic planning.

---

13 "Dual federalism" was also the dominant paradigm in the jurisprudence of the Australian High Court at this time, which construed a constitution remarkably similar to that of the United States. The High Court referred to the doctrine as "the reserved powers of the states" and dramatically overruled its earlier decisions embodying the doctrine in 1920. See Leslie Zines, "Federal Power to Regulate Economic Matters," *Publius* 20 (Fall 1990), 21–22.

14 Examples where this doctrine prevailed are: *Hodge v. The Queen* (1883–1884), 9 App. Cas. 117; *Maritime Bank of Canada v. Receiver General of New Brunswick*, [1892] A.C. 437; *Reference re Initiative and Referendum Act*, [1919] A.C. 935; and *British Coal Corporation v. The King*, [1935] A.C. 500.

15 *Edwards v. Attorney General of Canada*, [1930] A.C. 124; *Toronto Electric Commissioners v. Snider*, [1925] A.C. 356.

16 The period characterizations, "Unilateral Federalism," "Bi-Polar Federalism," and "Standardizing Federalism" are taken from Andree Lajoie, Pierrete Mulazzi, and Michele Gamache, "Political Ideas in Quebec and the Evolution of Canadian Constitutional Law, 1945 to 1985," in Ivan Bernier and Andree Lajoie, eds., *The Supreme Court as an Instrument of Political Change* (Toronto: University of Toronto Press, 1986).

17 Jacques-Yvan Morin, "A Constitutional Court for Canada," *Canadian Bar Review* 43 (1965), 546.

The Court's construction of the distribution of powers, claimed Quebec, in the thirty-three cases raising that issue during this period was even more centralist than Sir John Macdonald had intended in the *B.N.A. Act*.[18] The Court rejected the earlier approach of the Privy Council and moved both to restrict provincial and to expand federal jurisdiction.[19]

3. *Bi-Polar Federalism (1960–75)*. During this period the provinces, led by Quebec, then undergoing the Quiet Revolution, began to agitate for decentralization. Quebec demanded the constitutional room that would allow a positive role for the provincial government in secularizing and modernizing its society. By the early 1970s the Supreme Court was responding favorably to these initiatives. A major difference from the preceding period was the active participation of Quebec as a litigant before the Supreme Court. During the Duplessis regime, Quebec sought to achieve its goals through nonjudicial channels. In the 1960s and 1970s the province, following the path of racial minorities in the United States, turned to the courts to accomplish its political agenda, by means of direct litigation and intervention by the province's attorney general in cases originating from other provinces.[20] Whereas in the preceding period Quebec lost all cases on the distribution of powers at the Supreme Court, between 1960 and 1975, the Court decided two-thirds of the constitutional cases arising from Quebec in the province's favor. With regard to the other provinces, however, the Court still followed a basically centralist tack. The difference in treatment is explained by the Court's desire to deflect the separatist movement in Quebec.

4. *Standardizing Federalism (1976–85)*. Perhaps ironically, the election of the separatist Parti Québécois government in 1976 did not result in a continuation of concessions by the Supreme Court in order to keep Quebec within Confederation. On the contrary, the Court responded favorably to the Trudeau government's initiative to patriate the constitution and to centralize regulation of the economy and protection of individual rights. The justices may have been responding to the deep divisions within Quebec over sovereignty evidenced by the failure of the 1980 referendum. The English-speaking provinces, by contrast, fared rather well, winning a majority of their cases before the Supreme Court. The areas where the provinces were least successful were cases involving the criminal law, the environment, and the power to amend the constitution.[21] In fact, the Court emerged as the principal institutional brake on

---

18 Lajoie et al., "Political Ideas in Quebec," 7.

19 See, e.g., *Reference re Validity and Applicability of Industrial Relations and Disputes Investigation Act*, [1955] S.C.R. 529, and *Attorney General of Canada* v. *Canadian Pacific*, [1958] S.C.R. 285.

20 Lajoie et al., "Political Ideas in Quebec," 25.

21 Ibid., 60.

province-building, which threatened increasingly to distort the original design of the *Constitution Act, 1867*. In a case involving a challenge to the federal parliament's approval of an effort by New Brunswick to expand the jurisdiction of its provincially appointed judges at the expense of the federally appointed superior court judges, the Court stated, "Parliament can no more give away federal constitutional powers than a province can usurp them."[22]

5. *The Charter of Rights as an Instrument of Centralization (1985–Present)*. Since the first decisions interpreting the 1982 *Canadian Charter of Rights and Freedoms* began to issue from the Supreme Court in the mid-1980s, the Supreme Court has exerted strong integrative and centralizing influences on the provinces in the area of civil liberties. In fact, it was the Court that made possible the entrenchment of rights in a patriated constitution in a 1981 landmark decision.[23]

The entrenchment of individual rights meant that the Court would not simply act as an umpire between federal and provincial authorities but would place constitutional constraints on both. For instance, the Supreme Court's first fifteen *Charter* cases went against the positions of both federal and provincial governments. By the end of 1986, the Supreme Court had shifted toward more frequent support of the government party. By 1990 the Court was hearing some twenty-five *Charter* cases a year, about one-fourth of its total caseload. *Charter* claimants won about one-third of the time. The Supreme Court was more likely to favor *Charter* claimants than were provincial courts of appeal.[24] Supreme Court reversals of decisions of the Quebec Court of Appeals have been especially high, such as the 1989 Appeals Court's decision to sustain a Quebec Superior Court's injunction, issued at the request of the father, to a pregnant woman to prevent her from having an abortion.[25] Of all the provinces, Quebec has had the highest number of statutes struck down by the Supreme Court.[26] The Court, for instance, struck down Quebec language law provisions limiting access to English-language education for persons coming from other provinces.[27] It also held Quebec language

---

22 *McEvoy* v. *Attorney General of New Brunswick*, [1983] 1 S.C.R. 705.

23 *Re Resolution to Amend the Constitution*, [1981] 1 S.C.R. 753.

24 Carl Baar, "Judicial Activism in Canada," in Kenneth M. Holland, ed., *Judicial Activism in Comparative Perspective* (London: Macmillan, 1991), 59.

25 *Tremblay* v. *Daigle*, [1989] 2 S.C.R. 530.

26 See Alan C. Cairns, "Who Should the Judges Be? Canadian Debates About the Composition of a Final Court of Appeal" (Paper presented to the Fourth Berkeley Seminar on Federalism, 19–20 April 1990).

27 *Attorney General of Quebec* v. *Quebec Association of Protestant School Boards*, [1984] 2 S.C.R. 66.

laws prohibiting the use of languages other than French on commercial signs to be unjustifiable limits on freedom of speech.[28]

Section 33 of the *Charter*, which permits provincial parliaments to re-enact for a five-year period a statute found unconstitutional by the Supreme Court, permits the Court to be even bolder than its U.S. and Mexican counterparts in striking down provincial Acts.[29] Thus in 1988 the Bourassa government in Quebec invoked the notwithstanding clause to override the Supreme Court's decision in the *Quebec Signs* cases.

Whereas the U. S. Supreme Court's activism in the 1950s and 1960s was directed principally at the states, the Canadian Supreme Court's treatment of federal and provincial statutes is more evenhanded. In contests before the U. S. Supreme Court during the Warren Court era between the individual and government, state governments lost sixty-five percent of the time, while the federal government lost only thirty-five percent of the time. In Canada, since 1985, federal statutes challenged by individual claimants survive only slightly more often than provincial statutes (sixty-seven percent compared to sixty-three percent).[30] The difference is explained in part by the fact that in Canada enactment of criminal laws is entirely a federal responsibility.

The Supreme Court of Canada seeks to enhance national integration both by shifting the balance of power toward the federal government and by developing a uniform national law on civil rights and liberties.[31] Quebec's insistence on protecting provincial powers against federal encroachment and on the superiority of collective rights to individual rights flies in the face of both aspects of the Court's nation-building enterprise. The *Charter* contains equality rights that have raised expectations of many underprivileged groups, including women, the disabled, non-English and non-French ethnics, homosexuals, and religious minorities. On the whole, these "*Charter* groups," often led by members of the New Class—highly paid professionals with anti-business attitudes—favor uniform national policies and distrust the provincial governments.[32]

---

28 *Ford* v. *Attorney General of Quebec* [1988] 2 S.C.R. 712.

29 Baar, "Judicial Activism in Canada," 63.

30 F. L. Morton, Peter H. Russell and M. J. Withey, "The Supreme Court's First One Hundred Charter Decisions: A Statistical Analysis" (Paper presented at the Annual Meeting of the Canadian Political Science Association, Victoria, British Columbia, 27–29 May 1990).

31 Keith G. Banting, "Federalism and the Supreme Court of Canada: The Contradiction of Legitimation" (Paper presented to the Ontario Law Reform Commission Conference, 14–15 September 1989).

32 See R. Knopff and F. L. Morton, "Nation-Building and the Canadian Charter of Rights and Freedoms," Report of the Royal Commission on the Economic Union and Development Prospects for Canada, 1985, vol. 33, *Constitutionalism, Citizenship, and Society in Canada*, 133–82.

FEDERALISM AND THE MEXICAN SUPREME COURT OF JUSTICE

Throughout most of its history Mexico has had a constitution which rejected the unitary in favor of the federal system of government. Hence the polity's official name is the United States of Mexico.[33] The framers of independent Mexico's first constitutions in 1824 and 1857 admired the liberalism they associated with the United States and understandably embraced within the founding document a number of constitutional institutions they assumed to be the basis for economic and political freedom: a written constitution, representation, limited terms of office, bicameralism, separation of powers, judicial review, judicial independence, and federalism.

Neither the constitution nor the states as originally configured, however, survived the political and military turmoil that afflicted Mexico, with the consequence that it had a formally centralized political system during the periods 1836–47 and 1853–56. The abolition of federalism in 1836 precipitated a rebellion in Texas which had momentous consequences for Mexico's territorial integrity. The states even lost their representation in Congress with the abolition of the Senate by Benito Juarez, and the upper house was not reestablished until 1871.[34]

The Mexican commitment to federalism, however, survived these intermissions and is a conspicuous feature of the 1917 basic law, still in force, though much amended. Article 40 declares, "it is the will of the Mexican people to make themselves into a federal, democratic, representative Republic composed of free and sovereign States in all that concerns their internal affairs." Each state may levy taxes and legislate, and all powers not delegated by the Constitution to the federal government are reserved for the states. Hostility to centralized control is also evident in Art. 115 which enshrines the principle of the *municipio libre*, a concept of local self-government evocative of the New England town meeting.

Mexico has had much difficulty, however, in achieving a stable balance of federal and state power. Its history has been marked by wild fluctuations between assertion by the states of their sovereignty, resulting in civil war, and highly centralized government. There is, in fact, much cynicism regarding the sincerity of the federal government's commitment to a division of powers between the two levels of government. Mexico is often characterized as having a presidential system of government, with the federal executive exerting control over the election of federal deputies

---

33 Mexican Constitution, Art. 1.

34 Miguel Acosta Romero, "Mexican Federalism: Conception and Reality," *Public Administration Review* 42 (Sept.–Oct. 1982), 400.

and senators, state governors, state legislators—even occasionally mayors—and over the operation of state government. "What really exists in Mexico," says Supreme Court Justice Jorge Carpizo, "is a central government."[35] The main instruments at the president's disposal are, first, his position as leader of the ruling political party, the Party of Institutional Revolution (PRI), which has won the federal presidency and, with one recent exception, the governorship of every state since its founding in 1929. Second, the president, through his influence over the Senate as head of the majority party, can dismiss a recalcitrant state's governor.[36] Mexico's political instability and poverty have been so severe as to seem to justify centralized executive government, the constitution's commitment to federalism notwithstanding.

Unlike the Congress and state governments, the courts largely have maintained their independence and have made a small contribution to the evolution of federalism in Mexico. Under the constitution, the Supreme Court has the power of judicial review, including the right to protect the states from the encroachment of the federal government and vice versa. Given the Roman law foundation of Mexican law, it is not surprising that the Court's exercise of this power is more narrowly confined than in the United States or Canada. The courts can address the constitutionality of federal legislation interfering with the reserved powers of the states through the process of *juicio de amparo*, analogous to a combination of the English judiciary's injunction and writ of certiorari.[37] If the court finds that a state's legal rights have been adversely affected by a federal action then it can suspend the operation of that law or executive ruling as to that state but cannot declare the law generally null and void. However, five consecutive rulings to this effect constitute *jurisprudencia*, or binding precedent on the lower courts. The Supreme Court consists of twenty-six magistrates who are appointed for life by the president with the approval of the Senate. In 1934 the constitution was amended to provide for six-year terms for the judges, who were perceived as too independent of the president, but life tenure was restored in 1944. However, it is the custom for them to submit their resignations to each new president at the commencement of his six-year term.[38]

---

35 *Federalismo en Latinoamerica*, 1st ed. (Mexico City: Instituto de Investigaciones Juridicas, 1973), 78.

36 Article 76, s. 5 empowers the Senate to make a finding that "the constitutional powers of a State have disappeared" and to appoint a provisional governor from a list of three names proposed by the President. This power has been exercised several times in Mexican history.

37 Literally, *amparo* means protection, assistance, or refuge.

38 Craig H. Robinson, "Government and Politics," in James D. Rudolph, ed., *Mexico: A Country Study* (Washington, D.C.: GPO, 1985), 256.

The PRI monopoly on federal and state political offices has meant that "state governments have maintained a passive attitude . . . obedient to all types of decisions flowing from the central government."[39] Moreover, the federal ministries keep delegates in each of the state capitals to coordinate state-federal action.[40] When intergovernmental conflicts nevertheless do arise and reach the courts, the Supreme Court, staffed with members of the PRI appointed by the PRI president and confirmed by the PRI Senate, tends to rule in favor of federal power and the president's preferences. Although "between 1917 and 1980 one-third of some 5,500 writs of *amparo* involving the president and his secretaries as defendants were decided in favor of the plaintiff, the judiciary seldom attempted to thwart the will of the president on major issues."[41] The courts tend to treat such questions as "political" and therefore non-justiciable. For example, a district court rejected an *amparo* suit brought by former owners of a bank nationalized by President José Portillo even though the constitutional amendment giving the president that power postdated the action.[42] In fact, the Supreme Court has never invalidated any major policy of an incumbent president. In the words of a judicial reformer in Mexico City, "the Supreme Court does not interfere with matters that are of interest to the President."[43]

Nevertheless, the potential of the Supreme Court to play a much more active role in the future in adjudicating state-federal conflicts is quite high. In 1989, for the first time, the PRI lost a gubernatorial election, in the state of Baja California Norte. Party competition generates many of the cases involving the constitutional distribution of powers in Canada and the United States, where at least some of the provinces and states are always governed by a rival of the party controlling the federal government. In the 1988 elections, the leader of the PRI, Carlos Salinas, garnered only slightly more than fifty percent of the popular vote, the lowest in the party's history of contesting the six-year presidency, and opposition parties wrested 240 of the total 500 congressional seats away from the PRI. In the 1991 mid-term elections, the PRI won sixty-one percent of the congressional seats, in what was seen by many as fraud-marred balloting. In fact, two of the successful PRI candidates for state governorships stepped aside shortly after the election because of opposition charges of electoral fraud, and one of the two acting governors who replaced them

39 Romero, "Mexican Federalism," 404.

40 Martin C. Needler, *Mexican Politics: The Containment of Conflict* (New York: Praeger, 1982), 94.

41 Robinson, "Government and Politics," 256.

42 Ibid.

43 Carmen Carmona, Instituto de Investigaciones Juridicas, UNAM, Mexico, D. F. (interview with the author, 3 May 1991).

is from an opposition party.[44] Moreover, two of the sixty-four senate seats are now held by members of opposition parties.

The unprecedented policies of President Salinas stand to benefit both federalism and the judiciary. In a sharp break from his predecessors, he is seeking closer relations with the United States, which he hopes will culminate in a North American Free Trade Agreement that will form a single trading bloc from the Yukon to the Yucatan. He is liberalizing not only trade but the domestic economy and, more cautiously, politics. He has knocked down some of the major pillars of the 1910–20 Revolution by seeking economic integration with the United States, permitting peasants to sell or rent their *ejidos*, or communal farms, and normalizing relations with the Roman Catholic Church. The tax base of the states is benefiting from the *maquiladora* program, which has attracted scores of foreign manufacturers to the northern border states and from the policy of the Salinas administration of decentralizing new manufacturing plants to areas outside Mexico City, a policy whose urgency was made clear by the disastrous 1985 earthquake that struck the capital city.[45] One of the principal impediments to the vitality of the states has been their dependence on the federal government for revenue.[46] Mr. Salinas, in defiance of the teachers' union, one of the three most powerful constituents of the PRI, has taken steps to decentralize the educational system by transferring both responsibility for schools and the resources to administer them to the states.[47] The close association in the Mexican mind among liberalism, democratic participation, and federalism could result in additional devolution of functions and powers to the states. The center's grip on political power is also weakened by Mr. Salinas's attempt to shrink the role of government in general in pursuit of free market policies.[48] Thus, according to Miguel Romero, "as we enter the post-industrial age of advanced technoscientific complexity, Mexico cannot

---

44 Matt Moffett, "Governor-Elect in Mexico, the Winner in Fraud-Ridden Balloting, Drops Out," *Wall Street Journal*, 30 August 1991, A4; Tim Golden, "Mexican President Outlines Program for Changes," *New York Times*, 2 November 1991, 7.

45 Arthur Morris, "Decentralisation in Mexico," *Area* 22 (1990), 88–89.

46 "The fundamental essence of federalism can be questioned severely since the role of the states and municipalities, in levying, collecting, and managing their own revenue sources, has been seriously curtailed." Romero, "Mexican Federalism," 401. That states can exercise substantial power in policy areas, although in a position of fiscal subordination to the federal government, however, is well illustrated by the Australian example. See B. Galligan, O. Hughes, and C. Walsh, eds., *Intergovernmental Relations and Public Policy* (Sydney: Allen and Unwin, 1990).

47 Tim Golden, "Mexican President Outlines Program for Changes," *New York Times*, 2 November 1991, 7.

48 "Mexico: Salinas Shares Dream of 'New Nationalism' With Fellow Mexicans," *London Financial Times*, 4 November 1991, 2.

take its stand with the other developed nations of the world unless the notion of federalism . . . is a viable reality."[49]

Although the police, the civil service, and state courts are often associated with corruption in Mexico,[50] the higher federal courts are held in relatively high esteem. President Salinas reinforced the legitimacy of the Supreme Court as a bulwark of constitutional freedoms by appointing Justice Carpizo to chair a National Human Rights Commission charged with investigating rights abuses by the Mexican police reported by the international human rights monitoring organization America Watch. The Court must have a high degree of authority in order to umpire the constitutional division of powers, and every decision it renders in favor of the rights of individuals or the states enhances that authority. Such an active use of its power of judicial review is actually in the interest of the governing party, presently suffering a sharp decline in public confidence, since a publicly respected judiciary can give legitimacy to legislation challenged as unconstitutional.[51] Given the pace of political reform and the high degree of public confidence in the Mexican Supreme Court, the conditions are ripe for an increase in judicial activism, in the areas both of individual liberties and states' rights.

Skeptics, however, point to the long-term trend in Mexican politics, which undeniably has been in the direction of greater centralization. They also question the sincerity of President Salinas's commitment to the federal principle. If he respected the constitutional powers of the states, why, they ask, did he force the governors-elect of Guanajuato and San Luis Potosi to give up their posts even though they had been declared the victors by the appropriate state institutions?[52] On the other hand, one must recognize that the increasing integration of Mexico into the international economy, and especially the economy of the United States, which President Salinas is probably powerless to stop and which will proceed even if the NAFTA is not approved by the legislatures of each country, is exerting centrifugal influences on both Mexican business and politics. Thus in February 1991 the governors of the four U. S. and six Mexican border states met in Hermosillo to discuss ways they could cooperate to promote economic growth.[53] The devolution of education to the states

49 Romero, "Mexican Federalism," 402.

50 Guillermo Floris Margadant, *An Introduction to the History of Mexican Law* (Dobbs Ferry, N.Y.: Oceana Publ., 1983), 361.

51 James L. Schlagheck, *The Political, Economic, and Labor Climate in Mexico* (Philadelphia: University of Pennsylvania Press, 1977), 12.

52 David Clark Scott, "Mexico: Government Has Made Gains in Economic Reforms, But Falls Short on Political Openness," *Christian Science Monitor*, 3 September 1991, 3.

53 "Mexico: U. S., Mexican Border States' Governors To Talk Trade," *Reuters News Service*, 21 February 1991.

is proof of the president's sincerity, and his interference into the disputed gubernatorial elections can be regarded as part of a campaign to loosen the Mexico City-based PRI's traditional stranglehold on the states.

JUDICIAL FEDERALISM AND THE CRISIS OF LEGITIMACY

The articulation of the proper balance between central and local power in a federal regime is a daunting task. Federalism itself seems to have no fixed or static design governed by unalterable rules but presents itself as a process, a constantly evolving pattern of changing relationships.[54] Rationales for dividing power between levels of government are constantly changing. The various justifications for avoiding centralization of power have included the prevention of tyranny, administrative convenience, stimulation of economic growth, increased opportunities for civic participation, and preservation of community. The peculiar nature of judicial as opposed to legislative and executive power renders the courts a particularly rich source of alternative visions of federalism, for judges, unlike legislators, administrators, or founders, must justify their decisions by means of reason and argument. The comparative analysis of judicial efforts to umpire regional/central conflict in the United States, Canada, and Mexico can make an important contribution to our understanding of the nature and possibilities of the federal arrangement.

The Supreme Courts of the United States and Canada have played decisive roles in articulating the balance between national and regional power. Although it has been an important bulwark of individual liberty and the rule of law, the Supreme Court of Mexico has not been able to protect the reserved powers of the states against the centripetal forces that have dominated that country's politics since the end of the civil war in the 1920s. In part, this relative weakness is due to the Roman law's hostility to the power of judicial review. Mexican civil and criminal procedure in recent years, however, have reflected increasing influence of common law features, and the rule of *jurisprudencia* lends itself to transformation into a power analogous to judicial review. The current process of economic and political liberalization provides an unprecedented opportunity for the Supreme Court to play a leading role in the revival of a peaceful and constructive federalism.

The ultimate courts of neither the United States nor Mexico face the nation-maintaining challenge confronting the Supreme Court of Canada. When Quebec seemed in danger of loosening its ties to the federation, the Court tended to rule in its favor in its many contests with Ottawa. When public opinion in Quebec seemed sharply divided the Court forged ahead

---

54 Kenneth Wiltshire, *Planning and Federalism: Australian and Canadian Experience* (Australia: University of Queensland Press, 1986), 87.

with its effort to preserve the centralized federation implied by the *Constitution Act, 1867*. Its present attempt to enforce national standards under the *Charter of Rights and Freedoms* is reminiscent of the unitary vision of the Fathers of Confederation. The Court's dilemma is that if Quebec opinion rallies behind a coherent redefinition of Quebec's place in confederation any effort on the part of the Court to placate Quebec may contribute to the alienation of Alberta and the Maritimes.

The supreme courts in each North American nation enjoy, nevertheless, an advantage over their policy-making competitors—the courts have not suffered as much as other political actors from the crisis of legitimacy afflicting public institutions since the 1960s.[55] The one note of caution here is that the failure of the Meech Lake Accord in 1990 and the Charlottetown agreement in 1992, with their proposed reform of the judicial selection process, threatens to deprive the Supreme Court of Canada of much of its remaining authority within Quebec because its justices are still appointed by the federal prime minister, with no formal opportunity for participation by the provinces. On 24 September 1991, Prime Minister Brian Mulroney tabled a document entitled *Shaping Canada's Future Together* which puts forward twenty-eight proposals for constitutional reform. It became the basis for the constitutional proposals of August 1992, also known as the Charlottetown Accord, which were decisively rejected in an October 1992 referendum held simultaneously in each province. Proposal twelve would have provided a role for the provinces in appointments to the Supreme Court, guaranteeing a veto for Quebec over appointments to its three seats on the Court. The existing Canadian mode of federal judicial appointment stands in sharp contrast to that of Mexico and the United States, whose constitutions require confirmation of presidential nominees by a senate, where each state is equally represented. Either reform of the judicial appointing process or reform of the Canadian upper house along the lines of the U. S. and Mexican senates may be necessary to protect the Canadian Supreme Court's legitimacy vis-à-vis the provinces.[56]

CONCLUSION

The supreme courts of the United States, Canada, and Mexico have each adopted conceptions of federalism that pose no major obstacles to greater economic and political integration within North America. On the continu-

---

55 Kenneth M. Holland, "Introduction," in Holland, ed., *Judicial Activism in Comparative Perspective*, 10.

56 Jacques-Yvan Morin, "Vers un nouvel équilibre constitutionel au Canada," in P.-A. Crepeau and C. B. Macpherson, eds., *The Future of Canadian Federalism* (Toronto: 1965), 153.

um of degree of state/provincial sovereignty, each court falls on the minimal end. The delegated or reserved powers of the special governments no longer serve, within judicial constitutional interpretation, as effective restraints on the powers of the general governments. In the United States and Canada, the highest courts have not always taken such a restricted view of regional power. Only in the 1980s did the minimalist conception clearly come to prevail. The defeat of the Quebec referendum on "sovereignty-association" in 1980, followed by entrenchment of the *Canadian Charter of Rights and Freedoms* in 1982, seem to have been decisive in motivating the Canadian Supreme Court to pursue a nation-building agenda. The unworkability of the distinction made in *National League of Cities* (1976) between the "essential" and "non-essential" functions of the states in a federal system, accompanied by a sense of the anachronistic quality of the dual federalism doctrine, led the Supreme Court of the United States to adopt the broadest possible view of the scope of federal legislative powers in 1985. Subsequent conservative disenchantment with the redistributive and libertarian policies of many municipal and state governments mean that the current conservative nature of the Supreme Court's membership does not herald a return to a states' rights jurisprudence. The revival of federalism in Mexico expected to result from the liberalization policy of President Salinas will occur in the context of and be shaped by integration with the United States and Canada, widely regarded as the means by which Mexico will become the first nation in the western hemisphere to rise from the Third to the First World.[57]

---

57 See interview with Octavio Paz, winner of the Nobel Prize for Literature, in *Manchester Guardian*, 14 June 1991, 26.

III

The Politics of Rights

The Politics of Rights:
What Canadians Should Know
About the American Bill of Rights

F. L. Morton

> The debate about the Canadian Charter of Rights has not been very
> satisfactory. First . . . we have heard almost nothing of the old debates
> about natural law and natural rights. . . . Second, we have not looked
> very hard at the experience of other nations. It may be that . . . we will
> rely too heavily on the American example and [that it] will be somewhat
> misleading.[1]

Canadian legal commentators have portrayed the *Canadian Charter of
Rights and Freedoms* as a progressive force for justice, and the courts as an
appropriate instrument for mandating political and social reforms. This
sanguine portrayal of the *Charter*, what I shall call the "*Charter* myth,"
rests on a number of inaccurate and misleading arguments about constitutionalism and judicial review. Much of this misunderstanding stems from
an incomplete and distorted representation of the American Bill of Rights
experience. Canadian *Charter* experts have tended to systematically filter
out the problems and controversies associated with the American civil
liberties experience. The "*Charter* myth" has been built upon a sanitized
version of the American Bill of Rights. This paper attempts to chasten the
"*Charter* myth" by presenting the previously neglected darker side of the
American constitutional experience.

1. JUDICIAL REVIEW: FROM CONSERVATIVE TO PROGRESSIVE

Charter enthusiasts in Canada have portrayed the American Supreme
Court as a champion of the weak and oppressed, and a powerful agent of
social reform, and have held it up as a model for Canadian judges to
follow. There is considerable evidence to support this heroic vision of the
American Court. The Court played a leading role in eliminating state-

---

1 Donald Smiley, in William R. McKercher, ed., *The U.S. Bill of Rights and the Canadian
Charter of Rights and Freedoms* (Ontario Economic Council, 1983), 218.

sponsored racial segregation in the South.[2] The Court expanded the protections afforded criminal suspects (the "*Miranda* warning")[3] and defendants (the exclusionary rule, the right to free counsel),[4] and temporarily curtailed the use of capital punishment.[5] In 1973 the Court created a nationwide policy of abortion on demand in the name of the "right to privacy."[6] There seems to be almost no area of the progressive agenda where the Supreme Court has not played some role: the expansion of freedom of political speech and association;[7] restrictions on the censorship of pornography;[8] the elimination of government policies that discriminate on the basis of sex;[9] the expansion of freedom of religion;[10] decisions reinforcing the "wall" between church and state;[11] new rights for students,[12] welfare recipients,[13] prisoners,[14] and mental patients.[15] The list goes on and on.

---

2 See *Brown* v. *Board of Education*, 347 U.S. 483 (1954). More generally, see Richard Kluger, *Simple Justice* (New York: Knopf, 1976); and F.L. Morton, "Racial Injustice: The Roots of Result-Oriented Jurisprudence in the U.S. Supreme Court." Paper presented at the Annual Meeting of the American Political Science Association, New Orleans, Louisiana, 28 August–1 September 1985.

3 See *Miranda* v. *Arizona*, 384 U.S. 436 (1966).

4 See *Mapp* v. *Ohio*, 367 U.S. 238 (1961), and *Gideon* v. *Wainwright*, 372 U.S. 335 (1963).

5 See *Furman* v. *Georgia*, 408 U.S. 238 (1972). More generally, see Michael Meltsner, *Cruel and Unusual Punishment: The Supreme Court and Capital Punishment* (New York: Random House, 1973).

6 See *Roe* v. *Wade*, 410 U.S. 113 (1973).

7 For freedom of speech, see *Tinker* v. *Desmoines School District*, 393 U.S. 503 (1969); *New York Times Co.* v. *United States*, 403 U.S. 713 (1971); *Gooding* v. *Wilson*, 405 U.S. 518 (1972). For freedom of association, see *Yates* v. *U.S.*, 354 U.S. 298 (1957); and *Brandenburg* v. *Ohio*, 395 U.S. 444 (1969).

8 See *Roth* v. *U.S.*, 354 U.S. 476 (1957); *Memoirs* v. *Massachusetts*, 383 U.S. 413 (1966); and *Stanley* v. *Georgia*, 394 U.S. 557 (1969).

9 See *Frontiero* v. *Richardson*, 411 U.S. 677 (1973); *Craig* v. *Boren*, 429 U.S. 190 (1976). More generally, see F.L. Morton, "The Supreme Court's Promotion of Sexual Equality: A Case Study of Institutional Capacity," *Polity* 16:3 (Spring 1984), 467.

10 *Sherbert* v. *Verner*, 374 U.S. 398 (1963); *Wisconsin* v. *Yoder*, 406 U.S. 205 (1972).

11 *Everson* v. *Board of Education*, 330 U.S. 1 (1947); *Abington School District* v. *Schempp*, 374 U.S. 204 (1963); *Walz* v. *Tax Commission*, 397 U.S. 664 (1970).

12 *Tinker* v. *DesMoines*, 393 U.S. 503 (1969); *Goss* v. *Lopez*, 419 U.S. 565 (1975); *Wood* v. *Strickland*, 420 U.S. 308 (1975). More generally, see Richard E. Morgan, *Disabling America: The "Rights Industry" in Our Time* (New York: Basic Books, 1984), c. 3.

13 *Shapiro* v. *Thompson*, 394 U.S. 618 (1969).

14 *Hutto* v. *Finney*, 437 U.S. 678 (1978). More generally, see H. Frank Way, *Criminal Justice and the American Constitution* (North Scituate, Mass.: Duxbury Press, 1980), c. 13, "The Legal Rights of Prisoners."

15 See *Wyatt* v. *Stickney*, 325 F. Supp. 781 (1971); 344 F. Supp. 373 (1972).

The inaccuracy of the "heroic model" is not that the American Supreme Court has not served as an agency of social reform, but that this role is a very recent, indeed, a postwar phenomenon. Its proponents characterize it as the norm, while it may be more accurately understood as an exception. Prior to the 1950s, the Supreme Court had almost no role in defining the meaning and scope of civil liberties.[16] During the nineteenth century only nine federal laws were voided for violating the Bill of Rights. As recently as 1925, this figure was still only fifteen.[17] As for the fifty states, the original Bill of Rights did not even apply to the states.[18] Moreover, the Supreme Court has no jurisdiction over state law unless a "federal issue" is involved, i.e., an alleged conflict with a federal law, treaty, or the Federal Constitution. Together, these two factors effectively precluded any Supreme Court review of state laws and policies on civil rights and civil liberties grounds until the 1920s. Only then, through the process known as "incorporation," did the Supreme Court begin to enforce the provisions of the Bill of Rights against state laws and actions.[19] It was not until after the Supreme Court's 1954 School Desegregation Decision that any significant number of state laws were declared unconstitutional on civil liberties grounds. Today, however, almost all of the Supreme Court's constitutional workload consists of hearing allegations that state laws or practices violate Bill of Rights provisions. Prior to the 1950s, this would have been legally impossible and politically unthinkable. The "heroic model" of the Supreme Court as champion of civil liberties is thus of very recent vintage.

There is a second, more fundamental reason for the Supreme Court's traditional reluctance to play the role of political reformer. The original purpose of the Constitution and judicial review was to protect traditional rights and freedoms, not to create new ones. The American Constitution was based on a scepticism verging on pessimism about the wisdom of future generations. A reading of the *Federalist Papers* demonstrates that the "new science of politics"[20] with its array of "auxiliary precautions"[21] was motivated by a fear of simple majoritarianism ("pure democracy"),

---

16 Walter Berns, in McKercher, *Charter of Rights*, 94 at 95.

17 Ibid.

18 See *Barron* v. *Baltimore*, 7 Peters 243 (1833).

19 See *Moore* v. *Dempsey*, 261 U.S. 86 (1923); *Gitlow* v. *New York*, 268 U.S. 652 (1925); *Powell* v. *Alabama*, 287 U.S. 45 (1932).

20 *The Federalist*, No. 9.

21 *The Federalist*, Nos. 1, 9, 10, 15, 48, 51, and 78. The "auxiliary precautions" include a written constitution, separation of powers, checks and balances, federalism, an independent judiciary, judicial review, representative (rather than direct) democracy, the extended commercial republic encompassing a "multiplicity of sects and interests," and a written Bill of Rights.

especially future majorities. The American Founders were acutely aware of the tendency of democracies to degenerate into ochlocracies—mob-rule—that trampled upon the rights and freedoms of minorities. This was their understanding of classical political theory.[22] It was also their own experience under the Articles of Confederation.[23]

To guard against the threat of unjust political majorities in the future, the Founders used a written constitution to erect explicit barriers against the unjust use of legislative powers by both state[24] and national governments. While the text of the Constitution was silent on the practical issue of interpreting and enforcing constitutional limitations, Alexander Hamilton, in *The Federalist*, No. 78, ascribed this function to the Supreme Court. Some opponents of the new Constitution, the Anti-Federalists, also anticipated judicial review, and criticized it as a threat to the sovereignty of the states.[25] In 1803, Chief Justice John Marshall successfully claimed the power of judicial review for the Supreme Court in the celebrated case of *Marbury* v. *Madison*.[26] Hamilton, Marshall, and other Federalists characterized judicial review as a check on the inevitable excesses of democracy, and thus as a potential obstacle to political change. Most major legislative "reforms" were likely to be challenged by their political opponents, and would then have to pass the Court's constitutional litmus test. If anything, judicial review thus had a theoretical bias against democratic reform.

The Supreme Court's original role was thus conservative in the technical and politically neutral sense of "conserving" traditionally recognized rights and freedoms. It was intended to serve as a "brake" on the occasionally erratic and impulsive outputs of the new American democracy.[27] Over time, however, technological, economic, and political changes stripped the Supreme Court of its original political neutrality. The Court and judicial review came to be viewed as partisan bastions for the defense

---

22 *The Federalist*, Nos. 9 and 10.

23 Shay's Rebellion in Massachusetts being the leading example. See *The Federalist*, Nos. 6, 25, and 75.

24 Article 1, s. 10 enumerates specific limitations on state governments designed to protect individual rights. The most important was the clause prohibiting states from passing any "law impairing the obligation of contracts."

25 Consider the comments of Robert Yates: "The judicial power will operate to effect, in the most certain, but yet silent and imperceptible manner, what is evidently the tendency of the constitution:—I mean, an entire subversion of the legislative, executive, and judicial powers of the individual states." In Cecilia M. Kenyon, ed., *The Anti-Federalists* (Indianapolis: Bobbs-Merrill, 1966), 339.

26 1 Cranch 137 (1803).

27 See *The Federalist*, No. 78; and Christopher Wolfe, *The Rise of Modern Judicial Review: From Constitutional Interpretation to Judge-Made Law* (New York: Basic Books, 1986), cc. 1–3.

of corporate capitalism against the regulatory reforms advocated by the first American progressive movement.

In retrospect, the politicization of the Supreme Court and its siding with the forces of unregulated free enterprise was probably inevitable. American constitutionalism reflected the classic liberal mistrust of government and politics, and the celebration of society and economy. The latter is considered the private sphere, the realm of freedom and choice. The former is the public sector, the realm of coercion. The primary purpose of eighteenth-century constitutionalism was to enhance the one by limiting the other.[28]

This rather simplistic formula for just government was widely accepted in early nineteenth-century American society. It "fit," more or less, the relatively simple socioeconomic realities of a rural, agrarian, individualistic, frontier society. Against the European experience with absolute monarchs and state religions, it was reasonable to see the state as the principal threat to individual freedom. Locke's liberalism fit Jefferson's America.

Suffice it to say that as America increasingly became an urban, industrialized state, the "less government—more freedom" equation became increasingly inadequate. New and unprecedented concentrations of private economic power threatened the public interest. The American progressive movement was born, and successfully demanded government intervention to protect the public against the harmful consequences of the abuse of private power and the uncertainties of the market. Anti-combines and price-fixing legislation,[29] the right of employees to bargain collectively and to strike,[30] the regulation of child labor,[31] "sweat shops" and other unhealthy labor practices, minimum wage[32] and maximum hour laws,[33] preventing environmental pollution, zoning and safe housing regulations for the crowded new cities, social security and unemployment insurance for the workforce—all of these reforms required unprecedented government intervention in the "private" sector.[34] When business interests failed to stop such reforms in the political arena, they frequently turned to the courts. The anti-reform partisans argued that these novel extensions of

---

28 See Stuart A. Scheingold, *The Politics of Rights: Lawyers, Public Policy, and Political Change* (New Haven: Yale University Press, 1974), 25.

29 See *U.S.* v. *E.C. Knight*, 156 U.S. 1 (1895).

30 *Carter* v. *Carter Coal Co.*, 298 U.S. 238 (1936).

31 See *Hammer* v. *Dagenhart*, 247 U.S. 251 (1918); *Bailey* v. *Drexel Furniture*, 259 U.S. 20 (1922).

32 *Adkins* v. *Children's Hospital*, 261 U.S. 525 (1923); *Morehead* v. *Tipaldo*, 298 U.S. 587 (1937).

33 *Lochner* v. *New York*, 198 U.S. 45 (1905).

34 See Robert G. McCloskey, *The American Supreme Court* (Chicago: University of Chicago Press, 1960), cc. 5 and 6.

government regulation violated individual freedom, the sanctity of private property, and the Constitution. The Supreme Court was a receptive audience. Between 1899 and 1937, the Court invalidated 184 state laws on these grounds.[35]

Until the Court Crisis of 1937, the new American corporate interests successfully used the Supreme Court and the Constitution to stop, stall, or generally frustrate many of the legislative reforms listed above. While it has been politically and intellectually fashionable to blame the Court's anti-progressive decisions on the individual justices, the truth is that much of the problem lay with the American Constitution itself. The Constitution's foundation in the negative or "night-watchman" state placed it at odds with the emergent social-welfare, or positive state.

In retrospect the American Supreme Court justices can be criticized for failing to adapt the Constitution to the changing times—that is, for not adopting a "living constitution" approach to constitutional interpretation.[36] But this conveniently ignores the original purpose of judicial review—to keep the changing times in tune with the Constitution, not vice versa. Indeed, when the "living constitution" metaphor is stripped of its pleasant-sounding façade, it is really a demand that judges stay out of the way of Congress by ignoring much of the original meaning of the Constitution in the areas of federalism, regulation of commerce, and taxation. As such, it raises serious questions about the continued existence of judicial review and even a written constitution.

The American Supreme Court's four-decade struggle against the acceptance of the modern welfare state discloses a third error in the "heroic model." It is naive and unjustified to assume that judicial review is always exercised in a just or "progressive" manner. Power is power, regardless of who exercises it. Canadian commentators can be partially excused for this mistaken assumption since it is shared by so many contemporary American jurists.[37] There is a revealing analogy between the literature on the Supreme Court in the 1980s and the "textbook presidency" of the 1950s and 1960s. The latter refers to the tendency in post-war American scholarship to "seriously inflate presidential competence

---

35 Ibid., 151.

36 The "living constitution" doctrine is discussed below (see section 4).

37 Leading American exponents of the "heroic model" of the Supreme Court include Ronald Dworkin, *Taking Rights Seriously* (Cambridge, Mass.: Harvard University Press, 1977); Laurence H. Tribe, *Constitutional Choices* (Cambridge, Mass.: Harvard University Press, 1986); Jesse Choper, *Judicial Review in the National Political Process: A Functional Reconsideration of the Role of the Supreme Court* (Chicago: University of Chicago Press, 1976); Bruce Ackerman, *Private Property and the Constitution* (New Haven: Yale University Press, 1977); and Michael J. Perry, *The Constitution, the Courts, and Human Rights* (New Haven: Yale University Press, 1982). For criticisms of the "heroic judiciary," see Wolfe, *The Rise of Modern Judicial Review*, c. 14; and Richard Morgan, *Disabling America*, c. 7.

and beneficence," and to downplay traditional constitutional restraints on executive power.[38] The subsequent events of Vietnam and Watergate chastened this enthusiasm for unchecked executive power.

Like its executive and legislative counterpart, there is nothing inherently benevolent about the exercise of judicial review. The decisions of a judge may be as wrong and harmful as those of a president or a legislative majority. American history is full of examples. For every *Brown v. Board of Education*,[39] there is a *Dred Scott v. Sanford*,[40] or a *Plessy v. Ferguson*.[41] The Court's numerous anti-regulatory and anti-social welfare decisions confirm this point.[42] It must not be forgotten that the final constitutional acceptance of the Roosevelt New Deal occurred literally over the dead bodies of several obstructionist Supreme Court justices.

To conclude, both the theory and the practice of American constitutionalism prior to 1937 had a bias against reform. This bias was very evident to earlier generations of American reformers. Their dislike for both the Constitution and the Court was articulated by Senator Robert LaFollette, the presidential candidate of the American Progressive Party in 1924. Commenting on the Court's numerous vetoes of reformist social legislation such as progressive income tax, minimum wage, and child labor laws, LaFollette declared, "We cannot live under a system of govern-

---

38 Thomas E. Cronin, *The State of the Presidency*, 2d ed. (Boston: Little, Brown, and Co., 1980), c. 2, "The Textbook and Prime Time Presidency." A similar critique is developed by William G. Andrews, "The Presidency, Congress, and Constitutional Theory," in Aaron Wildavsky, ed., *Perspectives on the Presidency* (Boston: Little, Brown, and Co., 1975), 24–44.

39 347 U.S. 483 (1954). *Brown* v. *Board of Education* was the Supreme Court decision that declared racially segregated public schools a violation of the Equal Protection clause of the Fourteenth Amendment. It overruled the "separate but equal" doctrine established in *Plessy* v. *Ferguson* (see below, note 41). The case is widely recognized as a catalyst for the subsequent black civil rights movement in U.S. politics and as the archetype for judicially-led social reform. *Brown* v. *Board* is considered to be one of the Supreme Court's greatest decisions.

40 *Dred Scott* v. *Sanford*, 19 Howard 393 (1857). Chief Justice Taney ruled that slaves were no different from hogs or cattle, and thus Congress could not forbid their owners from taking them into the western territories. He went on to observe that Negroes were not and could not be citizens of the United States. *Dred Scott* is considered to be one of the worst decisions ever made by the Supreme Court.

41 *Plessy* v. *Ferguson*, 163 U.S. 537 (1896). The Court ruled that Louisiana's "separate but equal" train facilities for whites and blacks did not violate the equal protection clause of the Fourteenth Amendment. This decision conferred constitutional legitimacy on state-mandated segregation of the races, and ushered in the "Jim Crow" era in the American South. Like *Dred Scott*, *Plessy* v. *Ferguson* has been judged a legal and political disaster.

42 See above, notes 29–33.

ment, where we have to amend the Constitution every time we want to pass a progressive law."

The contemporary notion—that a constitutional bill of rights can serve as a vehicle for political reform—rests on a radical redefining of constitutionalism and judicial review. It also belies a change in the character of American progressivism.

2. THE POLITICS OF RIGHTS

The most enduring criticism of a *Charter*/Bill of Rights is that it is undemocratic, because it allows unelected and unaccountable judges to overrule the decisions of democratically elected legislators. Defenders of the *Charter* frequently respond by drawing a sharp distinction between law and politics, between questions of rights and questions of policy. Questions of policy are characterized as resulting from the conflict of economic interests. They are assigned to the electoral and legislative processes, where they are resolved through compromise and coalition-building.

By contrast, questions of right are portrayed as "above" politics. They are grounded in justice, not self-interest. They raise questions of right and wrong, not more or less, and thus should not be subject to bargaining and compromise. The beauty of a *Charter*/Bill of Rights is that it identifies these rights, and in so doing lifts them out of the political arena, the realm of interest, and into the courts, the realm of reason. Here, judges, exercising judgment, not will, can protect rights and liberties from the excesses of democratic politics.

There is no doubt about the enduring appeal of this argument. It was first made by Alexander Hamilton in the *Federalist Papers* two hundred years ago when he declared that "[Courts] may truly be said to have neither force nor will, but merely judgment."[43] It remains a proper starting point for a discussion of judicial review. However, two hundred years of experience cannot be ignored. That experience, plus a more realistic appraisal of what judges actually do, demonstrate that the Hamiltonian vision is as much myth as reality.

One might have thought that Canadians would have been more sceptical of the facile distinction between rights and policy, courts and legislatures. After all, Canada managed to survive its first hundred years without a constitutional *Charter*/Bill of Rights, and with a human rights-

---

43 *The Federalist*, No. 78.

civil liberties record that is arguably better than that of the United States.[44] The same could be said with even greater force for Great Britain, which still depends on its unwritten constitution (i.e., Parliament, not judges) as the best means of preserving its unparalleled heritage of civil rights and liberties. The American experience with racial segregation also demonstrates the converse: just as a society can protect its civil liberties without a *Charter*/Bill of Rights, so the existence of constitutional rights cannot "guarantee" that they will be respected in the face of sustained, hostile public opinion. Despite the post-Civil War adoption of the Fourteenth Amendment and the right to "equal protection of the laws," black Americans did not receive anything resembling "equal protection" for almost another century.

This was partly Peter Russell's message at the time the *Charter* was adopted. The most important effect of the *Charter*, he wrote, was not that it "guarantees" rights, but that it creates a new way of making decisions about rights in which the courts play a much more influential role.[45] The increased political influence of the courts, Russell predicted, would in turn have two important consequences: the judicialization of politics and the politicization of the judiciary.[46] We shall examine each of these concepts in turn.

The judicialization of politics describes first and foremost a simple increase in judicial influence over public policy. As, for example, the spate of Sunday closing litigation suggests, Canadian legislators must now tailor legislation to the constitutional standards defined by the Supreme Court.[47] But the judicialization of politics also denotes actual changes in the policy-making process itself. The creation of a new locus of power in the political system—the courts—attracts the attention of interest groups, who are always looking for ways to influence public policy.

---

44 While the Canadian record has its blemishes—especially against French Catholics and the Chinese minorities—these pale by comparison to the systematic mistreatment of blacks in the United States until the 1960s. Canada has also been more tolerant of political dissent—especially on the Left—than the U.S.

45 Peter H. Russell, "The Effect of the Charter of Rights on the Policy-Making Role of Canadian Courts," *Canadian Public Administration* 25 (1982), 1.

46 Peter H. Russell, "The Political Purposes of the Canadian Charter of Rights and Freedoms," *Canadian Bar Review* 61 (March 1983), 30 at 51.

47 These include the *Big M Drug Mart Case*, 18 D.L.R. (4th) 321, in which the federal *Lord's Day Act* was ruled unconstitutional; and *Edwards Book and Art Ltd.* v. *The Queen*, [1986] 2 S.C.R. 713, which upheld a "secular" Sunday closing law. Even after it was upheld in *Edwards Book*, the Ontario Sunday closing policy continued to be disobeyed by some Toronto merchants, who mounted a new challenge to its legality on s. 15 equality grounds. Apparently worn down by this ongoing campaign of noncompliance and *Charter* challenges, in 1988 Ontario Premier David Peterson proposed amendments to the Act that would allow Sunday opening for merchants. These proposals have met with considerable public opposition, and the outcome is still pending.

In the American context, this phenomenon has been appropriately described as the "politics of rights." The politics of rights "describes the forms of political activity made possible by the presence of [constitutional] rights in American society."[48] It is also intended as an antidote to the "myth of rights"—the traditional tendency to think of constitutional rights as judicially enforceable moral rules. Instead, constitutional rights function as a dynamic combination of political ideals and political resources:[49]

> [Constitutional rights] must be thought of, on the one hand, as authoritatively articulated goals of public policy and, on the other, as political resources of unknown value in the hands of those who want to alter the course of public policy.

Individuals and interest groups can try to exploit the gap between political reality and political ideal. They can appeal to the vague but powerful ideals enshrined in a *Charter*/Bill of Rights to legitimate their own policy interests. They can recast their policy goals in the rhetoric of rights, and then take them to the courts to be "enforced." Winning in the courts, however, is not necessarily the most important objective in the politics of rights. Litigation is only part of a larger political operation to change public opinion on an issue and mobilize support for it. For these purposes, legal defeats can sometimes be as effective as victories.[50]

In the United States, the most successful example of interest group use of constitutional litigation to change public policy was the NAACP's campaign to strike down segregated schooling in the American South.[51] The NAACP's success inspired a proliferation of "public interest" law foundations and "legal defense funds." During the protest politics of the 1960s, most of these groups were on the left, and there was scarcely a "cause" that lacked a legal arm.[52] Many of these groups literally lived to

---

48 Scheingold, *The Politics of Rights*, 83.

49 Ibid., 6–7.

50 Ibid., c. 9. This is what occurred in Canada in the 1976 *Bliss* case (*Bliss* v. *Attorney General of Canada*, [1979] 1 S.C.R. 183. The Supreme Court of Canada rejected a sex discrimination claim and upheld the exclusion of pregnant women from unemployment insurance benefits. Feminists used this defeat in the courts to publicize the issue, stir up public indignation, and mobilize support for pressuring the legislature to change the law. See L.A. Pal and F.L. Morton, "Bliss v. Attorney-General of Canada: From Legal Defeat to Political Victory," *Osgoode Hall Law Journal* 24:1 (Spring 1986), 141.

51 See Richard Kluger, *Simple Justice* (New York: Knopf, 1976). Also Clement Vose, "Litigation as a Form of Pressure Group Activity," *Annals of the American Academy of Political and Social Science* 319 (1958), 20.

52 In addition to the American Civil Liberties Union, which was active in a broad range of cases, prominent "public interest" litigators included the National Organization of Women (NOW), the Women's Equity Action League (WEAL), National Abortion Rights

litigate. By the end of the decade, causes had replaced clients on the Supreme Court's docket. During the 1970s, there was interest group participation as *amicus curiae* in more than half of all non-commercial Supreme Court decisions. If criminal cases are excluded, the participation rate is more than two-thirds.[53] This trend reached its apex in the 1976 Bakke Affirmative Action Case, when fifty-eight *amicus* briefs were filed by more than 100 organizations.[54] When politically conservative interest groups swallowed their scruples and began to adopt the same tactic in the late 1970s, interest group "lobbying" of the Supreme Court became an entrenched practice in the American political process.[55]

Such a "politics of rights" was not possible in Canada prior to the *Charter*.[56] Not only was it not possible, but most attempts in Canadian history to use the judicial process to achieve political purposes have failed. As recently as 1975, one of Canada's leading contemporary historians could write that "political action outside the party-parliamentary structure tends to be suspect—and not least because it smacks of Americanism."[57]

That era—and that attitude—of Canadian history ended with the *Charter*. The *Charter* has stimulated Canadian interest groups to adopt American-style litigation tactics to promote their objectives. Taking a page from their American "sisters," Canadian feminists successfully launched a legal defense fund.[58] Both sides of the abortion issue are pushing their positions through *Charter* litigation.[59] The conservative National Citizens'

League (NARAL), the Mental Health Law Project, the Children's Defense Fund, Committee for Public Education and Religious Liberty, The Ink Fund, to name only some of the most prominent.

53 Karen O'Connor and Lee Epstein, "Amicus Curiae Participation in U.S. Supreme Court Litigation: An Appraisal of Hakman's 'Folklore'," *Law and Society Review* 16 (1981–82), 311.

54 *Regents of the University of California* v. *Bakke*, 438 U.S. 265. Number of *amicus curiae* briefs reported in the *Chronicle of Higher Education*, 19 September 1977, 4.

55 See Fred Baldwin, "Rising Above Principle: The Conservative Public Interest Law Firm," *The American Spectator*, August 1981.

56 A "politics of rights" could have developed under the 1960 Canadian Bill of Rights, but the Supreme Court's self-restrained interpretation of the Bill and its deference to Parliament negated this potential. But see above, note 48 for an exception.

57 Kenneth McNaught, "Political Trials and the Canadian Political Tradition," in Martin M. Friedland, ed., *Courts and Trials: A Multidisciplinary Approach* (Toronto: University of Toronto Press, 1975), 137.

58 See M. Elizabeth Atcheson, Mary Eberts, and Beth Symes, *Women and Legal Action: Precedents, Resources, and Strategies for the Future*, Canadian Advisory Council on the Status of Women, 1985. More recently, see *Litigation Works: A Report on LEAF Litigation, Year Two*, Women's Legal Education and Action Fund (Toronto: Carswell Legal Publ., 1987).

59 See F.L. Morton, "The Meaning of Morgentaler: A Political Analysis," Research Unit for Socio-Legal Studies, University of Calgary, Occasional Papers Series: Research Study 4.2 (1988).

Coalition has successfully challenged the anti-PAC clause of the *Federal Elections Expenditures Act*,[60] and also labor union expenditures on political causes.[61] Organized labor has fought anti-strike laws as a violation of the freedom of association.[62] Surprisingly, the federal government has actually encouraged these developments by setting up a nine million dollar litigation fund to support "test cases" in the area of language and equality rights.[63]

My purpose here is neither to praise nor condemn the development of interest group use of litigation as a political tactic. Rather, it is simply to point out that a Canadian version of the politics of rights has been ushered in by the *Charter*, and that the traditional distinctions between law and politics, rights and policy, courts and legislatures, can no longer be taken at face value. There are still important differences, but the *Charter* has further blurred the boundaries. Discussions of the *Charter* and judicial review to be taken seriously must acknowledge this new reality.

3. REAGANIZING THE AMERICAN JUDICIARY

The counterpart to the judicialization of politics is the politicization of the judiciary. As judges become increasingly overt in their use of interpretive discretion to change public policy, affected parties will become more interested in who is appointed to judgeships. The process of judicial recruitment and selection, while nominally maintaining the forms of judicial independence, becomes the focus of sharp partisan competition and conflict. Political struggle over judicial appointments has reached new extremes in the United States. While this has not yet occurred in Canada, Canadians can benefit from the American experience. It provides further evidence that constitutional law does not develop "above politics" but within politics. It also suggests that there is a political price for using the courts as vehicles for political reform.

In 1987, the bicentennial of the American Constitution, the single most visible manifestation of constitutionalism was the bitter conflict between

---

60 *NCC, Inc. and Brown v. Attorney General of Canada*, [1984] 5 W.W.R. 436. For a detailed study of this case, see Janet Hiebert, "Fair Elections and Freedom of Expression Under the Charter," *Journal of Canadian Studies* 24 (Winter 1989–90):72–86.

61 The "Merv Lavigne Case." See *Globe and Mail* (Toronto), 8 July 1986, A10, "Top Court vetoes using union dues for political aims."

62 See *Public Service Alliance of Canada v. The Queen*, [1987] 1 S.C.R. 424; *Government of Saskatchewan v. Retail, Wholesale and Department Store Union*, [1987] 1 S.C.R. 460; and *Reference re Public Service Employees Relations Act of Alberta*, [1987] 1 S.C.R. 313.

63 For a more detailed discussion of interest groups and the *Charter*, see F.L. Morton, "The Political Impact of the Canadian Charter of Rights and Freedoms," *Canadian Journal of Political Science* 20:1 (March 1987), 31.

liberals and conservatives over President Reagan's recent nominations to the Supreme Court. In June 1986, President Reagan nominated the most conservative member of the Court, William Rehnquist, to replace the retiring Chief Justice, Warren Burger. Senate liberals, led by Senator Edward Kennedy, tried desperately to block the nomination. Despite a record-breaking thirty-three negative votes, Reagan ultimately succeeded in pushing the Rehnquist nomination through the Senate.[64]

Senate liberals were better prepared for Reagan's nomination of Robert Bork in June 1987. Senate Judiciary Committee Chairman Joseph Biden (Democrat-Delaware) took the unprecedented step of delaying his committee's hearings for two months to gain time for liberal interest groups to organize a campaign against the Bork nomination.[65] Assisted by Senate liberals such as Biden, Kennedy, Cranston, and Metzenbaum, liberal interest groups spent the summer campaigning against the Bork nomination. The anti-Bork coalition counted more than forty civil rights, black, feminist, and organized labor groups.[66] In an unprecedented step, they used paid political commercials on national television networks to rally public opinion against the Bork nomination. In September their strategy paid off. The extensive use of media turned the Senate Judiciary Committee hearings into "an emotional public referendum over the direction of the Supreme Court."[67] Public opinion polls overshadowed Bork's performance before the Committee. One by one, key southern Democrats whose support Reagan needed abandoned the Bork nomination. Many cited intense constituency pressure and fears of voter backlash in their next election. As syndicated columnist George Will protested, the Bork hearings had been transformed into a national plebiscite. The Judiciary Committee recommended against his nomination (9–5), but Bork refused to withdraw and forced a recorded Senate vote (58–42).

The Rehnquist and Bork controversies were only two more skirmishes in a political struggle that has been escalating for two decades. In 1968, then Republican presidential candidate Richard Nixon tried to exploit the unpopularity of some Warren Court decisions by promising to appoint Supreme Court judges who were "strict constructionists . . . who saw their duty as interpreting law and not making law." While Nixon eventually

---

64 See F.L. Morton, "Judicial Review and Conservatism in the United States and Canada," in Barry Cooper, Allan Kornberg, and William Mishler, eds., *The Resurgence of Conservatism in the Anglo-American Democracies* (Durham: Duke University Press, 1988), 163.

65 The *Sunday Globe* (Boston), 11 October 1987.

66 These included the American Civil Liberties Union, the National Association for the Advancement of Colored People, the Southern Christian Leadership Conference, the National Association of Women, People for the American Way, and the AFL-CIO.

67 "Losing Battle: How Reagan's Forces Botched the Campaign For Approval of Bork," *Wall Street Journal*, 7 October 1987, 1, 18.

made four new appointments to the Court, they did not reverse the liberal activist legacy of the Warren Court.[68] Indeed, the Burger Court's 1973 abortion decision, *Roe* v. *Wade*,[69] further extended the practice of judicially led social reform, and further alienated conservatives.

The 1980 Republican party platform, as rewritten by the conservative supporters of Ronald Reagan, called for the appointment of federal judges who believed in "the decentralization of the federal government and efforts to return decision-making power to states and local elected officials." In a not-so-covert criticism of *Roe* v. *Wade*, the platform also supported the appointment of judges "who respect the traditional family values and the sanctity of innocent human life."[70]

Once in office, Reagan acted to fulfil these promises. The O'Connor, Rehnquist, and Scalia appointments represent only the proverbial tip of the iceberg. In his first term, Reagan appointed 160 new federal judges. By the end of his second term, Reagan had appointed more than half of the entire federal judiciary, more judges than any previous president. To fill these judgeships, the Reagan Administration centralized the recruitment process in the White House to an unprecedented degree. The result was "the most consistent ideological or policy-orientation screening of judicial candidates since the first term of Franklin Roosevelt."[71] Reagan's strategy seemed to be paying off. Two different studies of the decisions of the Reagan judges found that they were fulfilling their patron's expectations of a more conservative jurisprudence.[72]

Liberals had reason to be upset with these trends, but their charge that Reagan was politicizing the Supreme Court—while true—was hypocritical. Liberals abandoned the "high ground" of a politically neutral Supreme Court three decades ago, and it was too late for them to reclaim it now. Reagan was simply taking a page out of the Democrats' own book. In the past, Republican presidents had viewed the Supreme Court as a law court and stressed judicial experience as a prerequisite for nomination.[73]

---

68 See Vincent Blasi, *The Burger Court: The Counter-Revolution that Wasn't* (New Haven: Yale University Press, 1983).

69 *Roe* v. *Wade*, 410 U.S. 113 (1973).

70 *Congressional Quarterly Weekly Report* (1980), 2046; and *Congressional Quarterly Weekly Report* (1981), 299.

71 Sheldon Goldman, "Reaganizing the Judiciary: The First Term Appointments," in *Judicature* 68:313 (1985), 315.

72 Jon Gottschall, "Reagan's Appointments to the U.S. Court of Appeals: The Continuation of a Judicial Revolution," in *Judicature* 70:1 (1986), 48. Craig Stern, "Judging the Judges: The First Two Years of the Reagan Bench," *Benchmark* 1 (1989):1–118.

73 This explains how it is that three of the four members of the "liberal bloc" on the Reagan Supreme Court were appointed by Republican Presidents: Justice Brennan by Eisenhower; Justice Blackmun by Nixon; and Justice Stevens by Ford.

Democratic Presidents have viewed the Court as a policy Court, and appointed men with political experience and loyalty to the Roosevelt New Deal.[74] Reagan, the ex-Democrat, simply did what the Democrats have done for decades: he stressed ideology and policy considerations—only more systematically.

Nor did this change with the end of the Reagan era in American politics. With the election of George Bush in November 1988, the Republicans maintained control of the White House and thus the power to nominate Supreme Court judges. Democrats, however, maintained control of the Senate (55–45), and thus continued to have the final say over President Bush's nominations. During the campaign, Bush declared that he would appoint "judges who are dedicated to interpreting the law as it exists, rather than legislating from the bench."[75] In his second debate with Dukakis, Bush went out of his way to repeat his support for the Bork nomination. The *Wall Street Journal* linked Bush's support for Bork with his repeated attacks on Dukakis's membership in the American Civil Liberties Union (a leader of the anti-Bork campaign), and suggested that "the presidential election has become the referendum that never was on the Bork nomination."[76] While this was an exaggeration, the Bush election campaign featured such issues as the "pledge of allegiance" and growing crime and abortion rates, all issues that the conservative wing of the Republican Party associated with past Supreme Court decisions.

With the three most liberal members of the Supreme Court—Brennan, Blackman and Marshall—all over eighty, it was inevitable that the judicial appointments issue would soon crop up again. When a mild stroke forced Justice Brennan to retire in 1990, President Bush tried to avoid a Bork-like confrontation with the Democratic Senate by nominating a little-known federal appeals court judge from New Hampshire, David H. Souter. Unlike Bork, Souter had no "paper trail" by which to measure his ideological and jurisprudential positions. At his hearing, he earned the nickname of the "stealth candidate" since so little was known about him. Despite protests from feminist groups, Souter easily won Senate approval.

This was not the case with Clarence Thomas, Bush's next nomination, following the retirement of Thurgood Marshall in 1991. Like Marshall, Thomas was an Afro-American. Unlike Marshall, he was a well-known and outspoken conservative. Thomas had been tapped early on by the Reagan administration, first to an appointment in the Department of Education, and later to head the Equal Employment Opportunity Commission

---

74 C. Herman Pritchett, "High Court Selection," *New York Times*, 12 January 1976. Reprinted in Walter F. Murphy and C. Herman Pritchett, *Courts, Judges and Politics: An Introduction to the Judicial Process*, 3d ed. (New York: Random House, 1979), 153–55.

75 *Judicature* 72:2 (1988), 77.

76 *Wall Street Journal*, 21 October 1988, A10, "The Vindication of Bork."

(EEOC). As head of the EEOC, Thomas had opposed the policy of racial (or sexual) "quotas" to increase representation of minorities in the workforce, a position that gained him the hatred of the civil rights establishment. Republicans, however, were pleased with Thomas, and the Bush administration subsequently rewarded him with an appointment as a federal district court judge. Once again, Democrats and liberal interest groups organized an all-out campaign to defeat the Thomas nomination, and nearly succeeded when a former employee of Thomas, Anita Hill, came forward with eleventh-hour accusations of sexual harassment. The Anita Hill–Clarence Thomas confrontation transfixed the nation for almost a week. In the end, Thomas was confirmed by the Senate, but the ideological wounds were laid open once again.

The Bork and Thomas affairs present a disturbing commentary on the current state of American constitutionalism. They suggest that the meaning of the American constitution can now be controlled by controlling judicial appointments to the Supreme Court. One of the central pillars of the "rule of law" tradition—judicial independence—seems jeopardized by such partisan wrangling over judicial appointments. Most Canadian observers have cautioned against similar developments in Canada.

In theory, there is no reason why the American pattern could not be duplicated in Canada, if Canadian judges follow the exhortations of *Charter* enthusiasts to use the *Charter* as a vehicle for social and political reform. At the level of principle, democratic theory does not tolerate governors who are not, sooner or later, accountable to the governed. For this reason Canadians do not expect—nor would they long tolerate—the independent exercise of power by the Senate or the Governor General. At a more practical level, pressure groups that are affected by the courts' decisions will seek to influence who makes those decisions. There is no reason to assume that what applies to other government actors—"Where power rests, there influence will be brought to bear."[77]—does not also apply to politically active judges. A court that acts as a policymaker will come to be treated as a policymaker. It will become the focus of partisan competition to ensure that "the right" (or the left) judge will be appointed.

There were some indications of such development in the wake of the Supreme Court's 1988 abortion decision, *Morgentaler* v. *The Queen*.[78] Angela Costigan, counsel for Choose Life Canada, a national pro-life lobby group, criticized the decision as "the expression of personal opinion by the judges," and indicated that in the future they would try to influence the appointment of judges who share their position. Norma Scarborough, president of the Canadian Abortion Rights League (CARAL), responded

---

77 V.O. Key, *Politics, Parties, and Pressure Groups* (Boston: Thomas Y. Crowell, 1958), 154.

78 Unreported, 28 January 1978.

by declaring that while her group had never tried to influence judicial appointments in the past, it would if necessary. "We are going to protect our position as much as possible," she declared.[79]

Two months later Justice Willard Estey announced his intention to resign from the Supreme Court. The search for Estey's replacement immediately attracted the attention of abortion activists. The *Globe and Mail* reported that "activists in the abortion debate and representatives of ethnic communities are lobbying hard. . . . Many members of the ruling PC Party's right wing . . . are putting pressure on PM Mulroney to appoint a conservative judge." MP James Jepson, one of the most outspoken pro-life Tory backbenchers, explained the importance of the new Supreme Court appointment. "We now have a chance to put men and women on the bench with a more conservative point of view." While emphasizing that he had never lobbied for a judicial appointment before, Jepson continued:[80]

> But this one seems to have caught the people's attention. Unfortunately, with the Charter that Trudeau left us, we legislators do not have final power. It rests with the courts. . . . You have seen the battling in the United States for the [most recent] Supreme Court nominee. Well, it doesn't take a rocket scientist to see we have the same situation here now.

In the end, the pro-life lobbying had no apparent effect on the government's appointment of Toronto lawyer John Sopinka to fill Justice Estey's seat on the Court. But the comments of MP Jepson were a political first in Canada, and are not likely to disappear as political elites become more sophisticated in their understanding of the politics of rights engendered by the *Charter*.

It should be noted that there are several countervailing factors that may limit the extent to which Canadian judicial appointments could become as politicized as in the American experience. Appointments to the Supreme Court of Canada are essentially the prerogative of the Prime Minister and his Justice Minister. There are no public hearings and no formal approval by the House of Commons or the Senate. The entire selection process is conducted in secret, the first public knowledge coming with the announcement of the appointment. There is thus little opportunity for interested parties to influence the process, and no opportunity to mobilize public opinion for or against a specific nominee.

---

79 "Public to demand say in court appointments?" *Lawyer's Weekly*, 12 February 1988, 1.

80 "Reduced role for politicians urged in naming of judges," *Globe and Mail* (Toronto), 16 May 1988, 1.

Also, the s. 33 "legislative override" mitigates the inducement for governments to try to pack the courts with ideologically sympathetic judges. Attempts by American presidents such as Roosevelt and Reagan to "pack the courts" were responses to a series of Supreme Court decisions that were judged wrong and/or as having unduly harmful consequences. Canada's s. 33 "legislative override" provides a much more direct and more narrowly tailored solution to "judicial mistakes." If a Canadian government became sufficiently disenchanted with a judicial decision based on the *Charter*, it could effectively negate such a decision by using the "notwithstanding clause" prescribed by s. 33. To make the same point somewhat differently, if either Roosevelt or Reagan had had something like the s. 33 "legislative override" power, they would not have been so preoccupied with judicial appointments.

To conclude, a court that acts politically will, in the long term, come to be treated politically. In the U.S., this has occasionally meant a highly partisan politicization of the judicial appointments process. Judicial activism in the interpretation of the *Charter* creates a similar potential, but such a "politicization of the judiciary," were it to occur in Canada, would likely take a different form.

4. THE PARADOX OF THE LIVING CONSTITUTION: THE REGRESSIVE PROGRESSIVES

Canadian commentators and judges have been almost unanimous in adopting what the Americans call a "living constitution" or "noninterpretivist" approach to interpreting the *Charter*.[81] This approach assumes that it is desirable that fundamental rights be given as broad an interpretation as possible, and thus holds that judges should be free to give new expanded meaning to these rights. The corollary to this approach is that judges should not be limited or tied down by the specifics of the constitutional text or fidelity to its original meaning. A constitution must change as the society changes, and responsibility for constitutional updating is vested with judges.

It is not surprising that Canadians adopted a "living constitution" approach to the *Charter*, as Canada already had its own indigenous (and more poetic!) formula for this kind of interpretation—the "living tree" approach.[82] Like its American counterpart, it evolved out of the law of

---

81 This assertion is supported in Morton, "The Political Impact of the Charter of Rights," 34–36.

82 The "living tree" metaphor was coined and made famous by Lord Sankey in his opinion for the Judicial Committee of the Privy Council in the famous *Persons Case* (*Edwards* v. *Attorney General of Canada*, [1930] A.C. 124 at 136): "The British North America Act planted in Canada a living tree capable of growth and expansion within its natural

federalism, and emphasized the necessity of adapting the law of federalism to the changing politics of federalism. The authority of the "living tree" approach in the law of Canadian federalism gave it an immediate legitimacy when applied to the *Charter*. Its application to the *Charter* was also a reaction against the Supreme Court's much-criticized self-restrained approach to the 1960 Canadian Bill of Rights.[83]

Unfortunately, the lack of any debate about applying the "living tree" approach to the *Charter* has obscured its political implications. In the United Sates, by contrast, controversy over the "living tree"/noninterpretivist method is at the heart of the conservative-liberal conflict over judicial appointments. An analysis of the evolving meaning of the "living constitution" doctrine in American jurisprudence and the controversy it has sparked can provide Canadians with a more critical understanding of their own "living tree" doctrine and its implications for judicial policymaking.

The original purpose of the "living constitution" doctrine was to enhance the legislative powers of the national government. The spirit of the doctrine can be traced back to Chief Justice John Marshall's famous admonition in the 1819 case of *McCulloch* v. *Maryland*. In rejecting a restrictive interpretation of the federal government's enumerated powers, Marshall declared:[84]

> We must never forget that it is a constitution we are expounding . . . a constitution intended to endure for ages to come, and, consequently, to be adapted to the various crises of human affairs.

The real genesis of the "living constitution" doctrine, however, was the growing confrontation between the Supreme Court and Congress that culminated in 1937. It was intended to encourage judges to expand the original meaning of the federal government's enumerated powers in order to "make room" for innovative legislative responses to new economic and social problems. Put more bluntly, it was intended to justify the evacuation of judicial review from the field of economic regulation and

---

limits. . . . Their Lordships do not conceive it to be the duty of this Board . . . to cut down the provisions of the Act by a narrow and technical construction, but rather to give it a large and liberal interpretation." Both the purpose and the wording of the "living tree" doctrine bear a strong resemblance to American Chief Justice John Marshall's dicta in *McCulloch* v. *Maryland* (1819) and *Gibbons* v. *Ogden* (1824). See below, note 84.

83 Justice Wilson has characterized the *Charter* as sending "a clear message to the courts that the restrictive attitude which at times characterized their approach to the Canadian Bill of Rights ought to be reexamined." *Singh* v. *Minister of Employment & Immigration*, [1985] 1 S.C.R. 177.

84 4 17 U.S. (4 Wheat.) 316 (1819). The same spirit is evident in Marshall's landmark interpretation of Congress' commerce power in *Gibbons* v. *Ogden*, 22 U.S. (9 Wheat.) 1 (1824).

social welfare legislation, thereby securing the constitutional legitimacy of the Roosevelt New Deal. The doctrine relegates the constitutional judge to the role of helpmate of legislative power and problemsolving. The doctrine finally carried the day in March 1937, when the Court made the famous "switch in time that saved nine."[85] Since that day, the Court has nullified only one federal statute for exceeding its federal jurisdiction.[86] In its 1985 decision in *Garcia* v. *San Antonio Metropolitan Transit Authority*, the Court subsequently overruled even this decision, and formally announced its intention to abdicate all judicial responsibility for policing federalism disputes.[87]

By contrast, when the focus of the "living tree" doctrine is shifted from the law of federalism to the law of civil liberties, the roles of courts and legislatures are reversed. Rather than expanding legislative powers, the "living tree" doctrine expands limitations on legislative power. Rather than accommodating legislative problemsolving, judges are encouraged to find better solutions. The constitutional judge is encouraged to read new meaning into the constitutional text in order to correct legislative errors. Courts are given the authority to dictate to the legislature what it may not do or even must do.[88] The political roles are reversed. The constitutional judge decides policy, and the legislator implements judicial choice. The essential meaning of the "living tree" doctrine is changed as its focus shifts from government powers to individual rights. The continued use of the same label of "living constitution" obscures the radical revaluation that has occurred. While the original version enhanced the process of majoritarian democracy, the new version obstructs it.

There is a second problem with the unreflective transfer of the "living constitution" doctrine from the law of federalism to the law of rights. In the first case, the "living constitution" is a pragmatic response to a practical problem—the problem of "updating" the law of federalism to adapt to social and economic change. The law of federalism cannot be changed

---

85 The implication was that President Roosevelt would have "packed the Court" by expanding its size and appointing enough "New Deal" judges to guarantee the Court's support. See McCloskey, *The American Supreme Court*, c. 6.

86 *National League of Cities* v. *Usery*, 426 U.S. 833 (1976). In this case, the Court struck down the 1974 extension by Congress of federal minimum wage provisions to cover state and local government employees.

87 *Garcia* v. *San Antonio*, 105 S. Ct. 1005 (1985). The Court forced San Antonio to abide by federal wage and hour laws.

88 The Warren Court pioneered the use of positive judicial remedies or "structural injunctions," whereby a judge actually takes over the administration of a school district or state mental hospital in order to ensure compliance with his decision. See Owen Fiss, *The Civil Rights Injunction* (1978). The structural injunction is foreign to Canadian jurisprudence, but has recently been advocated in the context of the *Charter*. See Robert Sharpe, "Injunctions and the Charter," *Osgoode Hall Law Journal* 22:3 (Fall 1984), 473.

unilaterally by either level of government. To expand the powers of the national government is to reduce the powers of the state governments, and this cannot be done without the latter's consent. The only way to change or adjust the boundaries of federal-state jurisdiction is through constitutional amendment. This proved to be a practical impossibility given the political difficulty of obtaining the approval of three-quarters of the states required by the amending formula. The solution, in the end, was the "living constitution"—which, despite its noble-sounding title, was really nothing more than an after-the-fact rubber stamp of judicial approval of Congressional policymaking. It wasn't pretty but it got the job done.

There is no analogous problem with the "updating" of individual rights. Since rights deal with *limitations* of government powers, a government (at either level) is always free to impose new statutory limitations on what it can or cannot do. That is, a government can unilaterally create new rights (against itself) in a way that it cannot confer new powers on itself. There is thus no analogous need for a "living constitution" doctrine in the realm of rights.

This transformation of the "living constitution" doctrine is at the heart of the contemporary American struggle between liberals and conservatives over judicial appointments. The "living constitution" or noninterpretivist approach has served as the foundation for the American Supreme Court's liberal reformist jurisprudence in the postwar era. Beginning with its race discrimination cases, the Warren Court read new and often unintended meaning into various provisions of the Bill of Rights in order to reach its civil libertarian results.[89] This noninterpretivist jurisprudence reached its high point in the 1973 abortion decision, which was based on the "right to privacy," a right nowhere mentioned in the Constitution.[90]

The conservative reaction has been described above. Beginning with Richard Nixon's call for "strict constructionists" in the 1968 presidential campaign, Republicans have campaigned against this kind of jurisprudence and the judges who practice it. Opposition to the noninterpretivist-living constitution approach has been the litmus test for the Reagan Administration's judicial appointments.[91] Both Chief Justice Rehnquist[92]

---

89 See Morton, "Racial Injustice."

90 See John Hart Ely, *Democracy and Distrust: A Theory of Judicial Review* (Cambridge: Harvard University Press, 1980), 2, 15.

91 See above, notes 64–67.

92 See, e.g., William H. Rehnquist, "The Notion of a Living Constitution," *Texas Law Review* 54 (1976), 693.

and Judge Bork[93] earned their reputations, and perhaps their appointments, as outspoken critics of the "living constitution" approach. Their liberal critics charge that "fidelity to original understanding" is really only a legal façade that allows conservatives to import their own policy preferences into constitutional interpretation.[94]

The transformation of the "living constitution" approach from a "pro-legislative" to an "anti-legislative" doctrine reveals a similar transformation of the American progressive movement.[95] It reflects, indeed embodies, American progressives' waning confidence in the process of democratic self-government. The first generation of American progressives were populists. They criticized the power of judicial review and the other anti-majoritarian elements of American government.[96] Progressives' sponsorship of the direct election of U.S. Senators, the use of primary elections to choose presidential and other candidates, the election of judges, the use of initiative and referendum procedures, the promotion of "presidential" rather than "congressional government"[97]—these were all reforms aimed at enhancing majoritarianism in American politics. The most famous of all American progressives—Woodrow Wilson—was so disillusioned with the "checks and balances" of the American constitution that he initially advocated that it be completely abandoned and be replaced by the "more democratic" parliamentary system of Great Britain.[98]

In legal circles, the leading progressive jurists of the day were unanimous in counselling judicial self-restraint and deference to Congress—the original meaning of the "living constitution" doctrine.[99] They agreed with James Bradley Thayer's influential teaching that, "the ultimate question is not what is the true meaning of the constitution, but whether legislation

93 See, e.g., Robert Bork, "Tradition and Morality in Constitutional Law," The Francis Boyer Lectures on Public Policy, American Enterprise Institute for Public Policy Research, Washington, D.C., 1984.

94 This was the thesis of Ronald Dworkin's scathing attack on Reagan's judicial appointments, especially Bork. "Reagan's Justice," New York Times Book Review 31:8 (1984), 27.

95 This transformation of the American Left is the subject of Aaron Wildavsky, The Revolt Against the Masses (New York: Basic Books, 1971). This is also the theme of Daniel Bell's concept of the "adversary culture," in The Cultural Contradictions of Capitalism (New York: Basic Books, 1975).

96 See comment by the Progressive Party's 1924 presidential candidate Robert LaFollette, pp. 113–14, above.

97 See James W. Ceaser, Presidential Selection: Theory and Development (Princeton: Princeton University Press, 1979), 170–213.

98 Woodrow Wilson, Congressional Government (Boston, 1885).

99 See Christopher Wolfe's discussion of the progressive influence of Woodrow Wilson, Oliver Wendell Holmes, and Benjamin Cardozo on U.S. constitutional law in The Rise of Modern Judicial Review, cc. 9 and 10.

is sustainable or not." Only if Congress made "a clear mistake . . . so clear that it is not open to rational question," was judicial nullification justified.[100] Likewise, Oliver Wendell Holmes protested against the "substantive due process" of his brethren by writing that a judge's "agreement or disagreement [with a law] has nothing to do with the right of a majority to embody their opinion in law."[101] Louis Brandeis pioneered the use of extrinsic evidence, or "social facts," in constitutional argument precisely to demonstrate the "reasonableness," and thus the constitutionality of new forms of economic regulation. Felix Frankfurter carried the progressives' jurisprudence into the realm of civil liberties in his eloquent plea for judicial self-restraint in the Jehovah's Witnesses Flag Salute Cases.[102] While affirming his own belief that the attempt to curb a man's conscience through legal compulsion was usually "vulgar . . . absurd . . . offensive," Frankfurter warned his colleagues (all Roosevelt appointees) that the Court must "avoid the mistake comparable to that made by those whom we criticized when dealing with the control of property."[103]

By contrast, the contemporary claimants of progressivism in American politics—the civil rights, civil liberties, feminist, environmental and gay rights groups—are the most enthusiastic defenders of the most anti-majoritarian institution in the Constitution—judicial review; and also its most anti-democratic expression, the "living constitution"/noninterpretivist approach to constitutional interpretation.[104] Their commitment to both can be measured by the zealousness of their attack on Judge Bork, a modern day apostle of judicial self-restraint. What is remarkable about this reversal is that while these groups sincerely claim to be the inheritors of the progressive tradition in American politics, they have abandoned the very foundation of American progressivism—faith in the democratic process and by extension faith in the American people. While most con-

---

100 James Bradley Thayer, "The Origin and Scope of the American Doctrine of Constitutional Law," *Harvard Law Review* (1893). Reprinted in Gary McDowell, ed., *Taking the Constitution Seriously* (Kendall-Hunt Publ., 1981), 49–69.

101 *Lochner* v. *New York*, 198 V.S. 45 (1905), per Justice Holmes, dissenting.

102 *Minersville School District* v. *Gobitis*, 310 U.S. 586 (1940); and *West Virginia State Board of Education* v. *Barnette*, 319 U.S. 624 (1943).

103 Letter from Justice Frankfurter to Justice Stone, 27 May 1940. Reprinted in Alpheus Mason and William Beaney, eds., *American Constitutional Law: Introductory Essays and Selected Cases* (Englewood Cliffs: Prentice Hall, 1978), 613.

104 See Richard E. Morgan's excellent documentation of this trend in his *Disabling America*. A variation on this theme is developed by Aaron Wildavsky, who notes that the ACLU "was once devoted to achieving individual freedom from governmental restraint, [but] has become a convert to the advocacy of government compulsion to achieve equality of condition." "The Reverse Sequence in Civil Liberties," *The Public Interest* 78 (Winter 1985), 32.

temporary claimants to progressivism would be reluctant to publicly acknowledge this reversal, it was conceded by Hodding Carter, a former White House advisor to President Carter. The Bork nomination, Carter conceded,[105]

> requires liberals like me to confront a reality we don't want to confront, which is that we are depending to a large part on the least democratic institution (with a small "d") in government to defend what it is we no longer are able to win out there in the electorate.

5. CONCLUSION

The myth of the *Charter* as an inherently progressive and democratic force in Canadian politics must be reevaluated in light of the American civil liberties experience. The "heroic" model of the U.S. Supreme Court as a vehicle for political reform is incomplete and misleading. So is the attempt to maintain a sharp dichotomy between rights and policy, courts and legislatures. The *Charter* has brought the politics of rights to Canada, and the Rehnquist and Bork nominations have shown how this process can erode the tradition of judicial independence. Canadians should rethink the application of the "living tree" doctrine to the *Charter* in light of the parallel American experience. The *Charter* and its supporters may well be progressives, but does progressivism still mean what it used to? Can we still accept Pierre Trudeau's characterization of the *Charter* as "the people's package," because it deals with the rights of individuals and not the powers of governments? At a minimum, Trudeau's individualistic version of democracy must be balanced against the caveat of G.K. Chesterton:

> What is the good of telling a community that it has every liberty except the liberty to make laws? The liberty to make laws is what constitutes a free people.

---

105 *Wall Street Journal*, 15 September 1987, 34.

The Impact of the American Constitution on Contemporary Canadian Constitutional Politics

Roger Gibbins

There are ample reasons to expect the American Constitution to have played a significant and perhaps even important role in shaping the constitutional development of the Canadian federal state. While the counter-revolutionary roots of Canada[1] would not lead us to expect the Canadian constitution[2] to mimic that of the United States, we should expect to find American reflections within the Canadian constitutional order.

This expectation stems in part from simple geographic proximity, and from the related fact that Canadian society, more broadly defined, reflects things American to an extensive and even, in the eyes of many Canadians, alarming degree. One would be hard-pressed to find two countries which have more in common than do Canada and the United States, and it would not be a surprise to find that the common ground shared by the two countries extends past language, an integrated economy, a shared mass culture and professional sports to include constitutional principles and practices. After all, if Canadians have adopted so much from the American mass culture, if Canadians have embraced "Saturday Night Live" and "The David Letterman Show," it would only be appropriate that they have also borrowed from the Americans constitutional principles which have left such a worldwide imprint on the evolution of democratic politics. Given what appears to be a pattern of convergence

---

1 Seymour Martin Lipset, *Revolution and Counterrevolution* (New York: Basic Books, 1968).

2 Throughout this discussion, the American "Constitution" will be capitalized while the Canadian "constitution" will not. This usage stems from the fact that American usage refers to a discrete document, whereas the Canadian usage refers to both a collection of documents (including but not limited to the *Constitution Act, 1867* and the *Constitution Act, 1982*) along with a substantial unwritten constitution. For a discussion of the Canadian case, see Alan C. Cairns, "The Living Canadian Constitution," *Queen's Quarterly,* 77:4 (Winter 1970), 1.

in the political cultures of the two countries,[3] it would be surprising to find constitutional divergence.

Certainly there are reflections of the American Constitution in the historical evolution of the Canadian federal state. After all, the American Constitution had been in place for more than seventy-five years before Canadians sat down in the mid-1860s to design the Canadian federal state and, as Jennifer Smith explains,[4] the federal aspects of the American Constitution were important, albeit not always positive, points of reference in the constitutional deliberations of Canada's Fathers of Confederation. In short, the mere precedence of the American Constitution ensured American influences in the Canadian debates, even if those influences were largely negative in character. Here it should also be stressed that Canadians and Americans, in their attempts to build transcontinental national communities, faced many similar problems of institutional and constitutional design. Both were sprawling, ethnically diverse societies and, at least partly as a consequence, both opted for federal forms of government.[5] When one takes into account how much of Canadian political life is built around federal principles, institutions and disputes, it is clear that Canada's adoption of the American federal innovation has led to a profound and lasting American influence. This conclusion holds even though American and Canadian federalisms differ significantly in their institutional articulation.

In short, the underlying social and geographical similarity of the two countries prompted a similar constitutional and institutional response. When federalism was combined with a common British tradition, a language held largely in common, and in many respects a continental democratic ethos, the stage was set for the American conditioning, although far from regimentation, of Canadian political life. Since Confederation, moreover, Canadian society has become progressively less British and more American, or at least more North American, in virtually every respect. British investment in and ownership of the Canadian economy

---

3 See Neil Nevitte and Roger Gibbins, *New Elites in Old States: Ideologies in the Anglo-American Democracies* (Toronto: Oxford University Press, 1990); and Gibbins and Nevitte, "Canadian Political Ideology: A Comparative Analysis," *Canadian Journal of Political Science* 18:3 (September 1985), 577.

4 Jennifer Smith, "Canadian Confederation and the Influence of American Federalism," in this volume.

5 However, it should be noted that, in the American case, federalism fit comfortably within, and indeed in some respects was a reflection of, other constitutional principles, such as the separation of powers embraced by the Founding Fathers. In the Canadian case, the adoption of federalism was a matter of necessity rather than choice, and the fit with other constitutional principles such as parliamentary supremacy and responsible government has never been an easy one. See Smith, "Canadian Confederation and the Influence of American Federalism."

has dropped sharply, to be replaced by American investment and ownership. American rather than British firms dominate the industrial sector, and American consumer products, including those produced in Canada, dominate the marketplace. The early British roots of the Canadian trade union movement have been overgrown by American models of industrial organization and trade union behaviour. With the development of electronic media, the British cultural impact on Canada has atrophied and has been almost totally obscured by the massive influence of the American mass media.[6] In general, then, Canadian society is even more open to American influence today than it was in the past. Thus one might expect American constitutional influences to have continued unabated since the 1860s, and perhaps even to have become more pronounced.[7] Certainly the Free Trade Agreement will act, for better or for worse, to increase the American impact on Canadian economic and social life.

All this preamble, however, has been in the cause of constructing an elaborate straw man, an admittedly plausible straw man, but a straw man nonetheless. When one looks closely at the evolution and contours of more contemporary Canadian political life, reflections of the American constitutional experience are difficult to find. The fundamental similarity between the Canadian and American societies has not increased Canadian receptivity to American political norms, institutions and values. If anything, it has made Canadians *less receptive*, as distinctive political institutions, and in particular the British (i.e., noncongressional) roots of those institutions, have come to be seen as the first and in some cases only line of defence for an independent national community. Canadians have been loath to borrow politically from the United States even when the American political experience may be of some immediate relevance,[8] and even when American political ideas and principles may be of greater intrinsic value than the American cultural and economic artifacts which are so readily absorbed by Canadian society.

Indeed, it can be argued that Canada and the United States are more distinctive politically than they are in any other way. This is particularly evident when one examines the period since 1945, a time when the

---

6 British television programs primarily enter Canada through the cable distribution of American public television rather than through Canadian stations per se. There is much greater British content on PBS than there is on CBC.

7 For the very reason we might expect American constitutional influences to be reflected within the Canadian political order, we should not expect any reciprocity in this relationship. It would be futile indeed to search for Canadian influences on the evolution of the American Constitution, or on the evolution of the American federal state, more broadly defined.

8 For a comparative discussion of Canadian and American attempts to contain the regional fragmentation of transcontinental societies, see Gibbins, *Regionalism: Territorial Politics in Canada and the United States* (Toronto: Butterworths, 1982).

Canadian constitutional order was destabilized by rapid political change, and when the resultant constitutional flux potentially opened up the Canadian constitutional order to American constitutional influences. As I will argue below, the American influence during this period was more apparent than real; during an extended period of constitutional instability and debate, the Canadian constitution remained surprisingly immune from American influence. Yet it will also be argued, in conclusion, that more recent political change in Canada may well open up the Canadian federal state to greater American influence than has been experienced in the past.

The following discussion will therefore examine Canadian constitutional change since the end of World War II, and will attempt to determine to what extent the course of constitutional change has evolved in response to constitutional principles and/or developments in the United States. While the historical overview upon which this examination is based will be necessarily brief, hopefully it will not also be cryptic.

CONSTITUTIONAL FLUX IN THE CANADIAN FEDERAL STATE

In the nearly five decades since the end of World War II, the Canadian constitution has come under a great deal of strain and, as a consequence, has experienced a substantial degree of both formal and informal change. In some important respects, the informal change has paralleled change in the United States. For example, the rapid postwar growth of government in both countries resulted in the progressive financial and programmatic entanglement of national and subnational governments. In Canada and the United States, the development of shared-cost and conditional grant programs blurred and obscured the federal division of powers; in both countries, the evolution of fiscal federalism strengthened the hand of national governments as more and more federal money came to be spent on social programs falling within the legislative domain of state and provincial governments. It is important to stress, however, that parallel developments need not and should not imply that the changes within the Canadian federal state were in response to, or were modelled after, changes occurring within the American federal state. (This conclusion is supported by the similar pattern of fiscal federalism that evolved in Australia during the same time, a pattern that neither drove nor was driven by the Canadian experience.) In the case of fiscal federalism, for example, there is no evidence to suggest that Canadian politicians paid any particular attention to or sought guidance from developments taking place south of the border. A common pattern of change appears to have resulted from similar fiscal and social conditions, and not from any direct infusion of American political ideas or models *per se*.

More importantly, the major engines of constitutional change in Canada during the postwar period were distinctively Canadian in character. While Americans wrestled with growing racial conflict and the often acute foreign policy strains brought on by an international presence and activism which Canadians did not share, Canada's constitutional order was destabilized by a vigorous nationalist movement in Quebec. This movement found forceful expression, not only through separatist organizations, but also through the relentless pressure of the Quebec provincial government to protect and then to expand its own jurisdictional domain, pressure that continued unabated through Liberal, Union Nationale and Parti Québécois administrations. Although some might be tempted to equate the constitutional strains induced by the black racial minority in the United States with those induced by the francophone linguistic minority in Canada,[9] such a temptation must be rejected. Francophones enjoyed a much more advantageous demographic environment than did American blacks, constituting as they did close to thirty percent of the Canadian population and over eighty percent of the population in Quebec. Francophones, moreover, were closely aligned with Canada's dominant political party of the twentieth century, the Liberal party, and through that party contributed three of the country's prime ministers—Wilfrid Laurier, Louis St. Laurent and Pierre Trudeau. Furthermore, it was the unique set of circumstances in which francophones controlled the government of the largest province in Canada—largest in size, second largest in population—that gave such a distinctive national spin to constitutional politics in Canada. These circumstances also ensured that the constitutional strategies of Quebec francophones were essentially federalist in character. Such strategies had no appeal or relevance for American blacks who were pursuing their own constitutional visions through the courts and national political institutions. The civil rights movement was centralist in character, and constituted an assault on the federalist underpinnings of the American political system, whereas Québécois nationalism was emphatically decentralist and federal.

Thus the linguistic debate in Canada established a distinctive constitutional agenda that bore little if any resemblance to the political agenda in the United States. National distinctiveness was further reinforced by the other engines driving constitutional change in Canada— by regional discontent on both the western and eastern peripheries, by increasingly acrimonious intergovernmental conflict, and by the need for constitutional patriation. These national differences have been explored at much greater length elsewhere;[10] here I would simply assert that

---

9 Note, e.g., Pierre Vallieres' *White Niggers of America* (Toronto: McClelland and Stewart, 1971).

10 See Gibbins, *Regionalism*.

Canadian political life at the time was marked by much sharper regional and intergovernmental conflict than was American political life, and that both regional and intergovernmental conflict found expression in the prolonged constitutional debate which Canadians began in the 1960s and have carried through to the 1990s. The final distinctively Canadian twist, and probably the least important, came from the need to patriate the country's basic constitutional document, the *British North America Act* of 1867, which remained an Act of the British Parliament until 17 April 1982. This anomalous and even embarrassing situation, far removed from the American revolutionary experience, was one of the factors which induced the need for constitutional change, and which thereby provided an opening for the constitutional expression of other, more serious political conflicts within the Canadian body politic.

Here it should also be noted that postwar constitutional evolution in the United States has taken place primarily through judicial reinterpretation by the Supreme Court; as the unsuccessful Equal Rights Amendment (ERA) campaign demonstrated so clearly, formal constitutional change has become very difficult to achieve, and in many respects may be unnecessary. In the Canadian case, however, the courts until recently have been no more than supporting players in the ongoing struggle over constitutional reform. At least until 1982, the constitution was seen by Canadians and their governments, and by the courts, as a document by and for governments, a document of little direct relevance for the rights and responsibilities of citizens. As a consequence, constitutional change was pursued primarily through an intergovernmental arena within which Canadians at large were at best passive spectators rather than active participants.[11] It was an arena that was relatively immune to judicial intervention, and an arena which in any event citizens did not assail through the courts. Also as a consequence, American judicial interpretation and constitutional experience were not as relevant as they might have been if Canadian constitutional change had been pursued through the courts. Federal and provincial politicians largely ignored the courts, preferring instead to use the intensely political and decidedly non-judicial forums provided by First Ministers' Conferences. Within those forums, there was little opportunity for the infusion of American constitutional experience or principles, and thus the Canadian constitutional debate was given once again a distinctively governmental and national cast.

All this is not to say that Canadians were completely immune to American constitutional influences. The passage of the *Canadian Bill of Rights* in 1960 reflected the rights-based political culture lying to the south of Canada, although the Progressive Conservative Prime Minister

---

11 A major exception to this generalization came with the referendum on sovereignty-association held in Quebec during the late spring of 1980.

at the time, John Diefenbaker, would have been appalled at the suggestion that his government was mimicking the American Bill of Rights. And indeed, such a reaction would have been warranted in that the Canadian Bill was not constitutionally entrenched, did not bind the Parliament of Canada in that it was a statute like other federal statutes, and did not apply to provincial governments and law. Moreover, the *Bill of Rights* had little significant impact on the unfolding of Canadian political life. It was seldom woven into Supreme Court jurisprudence, and served even less often as a point of departure for constitutional and political debate within the country. The *Bill of Rights* is analogous to a little stone tossed into the pond of Canadian political life; it produced a small splash and some minor ripples, then sank from sight within a national political culture that was still predominantly parliamentary and governmental in character.

The American constitutional emphasis on rights also spilled across the border in the wake of the civil rights movement. One finds, for example, some echoes of the civil rights movement in the early rhetoric of Pierre Trudeau's Liberal governments, and particularly in the Prime Minister's somewhat ill-defined vision of "the just society." More concretely, the civil rights movement found reflection in the efforts by the Trudeau government to address Canadian Indian issues. The 1969 "White Paper" on Indian affairs tried to recast the Canadian Indian situation along lines directly analogous to the situation faced by American blacks.[12] It is interesting to note, however, that the civil rights, assimilationist approach favoured by the White Paper was rejected by Canadian Indians and was subsequently abandoned by the federal government. While this episode illustrates the infusion of American constitutional thought, it also demonstrates the resistance that Canadians have displayed to any such infusion.

Thus, despite both a considerable degree of constitutional turbulence in Canada and the proximity of American constitutional models, there was in fact little American constitutional influence as Canadians steered an idiosyncratic course through the troubled waters of the 1960s and 1970s. In most important respects, the constitutional agenda was unique to Canada, and it was addressed through intergovernmental forums and models that were also distinctively Canadian. However, this separation of the Canadian and American constitutional experiences began to dissolve as Canadians moved into the 1980s.

---

12 For a discussion, see Sally Weaver, *The Hidden Agenda: Indian Policy and the Trudeau Government* (Toronto: University of Toronto Press, 1981).

THE CONSTITUTION ACT, 1982

The proclamation of the *Constitution Act* on 17 April 1982, marked the culmination of more than a decade of intense constitutional debate in Canada, a debate featuring the 1976 Quebec election of the Parti Québécois, the 1980 sovereignty-association referendum, and angry regional discord throughout as national Liberal governments, virtually devoid of elected western Canadian representation, faced powerful and assertive provincial governments. On balance, that extended debate did not draw extensively from American constitutional models or experience, in large part because it addressed distinctively Canadian problems of national unity and institutional design. It was not apparent, for example, that the American constitutional experience had much to offer with respect to the central problem of Quebec's place within the Canadian federal state,[13] and the American melting pot mythology was inapplicable to the position of Canadian linguistic and cultural minorities.

Nor, for that matter, did many of the elements of the *Constitution Act* reflect American constitutional experience or concerns. Certainly the matter of patriation was unique to the Canadian experience, the matter being one that had been addressed somewhat differently by Americans in 1776. The new amending formula was very much a response to the balance and disposition of political forces within the Canadian federal state, and bears little resemblance to the American formula. While the override provision of s. 33[14] reflected in part a wariness of judicial activism which stemmed from observing the American experience, it also, and more importantly, reaffirmed the British tradition of parliamentary sovereignty. The sections of the *Canadian Charter of Rights and Freedoms* that dealt with minority language rights addressed a specifically Canadian problem, and the sections of both the *Charter* and the broader Act[15] dealing with aboriginal peoples reflected a Canadian approach to issues surrounding aboriginal peoples in settler societies. The sections of the

---

13 In this respect, the *Constitution Act, 1982*, also had little to offer, as it was silent on Quebec's position within the Canadian federal state. While the linguistic rights of Canadians were addressed, the federal status of Quebec was not, except by silence.

14 Section 33(1) states that "Parliament or the legislature of any province may expressly declare in an Act of Parliament or of the legislature, as the case may be, that the Act or a provision thereof shall operate notwithstanding a provision included in section 2 or sections 7 to 15 of this Charter." A declaration made under this provision ceases to have effect after five years, although it may then be re-enacted.

15 The *Constitution Act, 1982*, contains 60 sections, of which the first 34 constitute the *Canadian Charter of Rights and Freedoms*.

Charter dealing with multiculturalism[16] and denominational schools,[17] and the section of the Act dealing with regional equalization payments,[18] addressed Canadian concerns which have no counterpart in American constitutional principles or documents.

In a more general sense, however, and certainly with respect to the symbolic role which constitutional documents play, the *Charter* did inject American constitutionalism into the Canadian constitutional culture and into Canadian political life more broadly defined. In a rather dramatic fashion, "rights" were infused into both the Canadian constitution and Canadian political discourse. Prior to 1982, the constitution was almost exclusively governmental in character; while it dealt with the distribution of powers and authority among governments, citizen rights and responsibilities were not mentioned. In this very important respect, the Canadian constitutional and political cultures differed significantly from their American counterparts. The *Charter*, however, blurs this distinction by embedding individual rights and freedoms into the heart of the Canadian constitution, and into the centre of Canadian political discourse. While this should not imply that, prior to 1982, a concern with rights had been solely an American preoccupation, there is little question that it was the American constitutional ethos, and not that of other countries, which influenced the Canadian *Charter*.[19]

To a degree, the American stress on rights had already entered the Canadian popular culture; Canadians talked of their rights, such as the "right" to make one phone call if arrested by the police, as if a Canadian counterpart to the American Bill of Rights in fact existed. In this sense, the *Charter* caught up with the popular culture; it put into the constitution what many Canadians had already assumed was there. Nonetheless, the entrenchment in s. 2 and ss. 7 through 15 of rights which roughly parallel those entrenched in the American Constitution will undoubtedly serve over the long run to "harmonize" the Canadian and American political cultures, as the former acquires a rights-based foundation which the latter has experienced for generations.

---

16 Section 27 states that "this Charter shall be interpreted in a manner consistent with the preservation and enhancement of the multicultural heritage of Canadians."

17 Section 29 states that "nothing in this Charter abrogates or derogates from any rights or privileges guaranteed by or under the Constitution of Canada in respect of denominational, separate or dissentient schools."

18 Section 36 states that the government of Canada and the provincial governments "are committed to (a) promoting equal opportunities for the well-being of Canadians; (b) furthering economic development to reduce disparity in opportunities; and (c) providing essential public services of reasonable quality to all Canadians."

19 For a more general discussion of this point, see Alan C. Cairns, *Charter Versus Federalism: The Dilemmas Of Constitutional Reform* (Montreal and Kingston: McGill-Queen's University Press, 1992), c. 1.

There are a number of other ways in which the *Charter* opens up the Canadian constitution to American theory and experience. At the same time that it encourages and indeed mandates Canadian courts to play a more active role in the political arena, the *Charter* also makes American judicial precedents more relevant to the interpretation of Canadian law and public policy.[20] The vast American experience with the interplay of constitutional rights and public policy will inevitably be brought into play as groups pursue political ends through judicial means, and as both lawyers and judges attempt to sort out the implications of the *Charter* for Canadian political life and public policy.[21] This is not to suggest that American precedents will be imported holus bolus, but rather that the *Charter* makes it more likely that Canadian interest groups will attempt to bring into play the litigious strategies long employed by their American counterparts.[22] While in the immediate term the impact is most likely to be felt in policy areas encompassing women's issues, abortion and aboriginal rights, the impact in the longer term will be much broader.

Parenthetically, it is worth noting that the gender equality rights embedded in ss. 15 and 28[23] of the *Charter* also reflect the American constitutional experience, even though American feminists were not successful in securing passage of the Equal Rights Amendment. The protracted and highly publicized ERA campaign in the United States prepared the Canadian soil so that when more sweeping constitutional change was required in response to quite different strains within the Canadian body politic, Canadian feminists were able to secure the constitutional entrenchment of gender equality rights without having to resort to the protracted public and legislative campaign that American feminists fought and eventually lost.[24] Feminists did not have to convince Canadians or legislators at large to amend the constitution; they simply had to ensure that when the constitution was amended, in response to a

---

20 For a useful comparative study, see Christopher P. Manfredi, "Adjudication, Policy-Making and the Supreme Court of Canada: Lessons from the Experience of the United States," *Canadian Journal of Political Science* 22:2 (June 1989), 313.

21 For an example, see Rainer Knopff, "What Do Constitutional Equality Rights Protect Canadians Against?", *Canadian Journal of Political Science* 20:2 (June 1987), 267.

22 For a discussion of how Canadian feminists have borrowed from the example set by American feminists, see Mary Eberts, "The Use of Litigation Under the Canadian Charter of Rights and Freedoms as a Strategy for Achieving Change," in Neil Nevitte and Allan Kornberg, eds., *Minorities and the Canadian State* (Oakville: Mosaic Press, 1985), 53.

23 Section 28 states that "notwithstanding anything in this Charter, the rights and freedoms referred to in it are guaranteed equally to male and female persons."

24 Roger Gibbins and Neil Nevitte, "The Ideology of Gender: A Cross-National Analysis," *Research in Political Science* 4 (1989), 109.

quite different set of concerns, the First Ministers "tacked on" gender equality rights. The point to stress is that Canadians were still guided by the American constitutional experience, even though in this case an American loss for feminists became a Canadian gain.

Finally, and as Alan Cairns has argued so persuasively,[25] the *Charter* has shifted the Canadian constitutional culture toward an acceptance of popular sovereignty, as citizens have come to see the constitution as theirs rather than the exclusive property of governments. Citizens, and particularly the "*Charter* Canadians" such as women, visible minorities, and minority language groups who identify with specific sections of the *Charter*, now have a sense of constitutional ownership. As Cairns explains, "the constitution that emerged from the battlefields of 1980–82, with the Charter's individual rights and various group recognitions, speaks past governments and directly to Canadians."[26] Cairns goes on to argue that:

> The political purposes of the Charter included the attachment of Canadians to the constitutional order by protecting their rights. In a surprisingly short time this has happened in English Canada; the Charter has taken root and generated a broad base of support. The various group recognitions and entitlements of the Charter have had their entirely anticipated consequence of inducing their possessors to believe that the written constitution is no longer an exclusive affair of governments. . . . Further, the possession of rights and recognitions logically generates a political culture increasingly sympathetic to constitutional participation by citizens. . . . This participant impulse is further stimulated by the general enhancement of the constitutional status of citizenship to which the Charter contributes, with its corollary of a diminished deference towards elites and governments.[27]

If Cairns is correct that the *Constitution Act, 1982* set in motion a pattern of change which will increase the constitutional participation of citizens and reduce citizen deference to governments and elites, it is also a pattern of change which will bring the Canadian constitutional culture more into line with that of the United States. While this was certainly not an intended consequence of the *Charter*, it is a likely consequence nonetheless. Although it is difficult to imagine a Canadian constitution which refers explicitly to "We the People," the *Charter* implicitly moves us in the direction of a more citizen-based and less government-based constitution.

---

25 A.C. Cairns, "Citizens (Outsiders) and Governments (Insiders) in Constitution-Making: The Case of Meech Lake," *Canadian Public Policy* 14 (September 1988), S. 121.

26 Ibid., 140.

27 Ibid., 142.

This drift in the constitutional culture was, if anything, accelerated by the Meech Lake debacle.

THE 1987 MEECH LAKE CONSTITUTIONAL ACCORD

Embedded within the *Constitution Act, 1982* was a rather profound irony, one which left an open wound in the Canadian constitutional order and thereby set the stage for the Meech Lake Accord, which was unveiled to a somewhat surprised Canadian public in April 1987. Simply put, the Act did not address the major concern which had driven the constitutional process since the late 1960s; it was silent on Quebec's place within the Canadian federal state. Minority language rights were addressed, but provincial powers and the status of Quebec were not, and thus the Quebec government and National Assembly refused to sign. Moreover, the Act did not address intergovernmental conflict, nor did it incorporate institutional changes which might have addressed perennial problems of regional conflict and alienation. In short, the Act did not address those items on the constitutional agenda which were distinctively Canadian, those items for which American constitutional experience was of little relevance. Instead, the major initiative of the Act came with the *Charter*, an initiative which opened the door to the infusion of American constitutional models and experience. The distinctively Canadian conflicts were left in abeyance, to be picked up again by the First Ministers at Meech Lake.

In many respects, the 1987 Meech Lake Accord was a quintessentially Canadian constitutional document, one that was virtually unmarked by American constitutional experience. It was hammered out by eleven men meeting behind closed doors until the early hours of the morning; it was then presented to the Canadian people as a seamless web, admittedly subject to legislative ratification and thus to a measure of public debate, but not subject to change or amendment.[28] While the Accord initially generated a significant degree of academic criticism,[29] the public reacted at first with acquiescence and even indifference. Here it is interesting to speculate on what the reaction of Americans might have been if a small group of men had emerged from behind closed doors to announce fundamental changes in the Constitution, changes that were not open to amendment, regardless of whatever weaknesses might be exposed in public debate. The difference between the initially deferential Canadian

---

28 In bringing the Accord forward for legislative ratification, the First Ministers declared that they would contemplate amendments only if "egregious errors" were discovered.

29 For example, see Cairns, "Citizens (Outsiders) and Governments (Insiders)," and Gibbins, ed., *Meech Lake and Canada: Perspectives from the West* (Edmonton: Academic Printing and Publishing, 1988).

reaction to the Accord, and the admittedly hypothetical American reaction, casts the national differences in political culture in bold relief.

As a constitutional document, the Meech Lake Accord was written by and for governments; it contained no provisions analogous to the *Charter*, no provisions which might have enhanced a sense of constitutional ownership or participation among Canadian citizens. The Accord bore no imprint from the American constitutional experience and, if it had been ratified, may have curtailed the infusion of American constitutional values, experience and models into Canadian political life. But the Accord was not ratified, and by the time it collapsed in June 1990, public opinion outside Quebec had swung decisively against it. The changes in constitutional culture described by Cairns, changes set in motion by the *Charter*, were strengthened and not derailed by the Meech Lake debate. If anything, the notions of citizen participation and popular sovereignty which took root in the Canadian constitutional culture with the implementation of the *Charter* continued to grow. Thus the *Charter* continues to ripple through the constitutional order and the Canadian body politic.

THE FREE TRADE AGREEMENT

In late 1988, after an emotionally charged federal election campaign in Canada fought almost exclusively against the backdrop of free trade negotiations, Canada and the United States signed the Free Trade Agreement. In principle, the FTA urges Canadians to adopt a more continental, and a more market-driven set of ideas, values and policies. While it would be alarmist to argue that the FTA will lead to the American domination of Canadian political life, it will further open up the Canadian political system to American influence, benign or otherwise. As Donald Smiley has observed,

> the thrust of any free trade agreement between Canada and the United States will be towards the harmonization of the public policies of the two countries. It is overwhelmingly likely that the direction of harmonization will be to bring Canadian policies into harmony with U.S. norms rather than the reverse.[30]

Although the Canadian constitution will be more resistant to "harmonization" than will public policies more broadly defined, any movement in this direction must be a matter of some concern. Here Smiley argues that "because Canada is essentially a political community rather than an

---

30 Donald Smiley, "A Note on Canadian-American Free Trade and Canadian Policy Autonomy," in Marc Gold and David Leyton-Brown, eds., *Trade-Offs on Free Trade: The Canada-U.S. Free Trade Agreement* (Toronto: Carswell, 1988), 442.

ethnic, cultural or religious one, free trade with the United States will fundamentally compromise Canadian distinctiveness and Canadian nationhood."[31] The extent to which such compromise occurs will depend upon how deeply "harmonization" reaches into the constitutional sinews of the Canadian federal state.

The general point to stress is that the FTA was designed to reduce and in many cases to remove barriers between the United States and Canada. While the initial barriers to be affected are economic, it would be naive to assume that political barriers will not be affected in turn.

THE CONSTITUTIONAL DEBATE OF THE 1990S

The Meech Lake debacle did not shut down the constitutional debate in Canada, but instead opened up an even more wide-ranging and heated debate, which is still raging and is far from settled at the time of writing. Given that the debate is unsettled, and given that the future character of the country is very much in doubt, it is difficult to draw any firm conclusions about the impact of the current debate on the themes of this essay. It is possible, however, to draw out a few observations which may provide a conclusion of sorts to the more general argument.

First, the current debate continues to display the Canadian timidity in examining, much less embracing, relevant aspects of American political and constitutional experience. For example, the debate on Senate reform is at best modestly informed by the American experience. In part, this is because the advocates of Senate reform realize that any positive reference to the American experience would hand their opponents the club of anti-Americanism, a club that could and would be used to beat back reform. To say that something works in the American context is still to imply that it would be inappropriate or even pernicious if applied to the Canadian scene. To take a second example, the current constitutional debate over aboriginal self-government draws little if at all from the vast American experience. The failure to do so is foolhardy at best, and irresponsible at worst. No one will be well-served by this attempt to reinvent the wheel.

Second, the growing popularity of the Reform Party is likely to lead to a more extensive injection of American ideas into Canadian political discourse. There is a greater receptivity to American ideas, and indeed to non-Canadian ideas in general, within the Reform Party than there is within the more established parties. In the short term, this greater receptivity will be used as an electoral club by Reform opponents who will argue, with some success, that to be open to non-Canadian ideas

31 Ibid.

borders on disloyalty. However, if the Reform Party survives, it will serve as a conduit for American ideas.

Third, and perhaps most important, the future impact of American ideas will depend a great deal on the outcome of the current constitutional debate. If the outcome is successful, then the opportunity for American influence will be curtailed. In part this will be because the constitutional debate itself will have been shut down, and thus the major playing field closed. Success will likely also mark the reinforcement of traditional Canadian values, including the centrality of Quebec and linguistic politics. However, if a successful end to the current debate includes Senate reform and the recognition of aboriginal self-government, then the door may be left ajar for at least a quick perusal of the American experience.

If the current constitutional debate ends in failure, then the door is thrown wide open for a much more extensive American influence. Canadians will be forced to design a new set of constitutional and institutional arrangements, perhaps exclusive of Quebec. In this event, Canadians would be foolish to ignore the American experience, and to fall back on traditional Canadian norms and values. Failure may and hopefully will force us to cast a much wider net in the search for new constitutional and institutional structures for the twenty-first century.

IV

The Judiciary
and Public Policy Issues

Two Supreme Courts:
A Study in Contrast[*]

The Honourable Madame Justice Claire L'Heureux-Dubé
of the Supreme Court of Canada

In this essay I would like to discuss a subject with which I am not altogether unfamiliar, the Supreme Court of Canada. Rather than rest within the boundaries of our own country, however, I propose to compare and contrast our institution with that of the United States, attempting to show that, insofar as constitutional adjudication is concerned, the function each Court performs is similar, although the manner in which each performs that function and the considerations brought to bear in doing so are quite different. A further attempt will be made to show that these differences may be attributed, in large part, to the constitutional document each court is required to interpret and apply.

A decade ago, the constitutional and legal landscape in Canada looked considerably different from what it does now. When a case came before the Court the principal question for constitutional purposes was usually limited to a determination of whether a given branch of government had stayed within its jurisdictional sphere in enacting a particular piece of legislation. The judiciary was not called upon to inquire into the merits of that legislation, or to subject it to any true scrutiny, apart from that fundamental question. This conformed with the notion of parliamentary supremacy, a governing principle of British constitutionalism. Under this principle, Parliament can make or abrogate any law it chooses without submitting its actions to the judiciary for *ex ante* or *ex post* approval. In this sense, the power of Parliament is limited not by a preordained set of precepts purporting to protect the individual member of society, but rather by that society itself, which is at complete liberty to exercise its democratic franchise and vote out the government the next time it has the chance to do so. And, although Britain now has bound itself to a number of international human rights documents, as a theoretical matter it is, I

[*] I wish to acknowledge the helpful collaboration of my law clerk Andrew Lenz in the research and preparation of this essay.

think, still possible to argue that constitutional authority is seen there as resting on the unfettered authority of Parliament.[1]

This is not so in the United States. There, constitutional liberty is perceived as being protected by a written charter with a Bill of Rights and the Civil War amendments. The charter prohibits the state from abridging the various rights which it contains. The judiciary is then charged with invalidating government actions which are inconsistent with those guarantees. In the words of Professor Cameron,

> In broad terms, liberty comprehends the right of individuals to be free from state authority; constitutional experience has institutionalized that conception of the state; and, in claiming the prerogative of review, the judiciary mediates conflicts between individual freedom and state authority, deciding which will prevail in any case.[2]

Note, then, that under the American model the individual is given a constitutional claim, or right of action against the government, and it is up to the judiciary (as opposed to Parliament under the British model) to decide how to reconcile the competing interests of the individual and that government.

As already indicated, prior to 1982 and the enactment of the *Canadian Charter of Rights and Freedoms*, the Canadian model was primarily that of Great Britain, although it must be remembered that the *British North America Act* of 1867 did contain some language rights and denominational school rights which, along with jurisdictional questions under the doctrine of *ultra vires*, were enforced by the judiciary. In general, however, it was Parliament, and not the judiciary, which decided how the competing interests of the state and the individual were to be resolved.[3]

A more Americanized view of the role of the judiciary was brought about by the enactment of the *Charter*, and Canadian courts openly welcomed the new challenges which the *Charter* presented. It is clear from the early jurisprudence that there was an immediate recognition that the judiciary in general, and the Supreme Court of Canada in particular, were to play an unprecedented role in the life of the country, and that

---

1 See J. Cameron, "Liberty, Authority, and the State in American Constitutionalism," *Osgoode Hall Law Journal* 25 (1987), 257 at 270–73. The essence of Parliamentary supremacy was described by Dicey in *Introduction to the Study of the Law of the Constitution*, 3d ed. (London: Macmillan, 1889) at 38 as: "neither more nor less than this, namely, that Parliament thus defined has, under the English constitution, the right to make or unmake any law whatever; and, further, that no person or body is recognised by the law of England as having a right to override or set aside the legislation of Parliament."

2 Cameron, "Liberty, Authority, and the State," 271.

3 Ibid., 272, n. 60. See also P. Hogg, *Constitutional Law of Canada*, 2d ed. (Toronto: Carswell, 1985), 257–58.

this role was greeted with both a sense of excitement and responsibility. I am thinking, for example, of the judgment of my colleague, Mr. Justice Estey, in *Law Society of Upper Canada* v. *Skapinker*,[4] where he speaks of

> a new dimension, a new yardstick of reconciliation between the individual and the community and their respective rights, a dimension which, like the balance of the Constitution, remains to be interpreted and applied by the Court.[5]

In the same case Mr. Justice Estey adopted the approach taken by the U.S. Supreme Court in *McCulloch* v. *Maryland*.[6] That is to say that the Court needed to leave the legislative body room to operate for the benefit of the people, but only within the scope permitted by the constitution.

A similar note was struck by Chief Justice Dickson in *Hunter* v. *Southam Inc.*[7] He stated that the judiciary had been made the guardian of the constitution and, in interpreting that instrument, we must bear in mind that it is a document which is intended to be adapted to the changing needs of a dynamic society. The Chief Justice also referred with approbation to the *McCulloch* case and the constitutional approach it advocated. Moreover, he went on to lay down the foundations for the now well-known purposive analysis whereby the individual provisions of the *Charter* would be interpreted in light of its larger objects and any governmental action inconsistent with those rights would be illegitimate and recognized as such by the Court.[8]

This new position has given rise to grave warnings about the Court's becoming a sort of "super-legislature" where the legitimate attempts of the elected representatives of the Canadian people to address current issues go to die. However, as my colleague, Mr. Justice Lamer, now the Chief Justice, remarked in *Reference re Section 94(2) of the British Columbia Motor Vehicles Act*,[9] this is an argument which has been heard on countless occasions, but which has been definitively settled by the enactment

---

4 [1984] 1 S.C.R. 357.

5 Ibid., 366–67.

6 17 U.S. 316 (1819). In *McCulloch* the U.S. Supreme Court, speaking through Marshall C.J., ruled unconstitutional state taxation on a branch of the Bank of the United States, a federal corporation. *McCulloch* established the doctrine that the national government possesses "implied powers" related to and flowing from its specifically delegated authority.

7 [1984] 2 S.C.R. 145.

8 Ibid., 154–60. See also M. Manning "The Role of the Supreme Court of Canada under the Canadian Charter of Rights and Freedoms," in G.-A. Beaudoin, ed., *The Supreme Court of Canada: Proceedings of the October, 1985 Conference* (Cowansville: Yvon Blais Ltée, 1986), 221 at 222–25.

9 [1985] 2 S.C.R. 486.

of the *Charter* itself, given that the decision to entrench this document in our constitution was made not by the judiciary but by those very same democratically elected representatives. They and they alone established the bounds of constitutional adjudication and, as such, the task of giving the *Charter* life must be approached without any lingering doubts regarding its legitimacy.[10]

This new role for the Court is, of course, far removed from the theoretical underpinnings of parliamentary sovereignty. This is not to say that all vestiges of our former role have been eradicated. The presence of s. 33 of the *Charter*[11] might well be seen as indicative of our British constitutional origins in allowing the legislative branch of government to play a legal "trump card" and legitimize otherwise unconstitutional legislation if it so chooses. Nonetheless, the function of our Court has been altered irrevocably and has caused the role we play in Canada to conform substantially with that which the United States Supreme Court plays in its country. Both institutions are engaged, at least for the purposes of the *Canadian Charter of Rights and Freedoms* and the American Constitution with its Bill of Rights, in a process of judicial review—acting as a buffer between the individual and the government, so that the actions of the latter do not unduly encroach upon the constitutionally protected rights of the former. In no way does this mean however, that the two institutions engage in this task in an identical manner.

Let me state at the outset that I am not going to discuss distinctions which might loosely be referred to as "institutional." These may be interesting but are not directly pertinent to what I would like to discuss in this article. For my purposes, it does not really matter, for example, that the United States Supreme Court is at the federal apex of a binary legal system and does not have the authority to hear cases bearing on matters of state competence, whereas we are a general court of appeal with much greater jurisdictional range, not fettered in the same way. Nor am I going to discuss other differences in jurisdiction, although it is interesting to note that the Supreme Court of Canada plays an entirely appellate role in our legal system, whereas the United States Supreme Court has origi-

---

10 Ibid., 497.

11 Section 33 provides, inter alia: "(1) Parliament or the legislature of a province may expressly declare in an Act of Parliament or of the legislature, as the case may be, that the Act or a provision thereof shall operate notwithstanding a provision included in section 2 or sections 7 to 15 of this Charter.

"(2) An Act or a provision of an Act in respect of which a declaration made under this section is in effect shall have such operation as it would have but for the provision of the Charter referred to in the declaration."

nal jurisdiction in some matters[12] and, in 1794, even held a jury trial between the state of Georgia and one of its citizens when the former sought to execute a debt from the latter.[13] Rather, in my opinion, the most fundamental differences and, I might add, those of which we must be especially wary when examining U.S. constitutional case law, stem from differences in the two documents which the Courts have been called upon to interpret and apply. The documents produce distinct considerations and methods of reasoning.

Let us begin with an examination of where the two institutions derive the necessary authority to carry out the exercise of judicial review. In Canada that authority is vested in the Court by virtue of ss. 52(1) of the *Constitution Act, 1982*[14] and 24(1) of the *Charter*.[15] Although there may originally have been some debate as to whether these sections in fact gave the Court the necessary authority in this regard, the debate was laid to rest in *The Queen* v. *Therens*[16] by Mr. Justice LeDain, who pointed to the "clear constitutional mandate" of the recently enacted *Charter* as a significant difference between that document and the *Canadian Bill of Rights*.[17]

South of the border, the Supreme Court was left to assert for itself the power to declare void federal or state laws which are contrary to the Constitution. Article III, s. 1 of the Constitution provides merely that "[t]he judicial power of the United States shall be vested in one supreme Court, and in such inferior courts as the Congress may from time to time ordain and establish," and says little regarding what the ambit of that

---

12 See E.G. Hudon, "Growing Pains and Other Things: The Supreme Court of Canada and the Supreme Court of the United States," *Revue générale de droit* 17 (1986), 753 at 760–63 and *The Supreme Court at Work* (Washington: Congressional Quarterly Inc., 1990), 6 ff. The circumstances in which the U.S. Supreme Court has original jurisdiction include cases in which a state is a party and occasions which involve an ambassador.

13 *State of Georgia* v. *Brailsford*, 3 Dallas 1 (1794). *Oswald, administrator* v. *State of New York*, 2 Dallas 401 (1792), is another example of a jury trial held by the U.S. Supreme Court. See generally H.L. Carson, *The History of the Supreme Court of the United States* (Philadelphia: P.W. Ziegler, 1902), 1: 155 ff. , cited in Hudon, at 761.

14 The text reads as follows: "52(1) The Constitution of Canada is the supreme law of Canada, and any law that is inconsistent with the provisions of the Constitution is, to the extent of the inconsistency, of no force or effect."

15 It provides: "24(1) Anyone whose rights or freedoms, as guaranteed by this Charter, have been infringed or denied may apply to a court of competent jurisdiction to obtain such remedy as the court considers appropriate and just in the circumstances."

16 [1985] 1 S.C.R. 613.

17 Ibid., 638–39. The Canadian Bill of Rights, S.C. 1960, c. 44, was enacted as an ordinary statute of the federal Parliament. This meant that not only did the document not apply to provincial laws but it could also be repealed at any time. See generally P. Hogg, *Constitutional Law of Canada*, 639 ff., and M. Manning "The Role of the Supreme Court of Canada under the Canadian Charter of Rights and Freedoms," 226–27.

power may be. The question remained unresolved until 1803, when the Court rendered judgment in *Marbury* v. *Madison*[18] and it was necessary for Marshall C.J. to defend his Court's power to declare unconstitutional the conferral by Congress upon the Court of original jurisdiction in a matter not contemplated by the Constitution itself. His argument rested more upon general principles of constitutional government than upon specific provisions of the Constitution itself.

First, he observed that the Constitution was the fundamental law of the nation. It follows from this premise that any law repugnant to the Constitution is void. Second, that it was the particular duty of the courts to interpret the law. It therefore falls to the courts to pass judgment upon the constitutionality of a law alleged to run counter to its norms, otherwise the legislature would be omnipotent and be able to do what is expressly prohibited.[19]

The fact that, in Canada, we are given an explicit mandate to declare unconstitutional laws void, whereas our American counterparts have been forced to read that mandate into their supreme law is not, I think, insignificant, and gives rise to important jurisprudential differences such as the "political questions" doctrine. *Operation Dismantle* v. *The Queen*[20] concerned a request by a group of people who claimed that the decision of the federal cabinet to permit the U.S. government to test the cruise missile in Canadian airspace violated s. 7 *Charter* rights to life, liberty and security of the person. At one point the issue of the "political questions" doctrine was raised.

Now, one theory of the American "political questions" doctrine defines political questions in terms of the separation of powers as set out in the Constitution.[21] And, given that the authority to make international agreements, as well as to make decisions relating to national defence, belongs to the Crown, it was probably quite natural for the respondent in *Operation Dismantle* to seek to rely on the "political questions" doctrine in arguing that the decision to allow the Americans to test their nuclear

---

18 1 Cranch, 137 (1803).

19 Ibid., 176–78. See also L. Tribe, *American Constitutional Law*, 2d ed. (Mineola, New York: Foundation Press Inc., 1988), 23–26.

20 [1985] 1 S.C.R. 441.

21 Ibid., 469–70. Mme Justice Wilson also identifies another theoretical basis for the doctrine which, in her opinion, "roots [it] in what seems to me to be a rather vague concept of judicial "Prudence" whereby the courts enter into a calculation concerning the political wisdom of intervention into sensitive areas." In actual practice, the doctrine, as it has evolved over the years in case law, has come to mean that even when the U.S. Supreme Court has jurisdiction over a properly framed suit, it may decline to rule because it decides that a case raises a political question that should be resolved by one of the other two political branches.

capability within Canadian boundaries was beyond the scope of judicial review.

Madam Justice Bertha Wilson, writing on her own behalf, rejected the argument. She acknowledged that since the executive and legislative branches of government had exclusive jurisdiction in the salient areas, if the Court were being asked to rule on the wisdom of the cabinet's decision it would have to decline. And, since the *effect* of the request was to challenge the wisdom of the government's defence policy, it would be tempting to say that the Court ought not to involve itself in the matter. However, given that the actual question upon which the Court was being asked to rule was merely whether the policy violated the appellants' rights under s. 7 of the *Charter*, s. 24(1) mandates the Court to exercise its proper function.[22] She states:

> . . . s.24(1) of the Charter, also part of the Constitution, makes it clear that the adjudication of that question is the responsibility of "a court of competent jurisdiction." While the court is entitled to grant such remedy as it "considers appropriate and just in the circumstances," I do not think it is open to it to relinquish its jurisdiction, either on the basis that the issue is inherently non-justiciable or that it raises a so-called "political question."[23]

She continues:

> If we are to look at the Constitution for the answer to the question whether it is appropriate for the courts to "second guess" the executive on matters of defence, we would conclude that it is not appropriate. However, if what we are being asked to do is to decide whether any particular act of the executive violates the rights of the citizens, then it is not only appropriate that we answer the question; it is our obligation under the Charter to do so.[24]

There is no need to speculate here as to what the result of *Operation Dismantle* would have been had it been heard in the United States. The mere fact that there is a "political questions" doctrine of some sort, and that there is ongoing debate as to whether the Court is acting legitimately, serves to illustrate my point. By virtue of our having been given explicit constitutional authority in Canada to carry out judicial review, whereas our American counterparts have not, the legitimacy of our engaging in such review is not contentious and every department of the

---

22 Ibid., 471–72.

23 Ibid., 472.

24 Ibid.

government must ensure that its actions are in conformity with the *Charter*.

I would now like to turn my attention to another constitutional distinction which, although less striking, may be of some significance in the future. In the wake of the Civil War, the U.S. Constitution was amended significantly. Arguably, the Civil War amendment which has had the most startling impact on the American legal system is the Fourteenth, enacted in 1868, which, as well as providing that no persons shall be deprived of "life, liberty, or property, without due process of law" also provides that no person within the jurisdiction of any state may be deprived of "the equal protection of the laws."[25]

In reference to this amendment I wish to note first that it enhances the presence of property rights in the American Constitution, rights which had already found their way into the text of the Fifth Amendment in 1791. Their presence may find their origins in the American Revolution, where so much rancor and bitterness seemed to stem from the fact that the colonists were taxed and otherwise deprived of proprietary interests in a way which they perceived as quite unfair. I am not an American historian and do not wish to spend too much time on this point, but wish only to note that these property rights were specifically left out of the *Canadian Charter of Rights and Freedoms*.

I wish to focus instead on the equal protection clause of the Fourteenth Amendment and the debate over whether affirmative action programs are able to find constitutional justification within its parameters. This has been a subject of enormous disagreement for our American neighbors.

Reduced to their simplest terms, the arguments in favor of the constitutionality of such programs generally take forms such as the following:[26] a) Despite the fact that the framers of the constitutional amendments left out any specific reference to race in the textual body of the Fourteenth Amendment, it was their express preoccupation in propounding it to ensure that Blacks would not continue to be relegated to an inferior position by Whites, despite the enactment of the Thirteenth

---

25 The entire text of s. 1 of the Fourteenth Amendment reads as follows: "All persons born or naturalized in the United States, and subject to the jurisdiction thereof, are citizens of the United States and of the State wherein they reside. No State shall make or enforce any law which shall abridge the privileges or immunities of citizens of the United States; nor shall any State deprive any person of life, liberty, or property, without due process of law; nor deny to any person within its jurisdiction the equal protection of the laws."

26 See J.H. Ely, "The Constitutionality of Reverse Discrimination," *University of Chicago Law Review* 41 (1974), 723.

Amendment[27] which had outlawed slavery; hence, such programs are entirely in line with the intent of the Constitution and should perhaps not even be subject to any heightened scrutiny. In the alternative: *b*) Racial classifications are suspect, and are subject to special scrutiny, but ultimately they may be justified on the basis of a compelling state interest, usually framed in terms of the promotion of racial integration.[28]

On the other side of the debate are those who maintain that such programs are manifestly unconstitutional, since the intent of the framers of the Fourteenth Amendment was not to benefit Blacks in particular, but rather to outlaw racial discrimination once and for all. Therefore, if anyone is being denied something on the basis of their race to which they would otherwise have access, that denial equals racial discrimination. They argue in this vein that a given institution would not be permitted to favor applicants because they are white, and to permit that same institution to favor minorities would be to countenance a double standard. Rhetorical support for this position is found in Justice Harlan's well-known dissent in *Plessy* v. *Ferguson*,[29] in which he states that the Constitution is "color-blind."[30]

When the U.S. Supreme Court is faced with these issues, it has precious little to guide it in terms of the specific wording of the Constitution itself. In *Regents of the University of California* v. *Bakke*,[31] the respondent had been denied access to the appellant's medical school, pursuant to an admissions procedure which reserved 16 of the 100 places in each year's class for disadvantaged members of certain minority groups, while permitting any and all candidates to apply for one of the other 84 positions. The Court ruled that although affirmative action programs are not unconstitutional *per se*, they are suspect and must be justified on the basis of a

---

27 The Thirteenth Amendment reads as follows: "Section 1. Neither slavery nor involuntary servitude, except as a punishment for crime whereof the party shall have been duly convicted, shall exist within the United States, or any place subject to their jurisdiction.

"Section 2. Congress shall have power to enforce this article by appropriate legislation."

28 Ely, "Reverse Discrimination," 723–28. Ely goes on to argue that such programmes are constitutional but for much different reasons. He maintains that although schemes where the majority attempts to advantage itself at the expense of a less-powerful minority must be subject to the strictest scrutiny, the same suspicion ought not to arise where the majority disadvantages itself to benefit that minority.

29 163 U.S. 537 (1896).

30 Laurence Tribe argues that the statement of Justice Harlan, when taken in context, does not necessarily support the view that the U.S. Supreme Court "should act as if race had to be excluded from all governmental and legal classification." See Tribe, *American Constitutional Law*, 1524 ff.

31 438 U.S. 265 (1978).

compelling state interest.[32] The Court affirmed the decision of the California Supreme Court which had directed that the appellant be admitted to the faculty.

Some of these debates have been and will be avoided in Canada by the enactment of s. 15(2) of the *Canadian Charter of Rights and Freedoms*.[33] It provides, of course, that the equality guarantees of s. 15(1) are not to be construed as precluding programs of the type which was at issue in *Bakke*. Although many questions remain unanswered with respect to this section, we may at a minimum expect to avoid many of the fundamental controversies which have been plaguing the U.S. Supreme Court for the better part of a generation. This section of the *Charter* represents an important distinction between the Canadian and U.S. Constitutions, and hopefully ensures that when our Court engages in judicial review it will not be in relation to cases like *Bakke*.

I now wish to turn to what is, in my opinion, the most significant difference between the two documents—the presence of s. 1 in our *Charter*.[34] This section is of vital importance because it means that in Canada we are able to give an extremely wide interpretation to the enumerated right as a substantive matter and then engage in the process of determining whether any limitation on that right may subsequently be justified by the party seeking to encroach upon it. The Americans, of course, find themselves without any such clause and have been forced to limit their rights at the level of the right itself. This results in radically different reasoning processes.

I will begin with the American position. Freedom of speech is protected by the First Amendment, the wording of which is anything but compromising in its tone.[35] It begins: "a Congress shall make *no* law . . . abridging . . ." and then goes on to enumerate a list of freedoms, including freedom of speech. It should be apparent that a society which permits its members to go about saying anything they want, whenever

---

32 Ibid., 314 ff. See also M.C. Daly, "Affirmative Action, Equal Access and the Supreme Court's 1988 Term: The Rehnquist Court Takes a Sharp Turn to the Right," *Hofstra Law Review* 18 (1990), 1057.

33 The exact wording of the section is as follows: "(2) Subsection (1) does not preclude any law, program or activity that has as its object the amelioration of conditions of disadvantaged individuals or groups including those that are disadvantaged because of race, national or ethnic origin, colour, religion, sex, age or mental or physical disability."

34 The text of s. 1 reads as follows: "1. The Canadian Charter of Rights and Freedoms guarantees the rights and freedoms set out in it subject only to such reasonable limits prescribed by law as can be demonstrably justified in a free and democratic society."

35 The text reads as follows: "Congress shall make no law respecting an establishment of religion, or prohibiting the free exercise thereof; or abridging the freedom of speech, or of the press; or the right of the people peaceably to assemble, and to petition the Government for a redress of grievances."

they want, will undoubtedly encounter some difficulties. As support for this proposition, one need only look as far as libel laws or the old law school hypothetical of whether or not it ought to be permissible to shout "Fire!" in a crowded theater.[36] The question for the American courts became, therefore, what kind of limits are justified when the wording of the section to be interpreted (namely, the First Amendment) speaks only in terms of absolutes?

Not surprisingly, the question has been contested for some time. It now appears that it is permissible for the government to abridge freedom of speech in certain instances, but the validity of the infringement depends to a great extent on the type of restriction the government pursues. If the government takes aim at information, ideas or actions, and attempts to control their dissemination either because of the specific message that is conveyed or because of the effects which may be produced by their dissemination, the Court will be rather strict. It will regard such regulation as unconstitutional unless the government can show that the message poses a "clear and present danger," constitutes a falsehood and also defames its object, or otherwise falls within the other categories in which regulation may occur with less onerous scrutiny by the judiciary. However, if the government is merely incidentally impairing the flow of ideas while pursuing other goals, by either limiting an activity through which ideas might be conveyed, or by enforcing rules which might otherwise hinder this flow, the Court has been much more lenient. In such a situation, the regulation will be presumptively constitutional, even if it applies to conduct which conveys a meaning, as long as the restriction is not "undue."[37]

The difference between these two schemes of constitutional adjudication is perhaps best seen through the example of hate literature. During

---

36 The hypothetical is trite but apt for the purposes of the discussion at hand. Its origins may be traced to the decision of Holmes J. in *Schenck* v. *United States*, 249 U.S. 47 (1919), in which the "clear and present danger" test of speech infringement was enunciated by the Court. The appellants had been circulating leaflets critical of conscription in contravention of the *Espionage Act* of 1917. At 52 Holmes J. argues: "We admit that in many places and in ordinary times the defendants in saying all that was said in the circular would have been within their constitutional rights. But the character of every act depends upon the circumstances in which it is done. The most stringent protection of free speech would not protect a man in falsely shouting fire in a theatre and causing a panic. It does not even protect a man from an injunction against uttering words that may have all the effect of force. *Gompers* v. *Buck's Stove and Range Co.*, 221 U.S. 418 (1911), at 439. The question in every case is whether the words used are used in such circumstances and are of such a nature as to create a clear and present danger that they will bring about the substantive evils that Congress has a right to prevent. It is a question of proximity and degree."

37 See generally Tribe, *American Constitutional Law*, 789–94 and K. Greenawalt, "Free Speech in Canada and the United States," *Law and Contemporary Problems* 55 (1992), 1.

World War II several state legislatures, in an effort to prevent the racism that marked Hitler's Germany, enacted group libel statutes. These statutes extended the rules of defamation against individuals to groups. In 1950 a resident of Chicago, Joseph Beauharnais, was convicted and fined $200 for running afoul of a provision which had been enacted by the State of Illinois. The statute prohibited, among other things, the distribution of material which portrays "depravity, criminality, unchastity, or lack of virtue of a class of citizens of any race, colour, creed, etc."[38] Mr. Beauharnais was apparently the leader of a group called "The White Circle League" and had supervised and participated in the distribution of leaflets which called for the mobilization of all "normal" white people on the basis that "if persuasion and the need to prevent the white race from becoming mongrelized by the negro will not unite us then the aggressions . . . rapes, robberies, knives, guns and marijuana of the negro, surely will." Attached to this diatribe was an application for membership in The White Circle League.

Now, if the statute under which Beauharnais was charged had been enacted under the rubric of some sort of outright prohibition against distributing pamphlets on the streets of Illinois because of the litter they produce then, assuming that the effects of the regulation did not overshoot the goal which they were seeking to achieve, the government could have argued that the law is more properly considered under the second scheme of restriction and should be the subject of more latitude on the part of the Court. However, the prohibition at issue here was specifically aimed at content and, as such, was seen as necessitating a more circumspect approach although, of course, that is not to say that constitutionality was necessarily precluded.

Mr. Justice Frankfurter, for the Court, noted that even when specific content is proscribed "there are certain well-defined and narrowly limited classes of speech, the prevention and punishment of which have never been thought to raise any constitutional problem,"[39] including obscenity, libel, and what has loosely been termed "fighting words." He reasoned that such words are more likely to cause a breach of the peace and that, given that they are so far removed from the rationale of First Amendment protection, any benefit that would otherwise be derived from their entry into societal discourse would surely be outweighed by the dangerous consequences they could conceivably have. As such, the material in question ought not to receive constitutional protection and the statute ought not to be struck down. Mr. Justice Frankfurter, of course, recognized the fundamental importance of the First Amendment and the Bill of Rights to American society, but was quick to point out that the liberties

---

38 *Beauharnais* v. *Illinois*, 343 U.S. 250 at 251 (1952).

39 Ibid., 255.

enshrined are not without limits, and that the danger posed by racist zealots was all too real, given the climate of the time. The Vinson Court accordingly upheld the provision by a 5–4 majority.

I should note that since *Beauharnais* the American view on hate literature has changed somewhat, and the courts are less likely to give their approval to such content-based speech regulation.[40] However, that is of less importance for my immediate purposes than the fact that, despite the wording of the First Amendment, there is no absolute right to say anything one wants in the United States—limitations had to be read into the rights by the judiciary.

The presence of s. 1 of the *Charter* permits our judiciary to give broader scope to the substantive right. This was specifically recognized by Chief Justice Dickson in *The Queen v. Keegstra*,[41] where the constitutionality of the hate literature provisions of our *Criminal Code* was at issue. After reviewing the jurisprudence which had been generated by our Court under s. 2(b), he noted that the established procedure for adjudication in this area involves two distinct steps. The first entails the determination of whether the form or act of expression comes within the scope of the interests protected by s. 2(b). Only if that question is answered in the affirmative does one move on to the next question of whether, in the final analysis, the expression deserves protection from state interference under the structure of the *Charter*.[42] This bifurcated approach, we are told, was made necessary by the presence of s. 1 and in *Ford*[43] "permitted the Court to give a large and liberal interpretation to s. 2(b), on the facts of the case, leading to the inclusion of commercial expression within its ambit."[44]

Having laid out the proper approach to be followed in cases of this kind, the Chief Justice went on to deal with the first question—namely,

---

40 See, e.g., *Collin v. Smith*, 578 F. 2d 1197 (1978), a well-known case in which the Court of Appeals for the 7th Circuit struck down a city ordinance in the City of Skokie which would have prohibited members of the American Nazi Party from marching through a neighborhood which was home to many holocaust survivors. The march was ultimately never held, however. Chief Justice Dickson examines the American jurisprudence in this area in *The Queen v. Keegstra*, [1990] 3 S.C.R. 697 at 738–44. See also Tribe, *American Constitutional Law*, 789–930 and T.A. Aleinikoff "Constitutional Law in the Age of Balancing," *Yale Law Journal* 96 (1986), 943 at 967–68. Aleinikoff argues that, instead of viewing all content-based regulation as prima facie unconstitutional and striking down such legislation unless it could be fitted into prescribed exceptions, the Court has now established a "sliding scale" of protection based upon the perceived value of the speech in question.

41 *The Queen v. Keegstra*, 743–44.

42 Ibid., 728.

43 *Ford v. Attorney General of Québec*, [1988] 2 S.C.R. 712.

44 *The Queen v. Keegstra*, 728.

whether the activity of the litigant falls within the scope of s. 2(b). Note the wide interpretation given to the right. Only if the activity in question does not convey or does not attempt to convey a meaning, or if it does so in a violent form, will the activity fall outside the purview of the section.[45]

This same methodology has been used in Canada in a litany of cases dealing with the issue of freedom of expression. I cite for the purposes of example the watershed case of *Irwin Toy*,[46] which ostensibly gave birth to the structure of adjudication we are currently discussing. Soon after that came the *Criminal Code Reference*[47] and *Rocket v. Royal College of Dental Surgeons*.[48] In none of these cases did the Court find it necessary to balance a myriad of interests at the level of the substantive right. In fact, this notion of balancing factors or of adjudicating according to a sliding scale of protection which, as we have already seen, was made necessary in the American jurisprudence by the absolute terms in which their rights are cast, is specifically rejected at this stage.

This leads us to consider the nature of s. 1 itself. We have seen that the presence of this section permits our Court to give a broad interpretation to the rights which follow on its heels. This gives rise to an interesting irony. The dominant theme of what I have been discussing has been the differences in reasoning which exist between our Court and that in the United States. The most important difference, in my opinion, is this last one—the existence of s. 1, which allows us to give wide scope to the rights of the *Charter* when engaging in judicial review of government activity alleged to infringe those rights. This fact, as well as the other differences already discussed, means that we must proceed with caution when looking to American jurisprudence for guidance in giving the *Charter* life. The Courts have been careful to heed this warning and have rejected the American approach where it has been seen as inapplicable in the Canadian context. Indeed, the Chief Justice, in *Keegstra*, refused to follow the American position on hate literature, noting:

> Where s. 1 operates to accentuate a uniquely Canadian vision of a free and democratic society . . . we must not hesitate to depart from the path taken in the United States.

---

45 Ibid., 729.

46 *Irwin Toy Ltd.* v. *Attorney General of Québec*, [1989] 1 S.C.R. 927.

47 *Reference re Sections 193 and 195.1(1)(c) of the Criminal Code (Manitoba)*, [1990] 1 S.C.R. 1123.

48 [1990] 2 S.C.R. 232.

In this vein, he saw the international commitment to the eradication of hate literature, as well as the special role given to equality and multiculturalism, as necessitating a stark divergence.[49]

In another example, *Reference re Section 94 (2) of the British Columbia Motor Vehicles Act,*[50] the meaning of s. 7's "principles of fundamental justice" was at issue. Mr. Justice Lamer (as he then was), on the basis of ss. 52, 33 and 1, not only found the American jurisprudence irrelevant to the issue at hand, but rejected its assistance in the anterior step of framing the issue into the distinction between substantive and procedural due process. In his view, it would have been doing our own constitution a great disservice to permit the American debate to define the issue for Canada, while ignoring what he called the "fundamental structural differences between the two constitutions." Incidentally, Mr. Justice Lamer went on to question the very nature of the dichotomy itself, arguing that besides being a foreign distinction and inapplicable to our own law, it creates difficulties by erecting artificial boundaries between concepts whose limits are inherently overlapping and unamenable to precise delineation.[51]

On one point I wish to be absolutely clear, however. I am not in any way saying that the Court ought never to look to American jurisprudence for guidance. To reject two hundred years of constitutional experience would be to reject an extremely valuable resource. As Professor Cameron has indicated:

> Our judiciary can contemplate the jurisprudential foundations for different constitutional solutions before adopting them, can realize the difficulties certain interpretations of the Charter may produce, and can improve doctrines which have produced problems of implementation in the United States. More important, awareness of the controversies which are inherent in rights review can alert our courts to the institutional consequences of over-zealous intervention.[52]

This brings me to the irony to which I alluded earlier. I mentioned that the very presence of s. 1 is one of the distinctive features of the *Charter* which must make us pause when considering the applicability of American jurisprudence. Yet, at the same time, that very section only

---

49 *The Queen* v. *Keegstra,* 743.

50 [1985] 2 S.C.R. 486.

51 Ibid. 498. See also (Hon.) G.V. LaForest, "The Use of International and Foreign Material in the Supreme Court of Canada," *Canadian Council on International Law* 17 (1988), 230 at 238 and J. Cameron "The Motor Vehicle Reference and the Relevance of American Doctrine in Charter Adjudication," in R. Sharpe, ed., *Charter Litigation* (Toronto: Butterworths, 1987), 69.

52 Cameron, ibid., 73.

guarantees the rights contained in subsequent provisions to such reasonable limits "as can be justified in a *free and democratic society*." In my opinion, this is tantamount to a directive to engage in a comparative exercise and research the position in other jurisdictions, for, and in saying this I am referring to lawyers and judges alike, we would be remiss in our duties as the trustees of the legal system in this country if we blindly accepted the Canadian experience as the last word on how a free and democratic society ought to conduct itself. This is not to say that we have to accept and adopt what we find elsewhere. If we arrive at the conclusion that the interests of our country would be better served by not following the examples set abroad, that is entirely acceptable and understandable. But we will still be better off for having engaged in the comparative process.[53]

By way of conclusion let me summarize what I have been discussing. Until 1982 and the enactment of the *Canadian Charter of Rights and Freedoms*, the Supreme Court of Canada functioned in accordance with the prevailing notions of British constitutionalism. Subsequent to the entrenchment of those rights, however, our Court took on a role similar to that of the highest court of the United States, and began to hold legislation up against strict norms. In engaging in this process of judicial review we may invalidate legislation which, for one reason or another, does not pass muster against those norms.

Nonetheless, although the role each Court performs in this regard is similar, there are significant differences in the way each carries out its role. These may be attributed to the respective constitutional documents each is called upon to interpret and apply. One of these differences, I remarked, was that the Supreme Court of Canada was given explicit authority to undertake the process of judicial review, whereas our American counterpart was forced to assert that mandate for itself, their Constitution being silent on the issue. I further argued that this has resulted in a type of "political questions" doctrine, a doctrine which has been shown to be inapplicable in the Canadian context.

I went on to discuss the relevance of s. 15(2) in the Canadian *Charter* and stated that its presence might in future preclude some of the rancor we see in the United States over the issue of affirmative action plans. I also submitted that the most significant difference in our two constitutional systems was to be found in the inclusion of a limitation section in our *Charter*—s. 1—which has allowed our Court to give an extremely broad interpretation to the rights and freedoms which follow it. This section, I said, led to an interesting irony, for it simultaneously caused us to be on our guard when examining American jurisprudence and instruc-

---

53 See LaForest, "Use of International and Foreign Material," 236–37.

ted us to look at other "free and democratic" societies when called upon to interpret *Charter* guarantees.

And so, I conclude with a reminder of my final point—that in interpreting this document we need to keep in mind the distinctions between the Courts and the constitutions with which each has been entrusted. We must, of course, avoid adopting American jurisprudence simply because it exists. But to reject the American experience out of hand and to refuse to engage in its examination, as at least a comparative exercise, would surely be as great a mistake—a mistake we as judges and lawyers cannot afford to make.

Public Policy and the Judicial Role

Madam Justice Rosalie Silberman Abella
of the Court of Appeal of Ontario

Judges have always been involved with public policy. And judges, in their role either in the interpretation of statutes or in the selective application of precedent, have always been involved in the development of law. Why then is there now an unfolding drama about the appropriate limits to judicial power and an intense curiosity about the backgrounds of the men and women who wield it?[1] The answer is, of course, the *Charter*.[2]

What the *Charter*'s klieg lights did as they illuminated the long-running play called "The Judicial Role" was to spotlight a participant whose talents the audience had not previously appreciated. That participant was public policy.

For centuries, and at least from the time of Montesquieu, public policy had been in all three of the play's acts in English-speaking Western democracies—in Act 1, as Common Law; in Act 2, as Statutory Interpretation; and in Act 3, as Constitutional Review. But it rarely had a speaking part, and was almost always billed far below the star, judicial neutrality. But when the *Charter* was added to this country's constitution, what came prominently into the nation's consciousness was the realization that public policy, far from playing a minor role in the judicial script, had in

---

1 In the United States and England, this generation in particular has spawned literature attempting to identify the relationship between the backgrounds and decisions of judges. See, e.g., M. Shapiro, *Law and Politics in the Supreme Court* (New York: Free Press of Glencoe, 1964), and R. Stevens, *Law and Politics: the House of Lords as a Judicial Body: 1800–1976* (Chapel Hill, N.C.: University of North Carolina Press, 1978). But the examination of the judicial role is neither a new preoccupation nor one fixated on constitutional issues. See O.W. Holmes, *The Common Law* (Boston: Little, Brown and Co., 1881), and B.N. Cardozo, *The Nature of the Judicial Process* (New Haven: Yale University Press, 1921).

2 *Canadian Charter of Rights and Freedoms*, Part I of the *Constitution Act, 1982*, being Schedule B of the *Canada Act 1982* (U.K.), 1982, c. 11 [hereinafter *Charter*].

fact been a co-star all along.[3] With the *Charter*, the public wondered whether policy wasn't being given too pronounced a form of recognition. It is one thing, after all, for the courts to enunciate policy in tort law, and even to revolutionize it as the judges did in cases like *Rookes* v. *Barnard*;[4] however, what to the legal profession may have seemed like Copernican revolutions in contract or tort seemed largely inconsequential to the wider public. The attribution to unelected judges of the responsibility for the final determination of fundamental issues no less controversial and political than human rights—frequently and essentially the equitable distribution of scarce commodities like opportunities[5]—brought upon us a tempest of inquiry into the judicial relationship with public policy. For some, the tempest revealed public policy as Caliban, a grotesque monster to be kept under control. For others, the tempest was a cathartic exegesis finally permitting public policy, like Prospero, to attain openly its proper status.

As the storm raged, two primary concerns swirled through the land: had the *Charter* compromised judicial neutrality by making public policy so conspicuously a partner in the determination of how rights and freedoms were to be allocated; and had the *Charter* compromised the historic jurisdictional division of lawmaking authority between the legislature and the courts? Once the tempest subsides, my own prognosis is that in the end it will be concluded that nothing has been inappropriately compromised with the *Charter*; it has simply spotlighted, rather than created, a judicial role, and what we are seeing, because of the public nature of the *Charter*'s impact and issues, is a difference in degree in judicial decisionmaking and the role of public policy, and not in kind.[6]

The first subject under review must necessarily be judicial neutrality, whose examination becomes vital if we are to prevent *Charter* adjudication from becoming an eternally frustrating Sisyphean task to lawyers and judges who may otherwise feel they are being made to present a play different from the one they rehearsed. The main fear, I think, is that an explicit judicial acknowledgment of the role public policy plays in decisionmaking invites accusations that the judiciary is usurping a

---

3 P.H. Winfield, "Public Policy in the English Common Law," *Harvard Law Review* 42 (1928), 76 at 77.

4 [1964] A.C. 1129 (H.L.).

5 L.G. Scarman, "Human Rights in a Plural Society," in R. Dhavan, R. Sudarshan, and S. Kharshid, eds., *Judges and the Judicial Power* (London: Sweet and Maxwell, 1985), 107.

6 L.L. Jaffe, *English and American Judges as Lawmakers* (Oxford: Clarendon Press, 1969), 5.

political function reserved to the legislatures, namely, the requirement to consider public policy when formulating law. The term "public policy" radiates a political heat judges fear will smother the light of their neutrality and independence. It therefore becomes important to define "public policy" and "judicial neutrality" in order to understand why policy considerations (as well as moral considerations) are an integral part of law, and therefore legal interpretation, and why judicial neutrality need not be, or need not be seen to be, or need not ever have been, impaired by the express or implied application of policy considerations to decision-making.

"Public policy" is the philosophical blueprint for the systems and rules that regulate social and political conduct.[7] It is both a strategy and an objective; that is, at any given time it may be either hortatory or derivative, inspirational or reflective of what is perceived to be in a community's optimal self-interest. It is the compendium of directives under which communities, of which judges are members, evolve. It may or may not enjoy a consensus. It has an inherent fluidity and may change within generations, from generation to generation, or may not change for several generations. Ultimately it defines a society's character. Despite the fact that it can rarely be empirically tested, it forms the basis of law. It has been described as an "unruly horse,"[8] though not a "Pegasus."[9] In its statutory incarnation, it may either represent a Faustian bargain between the legislature and the majority in exchange for continued electoral success where such a consensus is seen to exist; or it may represent a Kantian *a cappella* refrain, seeking daringly to redefine the social contract without benefit of majority accompaniment where the consensus is nowhere to be seen. It is, in short, an imprecise yet crucial progenitor of the rules we choose to live by.

Above all, however, the concept of public policy is value-laden.[10] Any given public policy stands for certain values or a code of morality with which we intend or expect most of society to abide. The legislature's basic function, whether it does so consciously or unconsciously, is to determine which values will be translated into statutory law based on a

---

7 R.S. Abella, "Public Policy and Canada's Judges: The Impact of the Charter of Rights and Freedoms," *Law Society Gazette* 20 (1986), 217 at 227.

8 Public policy "is a very unruly horse, and when once you get astride it you never know where it will carry you": *Richardson* v. *Mellish* (1824), 2 Bing. 229, 130 E.R. 249 at 252, *per* Burrough J.

9 Winfield, "Public Policy," 91: "But none, at any rate in the present day, has looked upon it as a Pegasus that might soar beyond the momentary needs of the community."

10 M. Schneiderman, "Toward a Public Policy Oriented Jurisprudence: 'Principles' as a Substitute for 'Rules' in the Legal Syllogism," *Saskatchewan Law Review* 34 (1969), 314.

perception of public interests, the importunings of constituents, the pre-vailing partisan ideology, collegial input, and perceived electoral risk.

In this legislative blender, the application of public policy is purely a political judgment. But this in no way detracts from its fundamental character as originating from values. It means, rather, that the values that originally inspired the statute are subject to political realities and may not emerge intact or unchanged. The final legislative product is still called public policy, but it is public policy as political compromise. It is political in the purest sense of the word: an accountable institution—the legisla-ture—assesses how best to balance societal values with the prospect of re-election. Essentially, the application of public policy is an exercise in the promulgation as law of selected perceived majority wishes.

The courts, in their relationship with public policy, are also involved in an evaluative process. The process, however, is interpretive and not blatantly political. It is impervious to electoral judgment, unrestricted by the constraints of partisan ideologies, and relatively immune to the requirement of compromise. The public policy values the court is there-fore free to evaluate are related to but independent from the political values which motivated the existence or absence of a statute. Parliament passes laws, courts decide what the laws mean,[11] and in so doing courts react, at least to some extent, either consciously or unconsciously, positively or negatively, to what they feel are the public policy values that underlie the statute. And if one feels that this interpretive role has the potential for interfering with the Parliamentary supremacy which emerged triumphant from the Glorious Revolution of 1688, overthrowing the obstructive Stuart Kings, it was ever thus.[12] The interpretive judicial function, whether of statute or common law, has always necessarily in-volved the sifting of normative considerations, not only because laws derive from and operate in a social system and culture of values,[13] but because judges are conditioned and operate in the same system.[14] Insofar as the sifting of legal choices is the sifting of policy values,[15] judges, in

---

11 "This flexibility and capacity for growth and adaptation is the peculiar boast and excellence of the common law": *Hurtado* v. *California*, 110 U.S. 516 at 530 (1884).

12 E. McWhinney, in *Judicial Review*, 4th ed. (Toronto: University of Toronto Press, 1969) at 238 refers to the "dynamic process of legal evolution" which keeps pace with society.

13 M. Shapiro, "Political Jurisprudence," *Kentucky Law Journal* 52 (1964), 294.

14 See, e.g., *Sommersett's Case* (1772), Lofft (Easter Term, 3 Geo. 3) 1, 98 E.R. 499, where Lord Mansfield rejected a slave-owner's claim for the return of his slave on the grounds that slavery was repugnant to English ideas. See also R. Hiers, "Normative Analysis in Judicial Determinations of Public Policy," *Journal of Law and Religion* 3 (1985), 77.

15 M.S. McDougal, *The Application of Constitutive Prescriptions* (New York: Association of the Bar of the City of New York, 1978).

interpreting law, do consider and always have considered, in addition to logic and precedent, the values or policy implications their legal conclusions represent.[16] But because judges tended to be wary about appearing to make policy judgments which some thought were more acceptably made in a political forum,[17] they have historically used ano-dyne terminology to shield the exercise of policy choice from conspicuous view. Policy-laden words like "reasonable," "arbitrary," "due process," "good faith," "unjustified," or "discretion" are what Learned Hand called a "protective veil of adjectives"[18] for insulating judicial policymaking from censure for violating the accepted spheres of policymaking. When judges interpret terms of art like "best interests," "discrimination,"[19] "unfair labour practice," or "responsibility for damage caused by his fault,"[20] are they not making policy judgments? Do not the areas of family law,[21] especially custody and support, sentencing, damages in tort, [22]contractual interpretation,[23] and the entire history of common law[24]

---

16 Hiers, "Normative Analysis," 78.

17 Winfield, "Public Policy," 86.

18 L. Hand, *The Bill of Rights* (Cambridge, Mass.: Harvard University Press, 1958), 70.

19 The results-oriented concept of "discrimination" sprang full-panoplied from judicial foreheads in *Griggs* v. *Duke Power*, 401 U.S. 424 (1971).

20 This article, Art. 1053 of the *Civil Code of Lower Canada*, provides the only legislative guidance for the development of the Quebec law of delict or quasi-delict (analogous to tort in the common law).

21 Consider the introduction, without benefit of statutory guidance, of concepts like joint custody, constructive trusts, or legal representation for children. In *Besant* v. *Wood* (1879), 12 Ch. 605, for example, a custody issue inspired the judge to observe, at 620, that it was "a branch of law which depends upon what is commonly called 'public policy,' which in turn was a matter of individual opinion, because what one man, or one judge, and . . . one woman . . . might think against public policy, another might think altogether excellent public policy." Is this case a mother lost custody because of the embarrassment she was causing her husband in using her married name to publish articles on "The Rights of Women."

22 *Rylands* v. *Fletcher* (1868), L.R. 3 H.L. 330, 19 L.T. 220; *Rookes* v. *Barnard*, [1964] A.C. 1129 (H.L.); *Overseas Tankship* v. *Morts Dock & Engineering Co.*, [1961] A.C. 388 (The Wagon Mound); *Overseas Tankship* v. *Miller Steamship Co. Pty*, [1967] 1 A.C. 617 (*Wagon Mound No. 2*); and *M'Alister (Donoghue)* v. *Stevenson*, [1932] A.C. 562. See also P.S. Atiyah, "From Principles to Pragmatism: Changes in the Function of the Judicial Process and the Law," *Iowa Law Review* 65 (1980), 1249 at 1254 and B.S. Markensinis, "Policy Factors and the Law of Tort," in D. Mendes da Costa, ed., *The Cambridge Lectures* (Toronto: Butterworths, 1981), 199.

23 See *Davies* v. *Davies* (1887), 36 Ch. D. 359, dealing with covenants in restraint of trade. The Court at 364 noted that the "doctrine on this subject is founded on 'public policy'," and at 365 said, "it was considered public policy to assist *England* to become a nation of traders."

represent processes whereby judges evaluated which values or policies ought to be operational?

This is not mere reliance on semantics to distract the public from observing the judicial trespass on Parliament's property. Considering policy is a function of the court's legitimate role in legal interpretation, a role necessarily evaluative of policy. The *Charter*, therefore, has allowed public policy to come out of the judicial closet and more openly to participate in a policy partnership it has in reality been a part of for centuries.[25]

Moreover, I do not think the neutrality of judges is at risk, partly because it may be that true neutrality is a myth,[26] and partly because I am not sure what neutrality really means. The usual antonyms in a judicial context for neutral are conservative and liberal. But what, for example, is supposed to be the liberal view of *in vitro* fertilization, the conservative one of separate school funding, or the progressive one of *Wisconsin v. Yoder*?[27] We must define more clearly what we are talking about and move away from the unproductive exercise of "label-pasting."[28]

Neutrality and impartiality are the words most often used to describe the primary virtue a judicial temperament should reflect. The importance of the virtue is obvious—the entire purpose of judicial and quasi-judicial adjudication is to provide a peaceful and civilized method of dispute resolution where the law[29] or the application of certain facts to it,[30] as between individuals or as between individuals and the state, is in

---

24 J. Stone, *Precedent and Law: Dynamics of Common Law Growth* (Sydney: Butterworths, 1985), 31. "The common law is an example *par excellence* of this flexible choicemaking process." See also ibid., 112; and J. Bell, "Three Models of the Judicial Function," in Dhavan, Sudarshan and Kharshid, *Judges and Judicial Power*, 57. Lord Devlin, in "Judges and Lawmakers," *Modern Law Review* 39 (1979), 1 at 13, feels that Lord Halsbury's prohibition against self-reversal, which lasted from 1898 to 1966, prevented the House of Lords from moving with the times and was "utterly antagonistic to the spirit of the common law."

25 For a slightly different approach, see W.R. Lederman, "Democratic Parliaments, Independent Courts and the Canadian Charter of Rights and Freedoms," *Queen's Law Journal* 11 (1986), 1 at 24, where it is argued that the *Charter* has changed the equilibrium point between the main functions of the legislature (i.e., law-making) and the courts (i.e., law application). It is nevertheless implied that each has had a part in performing the function of the other before the advent of the *Charter*. Only the balance has been altered. In any case, Lederman asserts that the "courts and legislatures are partners and not rivals" in the delivery of justice under the Rule of Law.

26 A.S. Miller and R.E. Howell, "The Myth of Neutrality in Constitutional Adjudication," in L.W. Levy, ed., *Judicial Review and the Supreme Court* (New York: Harper and Row, 1967), 198.

27 406 U.S. 205 (1972).

28 Hiers, "Normative Analysis," 82.

29 Atiyah, "Principles to Pragmatism," 1249; Devlin, "Judges and Lawmakers," 3.

30 Stone, *Precedent and Law*, 110.

dispute. In this role, it is fundamental that the people who decide the outcome are free from inappropriate or undue influence, independent in fact and appearance, and intellectually willing and able to hear the evidence and arguments with an open mind. If this is what neutral or impartial means, then all adjudicators should be it.

But neutrality and impartiality do not and cannot mean that the judge has no prior conceptions, opinions or sensibilities about society's values. It only means that those preconceptions ought not close his or her mind to the evidence and arguments presented. All law is about values,[31] values are about public policy, and public policy and laws are about morality.[32] We cannot pretend that judges are prohibited from being influenced by them, whether as "liberals" or "conservatives." Antonin Scalia admits that it is "foolish to deny the relevance of moral perceptions to law,"[33] Lon Fuller talks about law's "inner morality,"[34] Holmes implicitly acknowledges that values are the inarticulate major premise of judicial reasoning;[35] and Emmett Hall explains every decision as a "court's decision about how competing interests and values ought to be reconciled."[36] Lord MacMillan once said that "in almost every case, . . . it would be possible to decide the issue either way with reasonable legal justification."[37] In the area of disputed law, in other words, there is no right answer.[38] The answer or interpretation we choose, therefore, will be based to some extent on extra-legal premises like values.[39]

Judicial precedent is, of course, the major interpretive guide, but a judge can always choose from among different *rationes decidendi* in any

---

31 R.W.M. Dias, *Jurisprudence*, 5th ed. (London: Butterworths, 1985), 196.

32 H.L.A. Hart, *The Concept of Law* (Oxford: Clarendon Press, 1961).

33 A. Scalia, "Morality, Pragmatism and the Legal Order," *Harvard Journal of Law and Public Policy* 9 (1986), 123 at 123.

34 See L.L. Fuller, *The Morality of Law* (New Haven, Conn.: Yale University Press, 1969), 162, where Fuller equates the law's inner morality with dignity: "Every departure from Law's Inner Morality is an affront to man's dignity as a responsible agent."

35 *Lochner* v. *New York*, 198 U.S. 45 at 74–76 (1905).

36 E.M. Hall, "Law Reform and the Judiciary's role," *Osgoode Hall Law Journal* 10 (1972), 399 at 405.

37 Lord MacMillan, *Law and Custom* (Edinburgh: Thomas Nelson and Sons, 1949), 48.

38 Winfield, "Public Policy," at 88 observes that even in cases like *Egerton* v. *Brownlo* (1853), 4 H.L.Cas. 1, 10 E.R. 359, where public policy had to "fight for its life," two of the judges might agree that public policy was applicable, but they could still arrive at "opposite conclusions in applying it." More recently, see the range of interpretive possibilities evidenced by the different courts in *Chase* v. *R.*, 40 C.R. (3d) 282, reversed [1987] 2 S.C.R. 293, interpreting "sexual assault" in the *Criminal Code*, R.S.C. 1970, c. C-34, now R.S.C. 1985, c. C-46.

39 Stone, *Precedent and Law*, 29 and 109.

given precedent.[40] The outcome will depend on which *ratio* is selected. The same is true for the principle of *stare decisis*. In *stare decisis*, we draw legal conclusions by analogy,[41] not mimicry. Julius Stone has built an academic career on demonstrating compellingly that law is full of indeterminate categories,[42] that the application of *stare decisis* is selective, and that all adjudicators reflect in their decisions partly precedent, partly their experience[43] and partly their own notions of justice.[44]

An American judge in 1929 went so far as to write an article entitled "The Function of the 'Hunch' in Judicial Decision."[45] This public acknowledgment of judicial indebtedness to the role of instinct may be too cavalier, but it is hard to quarrel with Cardozo when he says that judges do not stand on "chill and distant heights" and that everyone, litigant or judge, is a complex of instincts, emotions, habits and convictions.[46] In other words, judges, like everyone else, receive information into intellectual baskets whose shape is partially formed by life experience, by legal knowledge, by culture and by personal vision. Inevitably, the information tends to take the shape of the cerebral basket, perhaps not determinatively but arguably presumptively. There is, after all, a critical difference between an open mind and an empty one. As Jerome Frank pointed out, "a mind containing no preconceptions . . . would be that of an utterly emotionless human being."[47]

Absolute justice, to paraphrase Bentham, may be unattainable—there is no absolute right or wrong answer in many cases[48]—but we can certainly attempt to reduce injustice by, among other things, acknowledging that judges have operational intellectual, moral, cultural and social perceptions which may guide, as opposed to dictate, their legal conclusions.[49] I consider this observation axiomatic and in no way derogatory of the judicial function, particularly when one appreciates that there are,

---

40 Ibid., 5.

41 R. Cross, *Precedent in English Law*, 3d ed. (Oxford: Clarendon Press, 1977), 24.

42 Stone, *Precedent and Law*, 113.

43 See also Holmes, *The Common Law*, 1.

44 J. Stone, *The Province and Function of Law* (Sydney: Associated General Publications, 1946), *Legal System and Lawyers' Reasonings* (Stanford: Stanford University Press, 1964), and *Precedent and Law: Dynamics of Common Law Growth* (Sydney: Butterworths, 1985).

45 J.C. Hutcheson, "The Judgment Intuitive; The Function of the 'Hunch' in Judicial Decision," *Cornell Law Quarterly* 14 (1927–28), 274.

46 Cardozo, *Nature of the Judicial Process*, 167–68.

47 *In re J.P. Linahan*, 138 F. 2d 650 at 652 (1943).

48 D. Pannick, "Judicial Discretion," in Dhavan, Sudarshan and Kharshid, *Judges and Judicial Power*, 50.

49 Lord Devlin, "Judges and Lawmakers," 3, argues that the "social service which the judge renders to the community is the removal of a sense of injustice."

in any event, many theories of the role of the judge. Chief Justice Marshall, in *Marbury* v. *Madison,* said the duty of a judge is "to say what the law is."[50] Devlin urged them "to do justice according to law," not to make law.[51] Jaffe said the function of the judge, at least in the minimum, is "the disinterested application of known law."[52] Mencken saw their role as being not to bring in the millennium, but to keep the peace.[53] Lords Denning, Wilberforce and Diplock thought judges should apply purposive analyses to statutory interpretation;[54] Viscount Simonds thought this teleological approach was a usurpation of the legislative function.[55] And Herbert Hoover said the business of the courts is to look out for business.[56] In my view, Stone's theory is the most seductive: judges do their duty by doing their utmost to make the best choice among possible premises.[57]

At heart, this is a debate characterized as either the difference between legal positivists and legal realists, between black-letter lawyers and what Dworkin calls instrumentalists,[58] or between judicial activism and judicial restraint. The legal positivists, black-letter lawyers and those in favor of restraint, are known for their literal or strict adherence to the language of statutes or to *stare decisis* and tend to deny that there is any moral component to decisionmaking. Their critics argue that judges cannot be "ventriloquial puppets"[59] to statutes and that *stare decisis* cannot realistically be seen, like Rumpole's wife, as emanating from one who must be obeyed.[60] The legal realists, instrumentalists and activists believe that courts are agents of society and cannot or should not function oblivious to social realities or the social consequences of their decisions. Their critics suggest that judges are not accountable, have no objective insight into the mind of the reasonable person, and therefore cannot permit their view of law to be determined by a subjective policy perspec-

---

50 5 U.S. 49 at 70 (1803).

51 Devlin, "Judges and Lawmakers," 11.

52 Jaffe, *English and American Judges,* 13.

53 Cited in S. Mosk, "The Common Law and the Judicial Decision-making Process," *Harvard Journal of Law and Public Policy* 11 (1988), 35 at 41.

54 See, e.g., Lord Diplock's comment in *Jones* v. *R.,* [1972] A.C. 944 at 1005, where he seeks "to ascertain the social ends [the Act] was intended to achieve."

55 *Magor and St. Mellons R.D.C.* v. *Newport Corporation,* [1952] A.C. 189.

56 See Hiers, "Normative Analysis," 110.

57 Stone, *Precedent and Law,* 9.

58 R.A. Dworkin, "'Natural' Law Revisited," *University of Florida Law Review* 34 (1982), 165 at 181.

59 Winfield, "Public Policy," 89.

60 Hiers, "Normative Analysis," 91.

tive. Moreover, multivariate and interlocking questions—those Fuller refers to as "polycentric"[61]—are unfit for adjudication and best left to the legislative forum. Judicial activists like Denning believe that judges, as policy partners, should fill in legislative gaps; those like Devlin in favor of restraint feel judges may only interpret and not create law.

Essentially, the debate is between those who feel, like Cappelletti, that in a modern democracy unaccountable people like judges ought not to overrule the majority will,[62] and those like Stone who argue that the judicial function has always been, through the interpretative, evaluative process that judging represents, intended either to advance or block certain values.[63] In nineteenth-century England, for example, judges relying on a literal rule of interpretation which they felt required them to glean the meaning of the statute from the words alone, so routinely declawed social welfare and labor legislation in England that the Prime Minister, Lord Salisbury, felt sufficiently moved to rebuke Lord Halsbury with the warning: "The judicial salad requires both legal oil and political vinegar, but disastrous effects will follow if due proportion is not observed."[64] We tend not to think of black-letter adjudicators as being activists, but their legal conclusions in this period were extremely interventionist.[65] In *refusing* to give the statute a "liberal" construction, these judges were being "activists" in creating conservative results. Simple labels, in other words, are meaningless. It is, in the end, the result that counts.

Nor are we even assisted by words like "progressive" or "traditional" in defining judicial approaches. Lord Denning, for example, who expansively developed the *Mareva* injunction,[66] is the same person who so restrictively interpreted labor legislation as to prevent secondary picket-

---

61 L.L. Fuller, "Adjudication and the Rule of Law," *Proceedings of the American Society of International Law* 54 (1960), 1 at 3.

62 M. Cappelletti, *Judicial Review in the Contemporary World* (Indianapolis: Bobbs-Merrill, 1971), 98.

63 Stone, *Precedent and Law*, 8.

64 Cited in G. Jones, "Should Judges be Politicians?: The English Experience," *Indiana Law Journal* 57 (1982), 211 at 213. Voices as ideologically disparate as Harold Laski, Jeremy Bentham and William Gordon-Harrison, a distinguished parliamentary draftsman, blamed British "judicial conservatism" for blocking social progress. See Jones, 215.

65 The pre-New Deal Supreme Court in the United States was similarly accused of "activism" for striking down industrial and social welfare legislation. It was only with the Warren Court in the 1950s that the "activist" label came to be associated with "progressive" policy choices. See the articles by E.V. Rostow and P.A. Freund in Levy, *Judicial Review*.

66 *Mareva Compania Naviera SA* v. *International Bulk Carriers SA*, [1975] 2 Lloyd's Rep. 509 (C.A.).

ing.[67] The same Privy Council which in 1929 chastised the Canadian Supreme Court for so narrowly interpreting the word "persons"[68] that it excluded one of this country's two official genders, in 1902 overruled the Canadian Courts, and declared legal the British Columbia Act denying the franchise to Chinese, Japanese and Indians.[69]

Since 1867, Canada has lived with the concept that the legislature, although supreme, is itself subject to the constitution. This was particularly true with respect to the authority of respective legislatures according to the division of powers. The *Charter* does not, therefore, introduce the novel concept of constitutional supremacy.[70] What it does is add the concept of constitutionally entrenched human rights to the content of that supremacy. The *Charter* is about human rights, not about judicial versus legislative roles, nor about judicial activism versus restraint, nor about the politicization of the judiciary. The *Charter*, introduced after all by the accountable legislature, represents the willing subjugation by the legislature of its conduct to the scrutiny and supremacy of certain principles of human rights—as interpreted by the judiciary. The morality of any law is now subject to the supreme morality of civil and human rights. The debate as to whether this is an appropriate role for the judiciary was held, and resolved in favor of the judiciary or, at the very least, in favor of the importance of declaring the reach of human rights and the values they represent to be beyond simple legislative grasp.

Judges have always reached legal conclusions based on their understanding of, sympathy, or antipathy for current social values. The *Charter* brings us nothing new in this regard. The judge who in 1873 said "the paramount destiny and mission of women are to fulfil the noble and benign offices of wife and mother,"[71] the judge who in 1915 thought admitting women to the legal profession would be a "manifest violation of the law of . . . public decency";[72] the judge who said in 1905 that fault-based support laws were desirable because wives "ought to be preserved from imminent temptation";[73] the House of Lords which said in 1959 that privative clauses ousting the jurisdiction of the courts were

---

67 *Express Newspapers Ltd* v. *McShane*, [1979] 1 W.L.R. 390; and *Duport Steels Ltd.* v. *Sirs*, [1980] 1 W.L.R. 142. In both cases the House of Lords reversed Lord Denning.

68 *Edwards* v. *Attorney General of Canada*, [1930] A.C. 124 (P.C.).

69 *Cunningham* v. *Tomey Homma*, [1903] A.C. 151 (P.C.).

70 *Lederman*, "Democratic Parliaments," 1.

71 *Bradwell* v. *Illinois*, 83 U.S. (16 Wall.) 130 at 141 (1873).

72 *Langstaff* v. *Bar of the Province of Quebec* (1915), 47 S.C. 131 at 139 (C.A.), affirming (1915), 25 C.B.R. 11.

73 *Squire* v. *Squire*, [1905] P. 4 at 8.

to be disregarded;[74] the court that said in 1975 that property rights take precedence over peaceful picketing;[75] the courts that said in 1949 that sanctity of the contract and restrictive covenants took precedence over the rights of Jews to purchase property;[76] the court that said in 1939 that freedom of commerce took precedence over the rights of blacks to be served beer;[77] and the court that said in 1959 that Duplessis had over-stepped the boundaries of permissible political behavior,[78] were all invoking or articulating, long before the *Charter*, their view of what public policy either required, prevented or permitted.

So what are we really talking about when we discuss judicial acti-vism versus restraint, the politicization or "Americanization" of the judiciary, or related concerns?[79] We are really talking about whether we agree with a court's result and what to do about it if we do not. If we favor the court's result we tend to applaud the approach, whether it be called restrictive or expansive. If our notion of justice is offended by the result, we chastise what we consider either too narrow or too broad an interpretation, as being either an abdication of the judicial role or an invasion of the legislative one. And this leads us into the question of whether, since there is always someone who disagrees with a court's decision, it was wise to have the capacity of correction removed from the legislature by the universality of the *Charter* and by virtue of the fact that judges have always articulated public policy. Is the public not entitled to indulge in some nervous anticipation now that in the field of rights and freedoms the court's role has changed from a penultimate to an authorita-tive one?

This may be true, but considering that in the traditional triumvirate division of legislative, executive and judicial branches, judges alone need fear no political consequences for an unpopular decision, they may be best suited to decide the kinds of controversial issues that *Charter* disputes involve.

---

74 *Anisminic Ltd* v. *Foreign Compensation Commission*, [1969] 2 A.C. 147.

75 *Harrison* v. *Carswell*, [1975] 2 S.C.R. 200, reversing Chief Justice Freedman of the Manitoba Court of Appeal, whose balancing list yielded the opposite result, as did Chief Justice Laskin's in his dissent.

76 *Re Noble and Wolf*, [1949], 4 D.L.R. 375 (Ont. C.A.).

77 *Christie* v. *York*, [1940] S.C.R. 139.

78 *Roncarelli* v. *Duplessis*, [1959] S.C.R 121.

79 A. De Tocqueville, in *Democracy in America*, trans. H. Reeve, rev. H. Bowen, ed. P. Bradley (New York: Alfred A. Knopf, 1945), at 290 said: "Scarcely any political question arises in the United States that is not resolved, sooner or later, into a judicial question." See also the discussion, ibid. 103–109. But Devlin, "Judges and Lawmakers," at 6, suggests that the American Supreme Court, "like the vines of France is not for transplantation."

In response to the argument that it is antidemocratic for unaccountable persons to impose their will on the majority, is the belief that there should be an institution in society which can independently and fairly and without fear of consequences safeguard against what Lord Scarman called "the modern menace of unbridled majority power."[80] Human rights essentially concerns the protection of minority rights from arbitrary erosion or violation by the majority. The legislature which relies on majority support cannot be expected routinely to risk political self-destruction by promulgating minority causes; on the other hand, the courts, which do not rely on any constituency, risk nothing in protecting them. What body can better attenuate the impact of majoritarian expectations when they may unfairly circumscribe minority ones, than one which does not depend for its survival on an appeal to popularity with the majority?

In a country as heterogeneous as Canada, it is in any event an illusory task to attempt to ascertain or define consensus;[81] but to the extent that this task is necessary, it is one the legislature must undertake in deciding whether to ignore, implement or redirect consensus statutorily. In interpreting human rights, the consensus may not only be ineffable, insofar as it represents a majority view, it may also be irrelevant, involving as it may the protection of rights *from* the majority's views. As Lord Scarman observed, human rights may be so fundamental that civilized man cannot survive without them,[82] but they are "more conspicuous in the mouths of men than in their practice."[83] As concerned, therefore, as one might be about an individual judge's skill in this role of interpreting and allocating human rights, institutionally there is no better guarantee that human rights will not be unduly compromised than by entrusting their protection to the "unaccountable" judiciary. The legislature has always, in any case, been subject to the jurisdiction of the constitution, and as Chief Justice Hughes once boldly said, "the Constitution is what the judges say it is."[84] In Chief Justice Dickson's words, the "judiciary is the guardian of the constitution."[85]

By pointing out that the *Charter* represents neither a new nor an undesirable variable in the judicial or political system, I do not mean to minimize the difficulty of the challenge. Definitive judicial constitutional interpretation of human rights issues is certainly different in degree from

---

80 Scarman, "Human Rights," 98.

81 Bell, "Three Models," 62.

82 Scarman, "Human Rights," 98.

83 Ibid.

84 Ibid., 96.

85 *Hunter* v. *Southam Inc.*, [1984] 2 S.C.R. 145 at 155.

the responsibility for definitive judicial constitutional interpretation of the division of powers. Issues of language, education, religion, equality, expression, association or liberty involve the most complex of legal assessments. They are core justice issues and will be affected by what judges read, know, experience, believe, understand, and above all, value. They are also supremely policy-oriented issues and require rigor in the acquisition and application not only of knowledge, but of greater empathy as well.

The *Charter* has been like a divining rod, attracting the attention of the public to the microscope judges themselves routinely use to examine their function and its appropriate execution. And members of the public, perhaps somewhat surprised by the impact of the *Charter* and feeling jolted from their historic inattention to the policy aspect of the judicial process, are beginning to put the role and composition of the judiciary on the defensive through persistent questioning and demands for accountability.[86] This, in turn, has come as somewhat of a surprise to members of the judiciary who, on the whole, had assumed that the *Charter* represented a more public version of a role they had always undertaken to the best of their ability.[87] Everyone, in short, has become sensitized, and the exercise has been a healthy one. The *Charter* has raised public consciousness about a number of things: who the judges are and the importance of what they do; political consciousness about territoriality, the policy partnership and the limits it imposes; and judicial self-consciousness about publicly declaring that the Emperor has no clothes.

The analysis of proper roles and casting will be an ongoing one. But whatever history judges to be its ultimate impact, the *Charter*'s high road over the public interest is certain to be a well-travelled one. It is a journey

---

86 Gareth Jones, in "Should Judges be Politicians?", at 233, advocating an entrenched Bill of Rights for England, nonetheless sees the main problem as being the judges: "[T]he English barrister, from whose ranks judges are chosen, is a professional, an expert in black-letter law, drawn . . . from the middle classes, apolitical, conservative and traditionalist. Not every supporter of a Bill of Rights will find that picture a comforting prospect." On the other hand, at 233, he observes that the "lawyer in the United States has always played a different, and more varied, role in society; floating in and out of law schools, Wall Street, and the Administration, he brings to constitutional adjudication a breadth of experience and a vision which a professional lawyer can never enjoy." His words are gently echoed by Lord Devlin in his acknowledgment that "judges, like any other body of elderly men who have lived on the whole unadventurous lives, tend to be old-fashioned in their ideas. This is a fact of nature which reformers must accept." This, plus his view that statutes are "not philosophical treatises and the philosophy behind them, if there is one, is often half-baked," forms a large part of his reasoned resistance to "purposive" or "creative" lawmaking: "Judges and Lawmakers," 14.

87 Stone observes that "the features common to constitutional review and to appellate . . . law generally are more important than the differences." In Stone, *Precedent and Law*, 8.

the judges, with their suitcases full of books and policy, are making with increasing ease and confidence. There have been no fatalities or serious injuries to date either to their neutrality, independence or credibility. As long as the task is clearly understood and undertaken, it need never be otherwise.

The *Charter*'s odyssey is destined to enhance everyone's understanding of what the Judicial Play is all about and why it has enjoyed such a long run. There will be some critical reviews, as there always have been, but there will be glowing ones as well. As long as the play is performed honestly and with respect for the pluralistic audience, then the public and public policy, the judiciary and the judiciary's role, will be history's fortunate beneficiaries.

V

Conclusion

Can the Canadians be a Sovereign People?*

Peter H. Russell

For me the most haunting lines in Canada's history were written in 1858. They are these: "It will be observed that the basis of Confederation now proposed differs from that of the United States in several important particulars. . . . It does not profess to be derived from the people but would be the constitution provided by the Imperial Parliament, thus affording the means of remedying any defect."[1] The words were written by three "Fathers of Confederation," George Etienne Cartier, Alexander Galt and John Ross, in a letter addressed to the Colonial Secretary, Sir Edward Bulver-Lytton. The aim of the letter was to begin to warm up the Imperial authorities to the project of a federal union of British North America. Cartier, Galt and Ross could think of no better way of beginning their sales pitch than by distancing their constitutional proposal from the Constitution of the American federal republic and, above all, by disavowing the heretical idea that a constitution should be derived from the people.

Now contrast the words of this mid-Victorian Canadian letter with those contained in a letter written on 15 January 1990. The contrasting words are these: "The Constitution belongs to the *people* of Canada—the ultimate source of sovereignty in the nation."[2] The author of these words was Premier Clyde Wells of Newfoundland, not exactly a Father of Confederation—indeed, he may even turn out to be a father of de-confederation. Wells was writing to Jack Pickersgill and Robert Stanfield, two staunch supporters of the Meech Lake Accord. His letter attacked not only the substance of the Meech Lake Accord but also the process through which

---

* Presidential address to the Canadian Political Science Association, Queen's University, Kingston, Ontario, June 1991.

1 Quoted in O. D. Skelton. *The Life and Times of Sir Alexander Tilloch Galt* (Toronto: McClelland and Stewart, 1966), 96.

2 Letter from Premier Clyde Wells to J. W. Pickersgill and R. L. Stanfield, 15 January 1990, 5 (emphasis in the original).

it had been reached, a process that was illegitimate because it denied the sovereignty of the Canadian people.

Between the two passages lies much more than the gulf of years. The two quotations express profoundly different views of what makes a constitution, and the regime based on it, legitimate. For the mid-Victorian Canadian constitutionalist, legitimacy flowed from the sovereign Parliament of the Empire. For Wells, the modern Canadian constitutionalist, legitimacy derives from the people. Although I have no empirical data to prove it, my strong belief is that both spoke for the great mass of their contemporaries.[3] Both evoked the constitutional spirit of their times.

How and when the ideological transition from imperial to popular sovereignty took place is not easy to ascertain. The insertion of a charter of rights in the Canadian constitution no doubt did much to consolidate the shifts from what Alan Cairns has characterized as a "governments' constitution" to a "citizens' constitution."[4] But the roots of this change in the normative assumptions of Canadian constitutionalism can be traced much further back in Canadian history. Notions of popular sovereignty were as integral to the Canadian nationalist spirit that worked for and welcomed Canada's independence from Great Britain as they were to the provincial rights movements which rooted the claims of provincial legislatures in the sovereignty of the people they represented.[5]

My concern is not with the details of the change in Canadian constitutionalism but with the simple fact that this fundamental transformation has taken place. The idea that a constitution, to be legitimate, must be derived from the people, a dreadful heresy to our founding fathers, has by our time become constitutional orthodoxy for Canadians. Indeed, it may be the only constitutional ideal on which there is popular consensus in Canada. We might celebrate this accord were it not for one crucial blemish when it is applied to the Canadian context. Not all Canadians have consented to form a single people in which a majority or some special majority have, to use John Locke's phrase, "a right to act and conclude the rest."[6] In this sense Canadians have not yet constituted themselves a sovereign people. So deep are their current differences on fundamental questions of political justice and collective identity that Canadians may now be incapable of acting together as a sovereign people.

---

3 The Fathers of Confederation did not speak for aboriginal inhabitants of the lands over which the British claimed sovereignty.

4 Alan C. Cairns, "Citizens (Outsiders) and Governments (Insiders) in Constitution-Making: The Case of Meech Lake," *Canadian Public Policy* 14 (1988), S121.

5 On the interaction of competing claims to sovereignty see Robert Vipond, *Liberty and Community: Canadian Federalism and the Failure of the Constitution* (Albany: State University of New York Press, 1991).

6 John Locke, *The Second Treatise of Government* (New York: Liberal Arts Press, 1952).

Popular sovereignty is not descriptive of the locus of actual political power. In polities of any scale, all the people, or even a majority of all the people, can never be the effective political sovereign. Popular sovereignty is a normative theory. It is a theory of political obligation which holds that political authority is legitimate and ought to be accepted only if it is derived from the people. Where popular sovereignty is the prevailing theory of political obligation the people can be said to be the moral sovereign, if not the political, legal, or coercive sovereign.[7]

In the course of history, highly elitist regimes have invoked the doctrine of popular sovereignty to justify their rule. This was surely the case in seventeenth-century England when the parliamentary party justified resistance to the royalists by pitting popular sovereignty against the divine right of kings. Here, popular sovereignty was not a product of popular demand. It was, as Edmund S. Morgan has so neatly put it, "a question of some of the few enlisting the many against the rest of the few."[8] When the parliamentary party finally prevailed at the end of the century it vested legal sovereignty not in a written constitution ratified by the people but in Parliament itself.

In the United States the advocates of popular sovereignty demanded and secured a more appropriate constitutional form. The pervasive political theory, first of state constitutionmaking and then of the constitution of the new American republic, conceived of a constitution as a compact or covenant drawn up by the people. Of course, there was plenty of fiction in the notion of "the people as a constituent power." The conventions that drafted and ratified these state and national constitutions excluded large elements of the population.[9] Indeed, the American people as a constituent body capable of intentional and coherent agency had to be invented by America's founding fathers. But the point is that the invention worked in that it produced a coherent and popular foundation myth—a myth which indeed gained credibility after the Civil War and the democratic evolution of the country.

There was scarcely a whisper of popular sovereignty in Canada's confederation movement. Canadian political leaders who believed in that theory had been thoroughly crushed in the abortive rebellions thirty years

---

7 For an analysis of the different aspects of sovereignty, see W. J. Rees, "The Theory of Sovereignty Restated," in Peter Laslett, ed., *Philosophy, Politics and Society* (Oxford: Basil Blackwell, 1956), 56.

8 Edmund S. Morgan, *Inventing the People: The Rise of Popular Sovereignty in England and America* (New York: W. W. Norton, 1988), 169.

9 There are many accounts. For a more recent one, see Richard B. Morris, *Forging the Union, 1781–1789* (New York: Harper and Row, 1987).

earlier.[10] By the 1860s their theories of democratic constitutionalism were in total eclipse. The political elites who put Confederation together were happy colonials. That is not to say that Confederation was imposed on the British North Americans in a totally undemocratic manner. For the federating colonies, the *British North America Act* was the first constitution in which the novel and creative elements were designed by the colonists themselves, not their Imperial masters. The positivist critics of the compact theory are no doubt right in contending that Confederation could not have been a compact in a strict legal sense. But they entirely miss the point that Confederation was a compact—a deal—first between the English and French political elites in the Canadas and then between the Canadians and the Maritimers.

Throughout this deal-making process Imperial officials continued to play an important role. They helped organize the meetings at Charlottetown and Quebec, serving somewhat clumsily and often half-heartedly as coaches and prods to the colonial politicians. Without their intervention the second North American federation would probably not have been put together. There were, to be sure, some democratic elements in the confederation process. The political elites who negotiated the deal were elected, albeit on a franchise confined to property-holding males of European extraction. Resolutions expressing the core principles of Confederation were debated in one elected legislature—the Canadian in Quebec City—and approved by a substantial majority. Politicians committed to Confederation did manage to win one election—in New Brunswick in 1866—prior to establishing the new constitutional arrangements. But throughout, the elites who managed the constitutional process were careful to keep public participation and debate to a minimum.

There are many examples of this. Donald Creighton records one which shows poignantly how the Fathers of Confederation sensed the danger of exposing their deal to public scrutiny. This was in the late spring of 1866, when the second election on Confederation was being fought in New Brunswick and Nova Scotia Confederates were looking forward to a conference in London which would throw out the Quebec Resolutions and virtually start afresh on constitutionmaking. In Canada, Macdonald and Cartier resisted the Governor General's call for an early meeting of the legislature, for they feared that they would be asked by Quebec members whether they were backing off the Quebec Resolutions. "If Macdonald and Cartier replied that nothing was settled and the Quebec Resolutions were

---

10 For the political theory of the French-Canadian rebels, see Denis Monière, *Ideologies in Quebec: The Historical Development*, trans. Richard Howard (Toronto: University of Toronto Press, 1981), c. 3. For the constitutional ideas of the Upper Canadian rebels see W. P. M. Kennedy, *The Constitution of Canada, 1534–1937*, 2d ed. (London: Oxford University Press, 1937), c. 11.

open to amendment, French Canada," Creighton writes, "would undoubtedly rise in violent protest. If, on the other hand, they answered that Canada was committed to the Quebec scheme as to a compact, the anti-Confederates in New Brunswick might exploit the assurance to [the Confederate leader] Tilley's complete undoing."[11] And so the lack of consensus within the confederation movement was papered over by the political elites, sixteen of whom, a few months later in a London hotel, did indeed make some changes in the constitutional scheme before turning it over for ratification by the Imperial Parliament.

Imperial stewardship of constitutional politics in the 1860s made it relatively easy to inaugurate Confederation. A new country could be founded without having to risk finding out if its politically active citizens agreed to the principles on which its constitution was to be based. But if this was a gift, it was a tainted gift. The Confederation compromise was sheltered from the strain of a full public review in all sections of the country, but at the cost of not forming a political community with a clear sense of its constituent and controlling elements. Thus, at Canada's founding, not only were its people not sovereign, but there was not even a sense that a constituent sovereign people would have to be invented.

Immediately following Confederation, questions of sovereignty were at the centre of constitutional politics. The sovereignty at issue was not sovereignty of the people but the sovereignty of governments and legislatures. Through three decades the provincial rights movement contested Macdonald's thesis that Canada's constitution vested "all the principles and power of sovereignty"[12] in the central government. In the end, the movement was successful not only legally, with judicial decisions cementing the concept of dual sovereignty into the bedrock of our constitutional law, but also politically, in building a solid popular foundation for the provinces as significant political communities.

The sovereignty claimed and won for provincial legislatures and governments within their allotted sphere of jurisdiction was, as Reg Whitaker has pointed out, primarily a top-down kind of sovereignty.[13] Canadian constitutional politics continued to be highly elitist, with provincial and federal leaders contending against each other in intergovernmental meetings and the courts. Still, traces of a more democratic constitutionalism were beginning to appear in the rhetoric, if not the reality, of the constitu-

---

11 Donald Creighton, *The Road to Confederation* (Toronto: Macmillan, 1964), 381.

12 These were the words Macdonald used in the Confederation Debates: P. B. Waite, ed., *The Confederation Debates in the Province of Canada* (Toronto: McClelland and Stewart, 1963), 156.

13 Reg Whitaker, "Democracy and the Canadian Constitution," in Keith Banting and Richard Simeon, eds., *And No One Cheered* (Toronto: Methuen, 1983), 240–60.

tional process. Robert Vipond has shown how exponents of provincial rights defended the sovereignty of provincial "parliaments" against federal incursions by emphasizing the right to self-government of local electorates.[14] On occasion provincial leaders even went so far as to refer to the rights of provincial legislatures as "the constitutional rights of those to whom the people have entrusted . . . with certain powers . . .,"[15] thus implying that the people were the true custodians of the constitution.

Out of this rhetoric and the political success of its authors was born the myth of Confederation as a compact of founding peoples. This myth had exceptional potency in Quebec, the one province in which it could be imbued with a sense of ethnic nationalism. Covenantal language in Canada's constitutional discourse spawned two potential antagonistic concepts of a founding compact: a compact of founding provinces and a compact of founding peoples.[16] Lurking within the core of these rival theories of the constituent elements of the Canadian political community is, of course, the dichotomy between the ideal of provincial equality and the concept of Quebec as a distinct society within Confederation.

So long as Canadians were uninterested in taking custody of their constitution into their own hands, this conflict over the nature of Canada as a political community was of no great political importance. It was bound, however, to become ever so much more salient once that condition changed. The time for that change arrived in 1926, when the Balfour Declaration declared Canada and the other self-governing Dominions to be "autonomous Communities"[17] and Canada's political leaders faced the task of arranging for Canada to become constitutionally self-governing.

As every first-year student of Canadian political science (once) learned, federal and provincial leaders, in a series of conferences that began in 1927 and extended over a great many years, could not agree on a formula for amending the constitution in Canada. And so, legal custody of Canada's constitution continued to lie with the Imperial Parliament. Underlying this tedious tale, which put generations of political science students to sleep, was as profound a question as can confront a people who aspire to constitutional self-government. The debate over a Canadian amending formula involved nothing less than the question of who or what should be constitutionally sovereign in Canada. If the written constitution is the country's highest law defining the powers of its governments and

---

14 Vipond, *Liberty and Community*.

15 Ibid., 235.

16 See Fillipo Sabetti, "The Historical Context of Constitutional Change in Canada," *Law and Contemporary Problems* 45 (1982), 11.

17 R.M. Dawson, *The Government of Canada*, 4th ed. (Toronto: University of Toronto Press, 1963), 63.

the rights of its citizens, then the combination of people or governments or legislatures which is empowered to change the constitution is sovereign.[18]

The amending formula issue was not discussed in these terms because Canadian constitutionalism at this time, philosophically speaking, was much closer to Burke than to Locke. Notions of parliamentary sovereignty rested uneasily with the legal reality of the written constitution as supreme law. And so, the debate over the amending formula was conducted by lawyer-politicians in dry technical terms as if they were drafting the patent for some newfangled contraption.

Nonetheless, beneath and behind the competing proposals for an amending formula it is possible to discern competing assumptions about the nature of Canada as a political community. There were those in national politics, mainly on the left, who pressed for a reasonably flexible formula—a majority of provinces—which would ease the way for needed reforms of Canadian federalism, reforms which in the circumstances of the depression and postwar reconstruction were assumed to be of a centralist nature. Advocates of this view appealed to an emerging sense of Canadian nationalism and the vision of Canada as a unified and majoritarian political community. Hard against this position were the heirs of the provincial rights movement, firmly entrenched now in provincial capitals. Because they viewed Canada as a thoroughly federal community, they insisted on the consent of all provincial governments to any changes in the "compact" of Confederation. Cross-cutting these positions were those who reflected a dualist conception of Canada by insisting on deep entrenchment for the rights of Ontario Catholics and Quebec Protestants and for those provincial powers, especially property and civil rights, regarded as essential for the preservation of the distinctive culture of Quebec's francophone majority.[19]

In retrospect, as we reflect on the seemingly unending constitutional turmoil Canadians have experienced over the last three-quarters of a century, we may well wish that the British had been more hard-boiled and had simply cast Canada adrift, constitutionally speaking, in the 1920s. However, their leaders and ours placed too much value on legal continuity to force the now autonomous community of Canada into an act of constitutional autochthony. And so Canada continued to lean on the legal crutch of Imperial sovereignty while its political and legal elites, in a long and fruitless series of meetings, trekked on in their quest for an agreeable amending formula.

---

18 Sovereign at least in a legal sense, but also, to the extent that the amending system is based on a genuine social consensus, sovereign in a moral sense.

19 For a discussion of the various proposals, see Paul Gerin-Lajoie, *Constitutional Amendment in Canada* (Toronto: University of Toronto Press, 1950).

One might question, however, whether Canada's democratic culture was sufficiently developed in the 1920s to permit anything approximating a genuine social contract. The style of our constitutional politics was thoroughly and complacently elitist. Occasional suggestions that the people, through referenda, might play a role in the amending process received little support.[20] The participation of women in Canadian politics had just begun, and the aboriginal people, discarded as military allies and economic partners, were in a condition of colonial subjection. The Canadians were scarcely in a position to constitute themselves a sovereign people when so many of the people were excluded from the constitutional process.

But there were signs of a more populist constitutional impulse on the rise. When the time came to review Newfoundland's constitutional status after World War II, there was no doubt or serious debate about the appropriate constitutional process. The people of Newfoundland, through an elected convention and two referenda, acted as a sovereign constituent people in making their decision to join Canada.[21] The country the Newfoundlanders were joining did not reciprocate this process. A simple resolution of the federal House of Commons was considered sufficient for accepting this addition to the Canadian body politic.

On through the 1950s and into the 1960s, Canada's constitutional politics was scarcely political but was more in the order of quiet meetings of federal and provincial constitutional technicians working out the terms of isolated amendments and burrowing away at the eternal puzzle of the amending formula. All this came to an end in 1964 when both the substance and style of Canadian constitutional politics changed dramatically.

On 15 October 1964, Canadians woke up to headlines proclaiming that their first ministers had agreed on the Fulton-Favreau amending formula—the constitution was coming home! This, as we now know all too well, turned out to be false news. Although the Fulton-Favreau formula, with its requirement of unanimous provincial approval for all important constitutional changes, did not lack for critics in English Canada, it was the premier of Quebec, Jean Lesage, who was pressured by public opinion in his province to reject Fulton-Favreau.[22] Lesage responded to a new

---

20 Even as liberal-minded a Canadian as Frank Underhill poured cold water on such suggestions: ibid., 234.

21 For an account of these events, see Peter Neary, *Newfoundland in the North Atlantic World, 1929–1949* (Montreal: McGill-Queen's University Press, 1988), c. 10.

22 For a brief but perceptive account, see Donald V. Smiley, *Canada in Question: Federalism in the Eighties*, 3rd ed. (Toronto: McGraw-Hill Ryerson, 1980), c. 3.

sense of political nationalism stirring the Québécois.[23] From the perspective of this Quebec nationalism, it would be a strategic mistake to consent to patriation with a rigid amending formula before Quebec had secured adequate constitutional recognition of its status in Canada as the home of a founding people.

Quebec's rejection of Fulton-Favreau plunged Canada into the first of five rounds of what I refer to as "macro-constitutional politics." Macro-constitutional politics is distinguished in two ways from ordinary or micro-constitutional politics.[24] First, macro-constitutional politics goes beyond disputing the merits of specific constitutional proposals and addresses the very nature of the political community on which the constitution is to be based. Macro-constitutional politics, whether or not directed towards comprehensive constitutional change, is concerned with reaching agreement on the identity and fundamental principles of justice of the body politic on which the constitution is to be based. The second feature of macro-constitutional politics flows logically from the first. Precisely because of the fundamental nature of the issues in dispute, and their tendency to touch citizens' sense of identity and self-worth, macro-constitutional politics is exceptionally emotional and intense. When a country's constitutional politics is at the macro level the constitutional issue tends to dwarf all other public concerns.

The first round of macro-constitutional politics began in earnest when three Quebeckers, Jean Marchand, Gérard Pelletier and Pierre Trudeau, reversed the path Jean Lesage had taken and moved from Quebec to Ottawa.[25] One of these, Trudeau, soon took over the leadership of the government of Canada and, against his earlier and perhaps his better instincts, joined the constitutional debate. But Trudeau endeavoured to refocus the debate on proposals designed to strengthen the unity of the Canadian nation. At the centre of his agenda were a constitutional bill of rights and national bilingualism. The future of the French Canadians was to be secured, not collectively through an autonomous provincial home-

---

23 Edward McWhinney, *Quebec and the Constitution, 1960–1978* (Toronto: University of Toronto Press, 1979).

24 To the best of my knowledge these terms are not used elsewhere in the literature. My distinction draws from Daniel J. Elazar, "Constitution-making: The Pre-eminently Political Act," in Keith G. Banting and Richard Simeon, eds., *Redesigning the State: The Process of Constitutional Change in Industrial Nations* (Toronto: University of Toronto Press, 1985). Elazar distinguishes constitutional politics which addresses "the existence of the body politic itself" from constitutional politics which may result in comprehensive rewriting of the constitution without addressing the fundamental nature of the political community itself.

25 For a recent account, see Stephen Clarkson and Christina McCall, *Trudeau and our Times* (Toronto: McClelland and Stewart, 1990).

land, but through participation as individual citizens in a Canada-wide regime of equal rights.

The Trudeau "vision" of Canada, as it has come to be called, gave birth to nothing less than a nation-building project rivalling that of Quebec nationalism. This was ironic, since Trudeau, in his 1964 address to the Canadian Political Science Association, had mused about the inherent incompatibility of federalism and nationalism.[26] In retrospect, we may now appreciate the merit of his musing, for the contest between the nationalisms of Trudeau and his Québécois adversaries came to be charged with the sense of moral righteousness which flows from competing ideologies of political justice and fundamental rights. A constitutional struggle of this kind in which both sides insist on a principled victory is, as the United States found in the middle of the last century, difficult, if not impossible, to contain within the accommodations of federalism. The secular religions of ethnic self-determination and individual rights could now divide Canadians as deeply as Catholicism and Protestantism had divided their nineteenth-century forebears.[27]

Although the constitutional debate in this period had deepened, participation in it was only beginning to broaden. The formal set pieces were still thoroughly elitist: government experts, attorneys general and first ministers negotiating through the procedures of what Richard Simeon aptly called federal-provincial diplomacy.[28] But there were signs of some cracks in the veneer of elite accommodation. The public was at least admitted via television as voyeurs to Ontario Premier John Robarts' Conference on Confederation for Tomorrow in 1967 and the subsequent constitutional conference in February 1968 which launched Trudeau's career as a constitutional reformer. And public opinion in Quebec was as decisive in ending this, the first round of macro-constitutional politics, as it was in initiating it. In June 1971, Quebec Premier Robert Bourassa, having negotiated at a first ministers' conference a set of constitutional proposals flowing primarily from Trudeau's agenda, returned to Quebec and, like Lesage a few years earlier, under the pressure of Quebec nationalist criticism withdrew his support for the Victoria Charter.[29]

---

26 See "Federalism, Nationalism and Reason," the final essay in Pierre Elliott Trudeau, *Federalism and the French Canadians* (Toronto: Macmillan, 1968).

27 For an analysis of the parallel between religious and nationalist conflict, see Rainer Knopff, "Quebec's 'Holy War' as 'Regime' Politics," *This Journal* 12 (1979), 315–31. For an account of the English-Canadian nationalism based on Trudeau's constitutionalism, see Kenneth McRoberts, "English Canada. and Quebec: Avoiding the Issue," Sixth Annual Robarts Lecture, York University, Toronto, 5 March 1991.

28 Richard Simeon, *Federal-Provincial Diplomacy* (Toronto: University of Toronto Press, 1972).

29 Smiley, *Canada in Question*, 74–79.

Following the Victoria failure, Canada's political elites were in no hurry to resume the great debate. The report of a parliamentary committee reviewing the entire constitution—and affirming, by the way, the right of the citizens of any part of Canada to self-determination—was greeted in 1972 with massive indifference.[30] Nonetheless, there were signs that the virus of constitutional discontent was creeping more pervasively through the Canadian body politic. The sudden and spectacular rise in the international price of petroleum quickened the interest of western provincial leaders in fortifying their provinces' constitutional powers to control their new-found wealth. Simultaneously, a groundswell of support was beginning to build, both in the West and in the Atlantic region, for the more effective participation of so-called "outer Canada" in the federation's central institutions.[31] And in 1973 Canada's highest court recognized what Canada's political leaders had long denied—namely, the foundation in law of aboriginal rights.[32] Fortified by this decision, the least empowered component of the Canadian community, its aboriginal peoples, would now at long last have an opportunity in the widening constitutional debate to insist that they too had a right to be subject to a constitution based on consent.

The second round of macro-constitutional politics did not get underway in earnest until Quebec, in 1976, elected a provincial government committed to achieving Quebec's political independence from Canada. This event greatly increased the sense of urgency among political elites about the need for major constitutional change. Many now contended that Canada must either have a total constitutional overhaul or must break up. And so Canada entered a period of new constitutionalism, when the little Solons which stir in so many of us produced a plethora of new constitutions which fluttered down on the country like autumn leaves.

Formal constitutional negotiations followed the traditional format of executive federalism. Now, however, the first ministers' agenda was cluttered with a contradictory collection of items representing the demands of all the provincial malcontents and the counterattack of the

---

30 The Special Joint Committee of the House of Commons on the Constitution of Canada (Molgat-MacGuigan Committee), *Final Report* (Ottawa: Information Canada, 1972), c. 7 on "Self-Determination" does not base this right on provinces but on contiguous, homogeneous communities.

31 For accounts of constitutional politics in the 1970s, see Smiley, *Canada in Question*, 79–88; Alan C. Cairns, "The Politics of Constitutional Renewal in Canada," in Banting and Simeon, eds., *Redesigning the State*; Michael B. Stein. *Canadian Constitutional Renewal, 1968–1981* (Kingston: Institute of Intergovernmental Relations, 1989).

32 *Calder* v. *Attorney General of British Columbia*, (1973), 34 D.L.R. (3d) 145. For the implications of this case for Canadian constitutional politics, see Michael Asch, *Home and Native Land: Aboriginal Rights and the Canadian Constitution* (Toronto: Methuen, 1984).

Trudeau nationalists.[33] Again, the constitutional process was opening up a little. Governments now packaged their proposals in glossy packages available, in the federal case, at the local post office.[34] A federal task force endeavoured to consult the people on the conditions of national unity.[35] And the second round concluded in May 1980 with that extraordinarily democratic event—the Quebec referendum.

For the Québécois, the referendum was, in the words of Christian Dufour, "the essence of sovereignty: the enjoyment of the right to self-determination."[36] For the first time since their abandonment by France and conquest by Britain, the Québécois were consulted directly, if not clearly, on their constitutional future. Their answer was ambiguous. While about half of French Quebec said "no" to sovereignty-association and "yes" to Canada, this was a conditional "yes." Many who voted this way, naively no doubt, read into the campaign promises of Trudeau, the effective captain of the pro-Canada team, a commitment to restructure the federation in a manner which would go some way to accommodating Quebec demands for a stronger and distinctive place in Confederation.[37] The one certain implication of that commitment was the immediate initiation of round three.

The third round of macro-constitutional politics began in the summer of 1980 with federal and provincial ministers going through the rituals of elite accommodation.[38] By this time Prime Minister Trudeau had lost patience with the tradition and soon turned to a more Gaullist approach. In October 1980, he appealed over the heads of the provincial premiers directly to the Canadian people. On national television he proposed a "people's package" of reforms, containing, of course, nothing for the Quebec nationalists, but instead the central ingredients of his own Canadian nationalist agenda—patriation, equalization and, above all, a constitutional charter of rights and freedoms. Trudeau's populism was

33 For a detailed account see Roy Romanow, John Whyte and Howard Leeson, *Canada . . . Notwithstanding* (Toronto: Carswell/Methuen, 1984).

34 The Right Honourable Pierre Elliott Trudeau, Prime Minister, *A Time for Action* (Ottawa: Government of Canada, 1978).

35 See the Task Force on Canadian Unity, *A Future Together, Observations and Recommendations* (Ottawa: Minister of Supply and Services, 1979).

36 Christian Dufour, *A Canadian Challenge* (Halifax: The Institute for Research on Public Policy, 1990), 85.

37 There are many accounts of the referendum. For a very balanced account, see Kenneth McRoberts, *Quebec: Social Change and Political Crisis*, 3d ed. (Toronto: McClelland and Stewart, 1988), c. 9.

38 For a detailed account of this period of constitutional politics, see Ronald J. Zukowsky, *Struggle Over the Constitution: From the Quebec Referendum to the Supreme Court* (Kingston: Institute of Intergovernmental Relations, 1981).

responded to positively by organizations representing some of the traditionally least empowered components of the Canadian community— notably women, the handicapped and multicultural interests. In televised hearings before a parliamentary committee these groups pressed success- fully for a stronger charter of rights. A new and important set of constitu- tional players was born with a perspective distinctly indifferent to federalism.[39]

A majority of the Supreme Court of Canada, as it turned out, found no foundation for Trudeau's populism, but rather a requirement of pro- vincial consent, in the traditions of Canadian constitutionalism and so forced an end game play to round three,[40] which employed the tradi- tional mechanism of elite accommodation—with two important modifica- tions. First, the federal and provincial leaders modified the deal they had made when women's and aboriginal groups protested the dropping of clauses entrenching their rights. Second, for the first time since Confeder- ation, constitutional changes affecting Quebec's powers were made with- out the consent of the government of Quebec.

In concluding with the *Constitution Act, 1982,* the third round of macro-constitutional struggle had at last produced formal constitutional changes. And significant changes they were indeed: the "people's pack- age" of patriation, a charter of rights and equalization—embedding the Trudeauian principles of the equality of rights and the equality of prov- inces in the law of the constitution—and the first formal constitutional recognition of the rights of aboriginal peoples.[41] However, significant as these changes were, they did not resolve the issue at the very heart of Canada's debate—namely the nature of the community which, in princi- ple, had been constitutionally self-governing since 1927 and had now taken legal custody of its constitution. Patriation was complete but the patria had not defined itself.

The fly in the ointment was, of course, the repudiation of the *Constitu- tion Act, 1982* by Quebec's National Assembly. This fact, according to the Supreme Court,[42] was of no legal consequence. Nor is it a matter of moral consequence to Canadians like Trudeau who have come to view their nation as a community of equal rights-bearing individuals expressing their collective will primarily through the majoritarian institutions of the federal government. However, the passage of the *Constitution Act, 1982* did not mean that the Trudeauian view of the Canadian people was now

---

39 Cairns, "Citizens (Outsiders) and Governments (Insiders) in Constitution-Making."

40 Peter H. Russell et al., *The Court and the Constitution: Comments on the Supreme Court Ref- erence on Constitutional Amendment* (Kingston: Institute of Inter-governmental Relations, 1982).

41 See David Milne. *The New Canadian Constitution* (Toronto: James Lorimer, 1982).

42 *Re Objection to a Resolution to Amend the Constitution,* [1982] 2 S.C.R. 793.

universally shared by the people themselves. Quite to the contrary! The very act of repudiation by the National Assembly strengthened the sense of many French Quebeckers—with the passage of time perhaps now most of them—that they are a people whose right to self-determination requires expression through the majoritarian institutions of Quebec.[43] Round three was over but a Canadian social contract had not been accomplished.

The Québécois were not the only component of the Canadian community which had difficulty believing that in 1982 they had consented to join what Pierre Trudeau apparently thought was a "federation set to last a thousand years."[44] The aboriginal peoples living on Canadian territory now had a small taste of having their right to government by consent recognized by the hegemonic recent arrivals. The *Constitution Act, 1982* itself mandated a process for clarifying the terms on which aboriginal peoples might share nationhood with Canadians,[45] although the four conferences which followed produced only the slightest clarification.[46] Nonetheless, these conferences solidified the entitlement of aboriginal peoples to be a party to the Canadian social contract. That fact was confirmed by the fatal consequences of their exclusion from the fourth round of macro-constitutional politics, which began formally in April 1987, just a month after the inconclusive fourth conference on aboriginal rights.

When the incompleteness of round three came to be recognized by the leadership of Canada's three major political parties and all of the provincial premiers, and when Quebec elected a government committed to satisfying Quebec's constitutional aspirations within Confederation, a fourth round of macro-constitutional politics became ineluctable.[47] In this round, the negotiating by federal and provincial elites which produced the constitutional proposals was as intense, but much more secretive, than the first ministers' meetings in the first three rounds.[48] All of the negotiating was, according to the negotiators, complete when their accord was unveiled at Meech Lake on the last day of April 1987. This, as we now—

---

43 Dufour, *A Canadian Challenge.*

44 Trudeau used this phrase in his May 1987 newspaper article attacking the Meech Lake Accord. See Andrew Cohen, *A Deal Undone: The Making and Breaking of the Meech Lake Accord* (Vancouver: Douglas and McIntyre, 1990), 165.

45 *Constitution Act, 1982*, s. 37.

46 See David C. Hawkes, *Aboriginal Peoples and Constitutional Reform: What Have We Learned?* (Kingston: Institute of Intergovernmental Relations, 1989).

47 David Milne, *The Canadian Constitution: From Patriation to Meech Lake* (Toronto: James Lorimer, 1989).

48 Cohen, *a Deal Undone*, and Patrick Monahan, *Meech Lake: The Inside Story* (Toronto: University of Toronto Press, 1991).

looking back—know so well, was hardly a fitting way to go about the completion of the Canadian social contract.

In the closed negotiations a compromise had been reached. An accommodation between Quebec's autonomist demands and the principle of provincial equality had been made by extending to all of the provinces four of Quebec's minimum conditions for accepting the 1982 constitutional changes: an extension of the veto power over constitutional amendments, entrenchment of bilateral immigration agreements, a role in Supreme Court appointments and protection against the federal spending power. The fifth condition, the recognition of Quebec as a distinct society within Canada, was hedged in by clauses ensuring that this recognition was not at the expense of federal power, aboriginal peoples or multiculturalism. Yet precisely because the public had not seen these accommodations being made, the Meech Lake Accord was not seen as a compromise but, in English Canada, as a total yielding to the demands of French Quebec.

Public opinion in English-speaking Canada defeated the Meech Lake Accord just as clearly as public opinion in Quebec had rejected the Fulton-Favreau formula and the Victoria Charter at the beginning and end of the first round. Writing provincial legislatures into the new all-Canadian amending system widened the opportunity for public debate and criticism of the constitutional products of executive federalism. The requirement of provincial ratification also exposed these products to the vagaries of the provincial election cycle.

The first ministers who negotiated the Meech Lake Accord were singularly unprepared for this change in Canada's constitutional process. When they submitted their Accord to the federal Parliament and provincial legislatures outside Quebec[49] after signing off on its final language, they compounded opposition to the substance of the Accord with opposition to the process which had produced it. Indeed, in the long term, the biggest casualty of the Meech Lake round may turn out to be not the Accord itself but the legitimacy of first ministers' meetings as the primary vehicle for reaching constitutional accommodations in Canada.

In the end, the Meech Lake proposals were approved by all but two legislatures—Manitoba's and Newfoundland's. To regard it as somehow undemocratic for the legislatures of two provinces representing just eight per cent of the Canadian people to have blocked constitutional changes ratified by legislatures representing all the rest is to miss the point that so many of the people were driven to through the Meech Lake round. That point simply is a loss of faith in the representative capacity of Canadian legislatures as they were seen to function. The primary exception may be

---

49 Quebec was the only province to hold hearings on the Accord between the agreement in principle at Meech Lake on 30 April 1987, and agreement on the final text at the Langevin Block in Ottawa on 3 June 1987.

Quebec's National Assembly. For the rest of Canada the Meech Lake experience may well have made reform of executive/government party domination of the legislature the most popular constitutional cause of the future.[50]

If, in the end, the Meech Lake proposals had been ratified by all the provinces, a fifth round of macro-constitutional politics would have followed immediately on the heels of the fourth. The very terms of the next round, which came within the whisker of Elijah Harper's vote and Clyde Wells's obduracy of salvaging Meech, contained commitments to launch a whole series of constitutional initiatives. The agreement unveiled by the first ministers on 9 June 1990, after a week of negotiating the conditions on which the hold-out provinces would agree to proceed with legislative ratification of the Meech Lake Accord, mandated the following:[51]

1. a House of Commons committee to consult the country on what should go into a "Canada clause" giving constitutional expression to the defining features of the Canadian community;
2. a commission composed of equal delegations from the provinces with appropriate numbers from the federal Parliament and the territories to conduct hearings and develop proposals for an elected Senate;
3. resumption of constitutional meetings with aboriginal peoples;
4. further constitutional amendments with respect to strengthening the entrenchment of sexual equality, the future of the northern territories and the protection of minority language rights; and
5. a commitment to review further the constitutional amending process.

Note here not only the substantial matters that would have to be resolved to win final acceptance of the Meech Lake Accord (which was designed to win Quebec's acceptance of the 1982 constitutional changes) but also the commitment, by the first ministers no less, to a much more open constitutional process to achieve this final resolution.

In one sense, all this became academic when the Manitoba and Newfoundland legislatures failed to ratify by the June 23 deadline and Meech died. Still, these conditions for getting Meech through are a measure of the breadth of the agenda in the post-Meech round. That round we entered soon after the death of Meech, when both the aboriginal peoples and the

---

50 In the Speech from the Throne on 13 May 1991, the federal government has made parliamentary reform a major element in its approach to constitutional reform (Canada, *House of Commons Debates*, 13 May 1991, 5).

51 *Globe and Mail*, 11 June 1990.

Québécois indicated their determination not to abandon their aspiration to live under a constitution to which they could freely consent.

It is in this, the fifth round, that history may finally answer the question posed in the introduction—can Canadians be a sovereign people?[52] Clearly the process in this round will be more open and democratic. Already the Meech order of proceedings has been reversed and this time we are having public discussion—buckets and buckets of it—before negotiations. There is more than a good chance that first ministers will not dominate the process that lies ahead but will have to tie their initiatives to procedures with more legitimacy such as legislative committees, constituent assemblies, referenda or some combination thereof.[53] This is indeed propitious, so far as process is concerned, for a round capable of concluding with a genuine political covenant.

However, when we move from process to substance, the prospects for a positive answer to my question are considerably less propitious. Reflect, for a moment, on the arguments which were so telling in turning public opinion outside Quebec against the Meech Lake Accord: rejection of English-French dualism as a fundamental feature of Canadian society; recognition of provincial equality as *the* principle of federal justice; insistence that the Québécois' collective right to cultural security be subordinated to the individual rights of the *Charter*; support for uniform national standards of social policy in areas of provincial jurisdiction. It is difficult to conceive how a majority of Quebeckers could be induced to join a constitutional covenant based on these precepts. By the same token, it would seem equally unlikely that a majority of Canadians could be persuaded to support constitutional changes designed to accommodate the extreme nationalist demands which have issued thus far from the constitutional discussions within Quebec.[54] These demands reduce the meaning

---

52 Already a number of books have been published on the post-Meech round. They include: Pierre Fournier, *A Meech Lake Post-Mortem*, trans. Sheila Fischman (Montreal: McGill-Queen's University Press, 1991); Philip Resnick, *Toward a Canada-Quebec Union* (Montreal: McGill-Queen's University Press, 1991); David Smith, Peter McKinnon and John Courtney, eds., *After Meech Lake: Lesson for the Future* (Saskatoon: Fifth House, 1991); Ronald L. Watts and Douglas Brown, eds., *Options for a New Canada* (Toronto: University of Toronto Press, 1991); and Robert Young, ed., *Confederation in Crisis* (Toronto: James Lorimer, 1991).

53 Quebec and British Columbia are both committed to including referenda as part of the constitutional process. For Quebec, see *Report of the Commission on the Political and Constitutional Future of Quebec* (Belanger/Campeau Commission) (Quebec: Secrétariat de la Commission, 1991). In the Speech from the Throne, 13 May 1991, the federal government announced its intention to introduce "enabling legislation to provide for the greater participation of Canadian men and women in constitutional change" (*Debates*, 3).

54 See, in particular, *A Quebec Free to Choose: Report of the Constitutional Committee of the Quebec Liberal Party* (Allaire Report) (Montreal: Quebec Liberal Party, 1991).

of Quebec's participation in a Canadian political community to merely a commercial convenience.

Indeed, if clear nationalist ideology and uncompromised principle are to be the touchstones of our political covenant, Canadians would seem destined to reorganize themselves as two or more distinct peoples in separate states, enjoying only international relations with one another. Such an outcome could result in more coherent, unified and socially homogeneous nation-states very much in keeping with the receding age of the autonomous nation-state.

The alternative outcomes are some restructuring of the existing federation or a new, more confederal arrangement. To be viable, both of these outcomes would require that Canadians agree to be a federal people accepting what that great teacher of federalism, Carl Friedrich, once called "the federal spirit":

> a highly pragmatic kind of political conduct, which avoids all insistence upon "agreement on fundamentals" and similar forms of doctrinaire rigidity. Such behaviour proceeds in the spirit of compromise and accommodation. It is molded by the knowledge that there are many rooms in the house that federalism builds.[55]

An outcome based on the federal spirit, so defined, would, I submit, be more in keeping both with the Canadian political genius and with the forms of political organization which will be the pace-setters in the twenty-first century.

Whether or not, in the fifth round of macro-constitutional politics, we Canadians get the outcome we want or deserve, we should at least agree that five rounds is enough. No other country in the world today has been engaged so intensively, so passionately, or for so long, in searching for the constitutional conditions of its continuing unity. This inward navel-gazing has drained the creative energy of our leaders. It has frustrated, demoralized and yes, even bored, our people.[56] It has undermined Canada's ability to deal with pressing practical problems within and to respond effectively to global opportunities without. We simply cannot afford to let our great constitutional debate—addicted to it though we may be—drag on interminably. It is time to bring it to an end.

---

55 Carl J. Friedrich, *Trends of Federalism in Theory and Practice* (New York: Praeger, 1968), 39.

56 The frustrating nature of constitutional politics is further elaborated in Peter H. Russell, "The Politics of Frustration: The Pursuit of Formal Constitutional Change in Australia and Canada," in Bruce W. Hodgins, John Eddy, S.J., Shelagh D. Grant and James Struthers, eds., *Federalism in Canada and Australia: Historical Perspectives* (Peterborough: Broadview Press, 1989).

Notes on Contributors

Madam Justice Rosalie Silberman Abella was elevated to the Court of Appeal of Ontario in 1992. Between 1976 and 1987, she served as Judge of the Ontario Provincial Court (Family Division). Subsequently, she was Boulton Visiting Professor in the Faculty of Law, McGill University (1988–92). Some of her previous roles include chairing the Ontario Labour Relations Board (1984–89), Sole Commissioner of the Royal Commission on Equality in Employment, which created the term and concept of "Employment Equity," and Commissioner from 1975 to 1980 of the Ontario Human Rights Commission. Her directorships include the Institute for Research in Public Policy (1987–92) and, since 1983, the Canadian Institute for the Administration of Justice. For the latter, she is at present and since 1989 honorary director.

    Justice Abella is the holder of fifteen honorary doctorates. She has written four books and over sixty articles on such subjects as the *Charter*, labour law, family law, public policy and the judicial role.

Roger Gibbins is Professor and current Head in the Political Science Department at the University of Calgary. He received his Ph.D. from Stanford University the year after he was appointed to the University of Calgary in 1973.

    Dr. Gibbins has since pursued a variety of research interests spanning western alienation, Canadian constitutional politics, political belief systems, Senate reform, and American, Australian and aboriginal politics. He is the author or editor of ten books and over fifty articles and book chapters. His publications include: *Prairie Politics and Society* (1980); *Regionalism: Territorial Politics in Canada and the United States* (1982); *Conflict and Unity: An Introduction to Canadian Political Life* (1985, 1990); *Canadian Political Life: An Alberta Perspective* (with Keith Archer and Stan Drabek, 1990); and *New Elites in Old*

States (with Neil Nevitte, 1990). Currently, Dr. Gibbins is the English language co-editor of the *Canadian Journal of Political Science*.

The Honourable Madame Justice Claire L'Heureux-Dubé took her seat as Puisne Judge on the Supreme Court of Canada in 1987. Prior to that she served from 1979 as Judge of the Court of Appeal of Quebec. After being admitted to the Bar of Quebec in 1952, she went into private practice until her appointment in 1973 as Puisne Judge of the Superior Court of Quebec.

In addition to her work for the General Council and several committees of the Bar of Quebec, Madame Dubé was Vice President of the Canadian Consumer's Council (1970–73), and of the Vanier Institute of the Family (1972–73). She was President of the International Commission of Jurists (Canadian Section 1981–83) and is currently Vice President of its International Board. From 1985 to 1988, she chaired the editorial board of the *Canadian Bar Review*.

She holds doctorates from the universities of Dalhousie, Calgary, Montreal, Laval, Ottawa and Quebec at Rimouski, where she spent her childhood. Publications include a chapter "Deciding on Child Custody," in *The Child and the Courts*, Ian F.G. Baxter and Mary Eberts, eds. (1978), and *Family Law: Dimensions of Justice* (with Rosalie S. Abella, 1983).

Kenneth M. Holland is Professor and Chair of Political Science at Memphis State University in Tennessee. He received his M.A. from the University of Virginia and his Ph.D. from the University of Chicago. Before going to Memphis State, he held academic positions at the University of Vermont, the University of Wisconsin at Madison, and at Luther College. He was a Fulbright Visiting Professor at Tohoku University in Japan.

Professor Holland is the author of *Judicial Activism in Comparative Perspective* (1991) and co-editor (with Jerold L. Waltman) of *The Political Role of Law Courts in Modern Democracies* (1988). He has contributed numerous articles on judicial politics to such periodicals as *Justice System Journal*, *Law and Policy Quarterly*, and *Canadian Journal of Law and Society*. He has been the recipient of several research grants from the Canadian government and the government of Quebec, as well as from the National Science Foundation and the American Political Science Association.

J. Woodford Howard, Jr. is the Thomas P. Stran Professor of Political Science at the Johns Hopkins University in Baltimore, Maryland. He received his A.B. degree from Duke University and M.P.A., M.A. and Ph.D. degrees from Princeton University, where one of his mentors was the distinguished political scientist, Alpheus T. Mason. Professor Howard has taught at Lafayette College and Duke University and has delivered papers at numerous national and international conferences. He has served on the editorial boards of the *American Political Science Review*, the *Journal of Politics*, and the *Law and Society Review*.

His publications include: *Mr. Justice (Frank) Murphy: A Political Biography* (1968) and *Courts of Appeals in the Federal Justice System* (1981). Currently he is writing the authorized biography of Judge Harold R. Medina under the auspices of Princeton University.

Marian C. McKenna is Professor of History at the University of Calgary, where she teaches American Legal and Constitutional History and courses in the American Civil War. She has published a number of articles on politics and constitutional issues in the *Canadian Annual Review*, *Pacific Historical Review*, *Sociology and Social Research*, and the *Canadian Journal of History*. Her most recent publication is *Tapping Reeve and the History of the Litchfield Law School* (New York: Oceana Press, 1986). Currently, she is working on a book-length study of Franklin D. Roosevelt and the United States Supreme Court.

Frederick L. Morton is an Associate Professor of Political Science at the University of Calgary and Co-Director of its Research Unit of Socio-Legal Studies. His articles for periodicals in Canada and the United States reflect his specialization in Canadian and American constitutional law and Charter issues. His books include *Law, Politics and the Judicial Process in Canada* (University of Calgary Press, 1992); *Morgentaler v. Borowski: Abortion* (Toronto, 1992); *The Charter, and the Courts: Charter Politics* (Toronto, 1992); and *Federalism and the Charter: Leading Constitutional Decisions* (with Peter Russell and Rainer Knopff, 1989). His article, "The Political Impact of the Canadian Charter of Rights and Freedoms," *Canadian Journal of Political Science*, 20 (March, 1987) has special relevance for this volume of essays.

Thomas Pangle is Professor of Political Science at the University of Toronto. He has also taught at Yale, Dartmouth, the University of Chicago and L'École des Hautes Études en Sciences Sociales, Paris. In recent years, he has held three National Endowment for the Humanities Fellowships and a Guggenheim Fellowship.

Professor Pangle's publications include: *Montesquieu's Philosophy of Liberalism* (1973); *The Laws of Plato* (in translation with an Interpretive Essay) (1980); *The Roots of Political Philosophy: Ten Forgotten Socratic Dialogues* (1987); *The Spirit of Modern Republicanism: The Moral Vision of the American Founders* (1988); *The Ennobling of Democracy: The Challenge of the Post-Modern Era* (1992); and *The Learn-*

ing of Liberty: The Educational Ideas of the American Founders (with Lorraine Smith Pangle, 1993).

Peter H. Russell is Professor of Political Science at the University of Toronto. He has written numerous articles and books on politics, nationalism, the Charter, and more recently on the constitution in the context of the current debate. He is a past president of the Canadian Political Science Association. Some of his publications include: "The Supreme Court's Interpretation of the Constitution since 1949," Paul Fox, ed., *Politics in Canada* (Toronto, 1966); *The Court and the Constitution: Comments on the Supreme Court Reference on Constitutional Amendment* (1982); *The Judiciary in Canada: The Third Branch of Government* (Toronto, 1987); "The Politics of Frustration: The Pursuit of Formal Constitutional Change in Australia and Canada," *Australian-Canadian Studies*, 6:1 (1988): *Federalism and the Charter* (with Rainer Knopff, 1989); and *Constitutional Odyssey: Can the Canadians Become a Sovereign People?* (Toronto, 1992).

Jennifer Smith is Associate Professor of Political Science at Dalhousie University in Halifax, Nova Scotia. She received her B.A. (Hons.) from McMaster University, and her M.A. and Ph.D. from Dalhousie. In 1991–92, she served as Commissioner for the Province of Nova Scotia on its Electoral Boundaries Commission, and in 1991 chaired the Province's Advisory Committee on the Division of Powers and Government Institutions. She was a participant in 1992 in the "Renewal of Canada" Constitutional Conferences. Her recent publications include "Representation and Constitutional Reform in Canada," in J. Courtney et al., *After Meech Lake: Lessons for the Future* (1991); and *Democratic Rights and Electoral Reform in Canada*, Vol. 10 of the research studies of the Royal Commission on Electoral Reform and Party Financing (1992).

Table of Cases

Index